Her Master's Voice

Mignon Allen, racing in a Blean Beagles Point-to-Point in 1922

Anne Edgar

Her Master's Voice
The life of Betty McKeever

© Anne Edgar 2000

Published 2000 by Anne & Colin Edgar

Designed & typeset by Robert Banham
student in the Department of
Typography & Graphic Communication
The University of Reading

ISBN 0-9538388-03

Printed and bound in Great Britain
by Geerings Printers, Ashford, Kent

Map inside front cover: reproduced with kind permission of the Ordnance Survey
Map inside back cover: Bartholomew Ltd. 2000 reproduced by kind permission
of Harper/Collins Publishers. www.bartholomewmaps.com

Contents

Author's acknowledgements

I would like to dedicate this work to my father, John Dawes, who suggested that I write it, and who gave me so much support and help. (He is shown overleaf, with his governess Scottie.)

My sister Janet was superb. She remembered so many stories off the top of her head and kept coming back with more. Janet spent much time with Betty and Jean, in the '70s and early '80s and her memory is phenomenal.

John Dawes with his governess, Scottie

Foreword

We think of Betty McKeever as Edwardian, when in actual fact she was twentieth century, having lived through the heart of it, the first nine decades, 1901–90.

I have always thought that her generation had the most interesting technical breakthroughs in their lifetime. From the horse and cart, via motor-car and aeroplane. Through the mechanized First and Second World Wars, up to the jet age with space travel, supermarkets and the microchip. Betty met new events with intelligence and resiliance. She remained robustly Edwardian in her outlook. She was always interested in people, especially the young.

I haven't put in the hoots of laughter that accompanied the telling of most of her stories in this book. Trying to interview people has been interesting. When playing the tape-recorder later, it is hard trying to make sense of stories told against the sound of beagle puppies barking loudly, motorway noises or pouring rain. Or at Jenny Dawes's wedding with the Hernhill Church bells ringing.

My position in the famliy is set. I am Aunty Betty's great-niece and like her started off as a Miss Dawes. So when mentioning relatives, many people are both my father and her nephew, or my grandfather and her brother. Life gets a little complicated at times – too many relations. I have for the most part, tried to show their relationship to Betty rather than to myself. I realize that the 'voices' from my side of the family come over loud and clear – perhaps dominating the story, but one gets facts where one can. As a genealogist, I have to be dragged kicking and screaming into this century! All my life I remember the flavour of all those old hunting stories – most of the details forgotten – and the feeling of a strong family whose cousins all knew each other and did things together. Even then this felt unusual.

The stories told about other people and events were all Betty's stories, as told by her and remembered by someone else.

Chapter One
A celebration in Kent

Eighty years a Master! This was an achievement in personality, not just in longevity.

Betty McKeever was eighty-eight. She dressed as she always had done, in her tweed coat and skirt and a tweed hat, with a hunt button on her lapel. Stout shoes and thick stockings completed her outfit.

A celebration was taking place – there had been many others. One to commemorate fifty years, one at each decade since, and a precautionary event at seventy-five years. Today's event, however, held on 14 October 1989 was the culmination.

This Opening Meet of the Blean Beagles, celebrated the fact that Betty had been Master of the pack for an unimaginable 80 seasons.

The Meet was held at Mount Ephraim, which was fitting as it was Betty's childhood home. In her lifetime it had housed her grandfather, father, brother, nephew and now great-nephew. Another generation was growing up at the Mount and keeping up the continuity. Throughout her life Betty had visited Mount Ephraim constantly, sometimes for long periods. Her great-nephew, Sandys Dawes, and Lesley his wife were hosting this occasion.

Around Betty were crowds of people. She was very much the heart of Kent, she knew the people and the land – and stayed close to both.

Her pack of hounds naturally had pride of place at the Meet. She had 24 couple of beagles, most of which were present. They were accompanied by her huntsman, Chris Hill and several whippers-in, who were all smartly dressed in their distinctive Blean Beagles green jackets, green stockings, white knee-britches and stocks, some of whom wore green caps.

By now Betty McKeever's sight was deteriorating, so when people came up to her, they had to introduce themselves, after which she was spot-on and entirely homed in on to whoever it was.

Arthur Finn ran the event. A beagler since the 1950s, he had given the Blean Beagles stalwart support and was now chairman. *'There was no organized subscription'*, he said, *'but a book of those that*

attended, and no presentation – at her request.' Arthur made a speech
for the occasion that day and so did Maurice Berry, a local farmer.

Two hundred and sixty-six people attended the Meet. They
had all been invited as it was an invitation-only meet. Drinks were
handed around. Even for those who had been present at other land-
marks in Betty McKeever's Mastership, this was an awesome occasion. Many of her generation by now had died, but Joan Sayer was
there, beagling still, as a family friend. She had hunted since the
beginning.

The horn was sounded. It was 1989 and the start of Autumn.
The field of 266 people started following the hunt, which went
down through the orchards and woods of Hernhill. Betty went
with them to start her 80th season as 'Master'.

Betty was entered into the 1980 edition of the *Guinness Book of
Records* as being at that time (1979) the longest-serving Master
of Hounds – for 70 years. Her entry was kept in the Record Book
until 1997 – well after her death. Our 1987 edition has:

FIELDSPORTS – Foxhunting Longest Span
Jean Bethel 'Betty' McKeever (nee Dawes). (b. 26 Feb 1901)
has been Master of the Blean Beagles in Kent since 1909.

Betty McKeever had been about 5 foot 4 inches tall, then shrank
in old age. **'Precious things come in small parcels.'**

When young she had had sandy red hair and it retained its
sandy colour into old age. She wore it in a bun – from the time
it went up (as a young woman) until the end of her life.

She had fair skin and huge pale blue eyes, with a blunt sturdy
(Dawes) nose in a strong face. Betty had small hands and feet and
was very proud of the fact that her hands were Simpson hands with
saddlers' thumbs which could bend right back. (This trait was also
shared by other family members, such as John Dawes and Mary
Houstoun.)

Betty was of solid build. **'Short and stoot, just like a hayrick.'**
In advanced years she was shapeless but always very strong, whether
following hounds all day, shooting, fishing or doing whatever she
wished.

Her voice was deep and masculine. If a man answered her telephone, one always said, *'Hello, Aunt Betty.'*

She had a Victorian English Gentry accent. She would pronounce off as 'orf' and would say: 'Gorne away', or 'He lorst a quid.' Very down to earth. Betty was great fun and always interesting.

There was an inexhaustible fund of stories. She used to eat, drink, smoke and breathe in the middle of a sentence so no one could interrupt.

Betty was very English in England – a woman of Kent, and very Scottish in Scotland.

Her knowledge was extensive of history – and local history. She knew four generations of most Hernhill families, and was interested in art and knowledgeable on furniture, china, architecture, jewellery and paintings. She loved her garden and was good on her botany. Most especially Betty was skilful at all field sports. She was no mean nagsman, and knew her horses, cattle and sheep.

Neither she nor her brother Slotty had been to school and were never team members, but individual players, with great desire to win. She played tennis effectively – and to win.

Attending The Horse of the Year Show, one year, Betty was able to describe the grandparents of each rider and each horse that was competing that day. She was widely read and an intense reader. Betty really did learn – perhaps because she never went to school.

NORMA CURLING: *She was a fantastic reader. She really did read and read and read. Her house was full of books and she would get books. She took it all in and it stayed in. She had all the refinements like sewing, knitting and drawing – as well as going outside and mucking out the horses.*

The accomplishments had not passed Betty by. She was skilled in painting water-colours (of flowers and scenes) and sewing. Knitting was an occupation all the time, and accompanied her story-telling. Drawing, making shoes and gardening were other pursuits.

So what made this elderly country lady special? One thing was her tremendous stories. Indeed, an inexhaustible supply. Stories back through the generations. She had a superb oral memory. One family story that Aunty Betty told us, went back to the time of George IV, who was crowned in 1821 – told from stories she remembered her grandparents telling her – good stories too.

JOE BUTLER: *She could tell a good yarn. It's one thing knowing about something, but it's another thing to put it into something that's attractive, which she could do. She'd always embellish it and make it sound more than what it actually was. But I think that is the art of telling a good story.*

Betty would start with one story, then tell another and another, and would make them dovetail together to make some particular point.

An unusual character – Betty was a true eccentric. How many women do you know who kept their circular saw in their elegant Edwardian bedroom? Tools lay on her dressing-table between her silver backed dressing-table set, with sawdust and all. One of her bedside chairs had saw marks on it.

Betty was an excellent carpenter and made, indeed, a couple of intricate drinks cabinets and several cradles. She also was the leader in the building of Hernhill Village Hall, designing the stage herself.

She had a terrific interest in people – especially the young. She always had a bevy of young men around her, often in a beagling capacity, but for other reasons too. Hoards of youths were fascinated by her over the years.

Betty was a true Edwardian sportsman. She remained so long after that way of life had generally ceased to be. Her beagle pack was settled on her at the age of 8, true, but this was because even at that young age, she showed potential. That pack was kept going through thick and thin, through two World Wars and 80 long years – due to her character and determination. She remained attached to the great sporting traditions of her youth. At that stage of the late 1980s she was one of the last representatives of a dying breed – a sturdy, vital person, holding her own in a man's world.

Betty rode side-saddle. She eventually gave up around 1960. But she had ridden in Point-to-Points, in the days before Ladies' Races. And she hunted, several days a week – all day in the saddle, mostly in Kent and in Ireland, but she also hunted a season in Yorkshire. **'We had 20 hunting horses and I hunted at least four times a week,'** Betty told Mike Field of *Horse and Hound*, just before this celebration event. **'I didn't go to school. I was taught at home by a governess, so there was plenty of time for hunting.'**

MIKE FIELD: *She graduated as a skilled worker in wood, leather, metal and stone, a farmer who was ultimately to manage over 500 acres of orchards, arable and pasture, and the possessor of a retentive memory, a vivid turn of speech, a strong sense of the ridiculous and a lively and sympathetic interest in each and every one of the hundreds of young and old who have the good fortune to be among her friends.*

Betty was a very competent fisherman, and fished annually, mostly on the Deveron in Banffshire, Scotland, for salmon and sea-trout.

Shooting was a lifetime's and very natural sport for Betty. She boasted a shooting record of rabbits for herself in 1917. She was a good enough 'shot' to be asked out to 'smart' shoots. Not something that always happened automatically to a woman.

Betty always drummed in 'safety' as of maximum importance to the younger generations of guns. But in 1978 her safety maxim did not prevent an accident happening in which she shot herself with her own gun – and survived; undoubtedly a great survivor – a very tough lady.

There was tremendous charisma. Nobody ever forgot her who had met her. She became a legend in her own lifetime in Kent.

Betty farmed from 1931 onwards. Different specializations at different times were award-winning poultry in the '30s. Prize Sussex cattle in the '50s and Large White pigs. Pure-bred Kent sheep in the '60s and Welsh Mountain Ponies from the '60s onwards.

Betty's dress style didn't tend to change. She always wore a blouse and tweed coat and skirt, sometimes with an anorak. She knitted her own thick woollen stockings – from the toe outwards, on four needles so that there was no seam. These she would wear with beige bloomers – as was obvious to anyone sitting opposite her!

My uncle, Harry Mitchell, returning once from India, told of having met someone out there who knew her sitting position, so quoted that she was known *'from the Indies to the Andes by her undies'.*

On her feet Betty wore brogues, latterly made for her by the National Health Service as she had very flat feet. She regularly wore these out on long walks beagling, going shooting and actively farming. The Health Service found it unusual that someone wearing medical shoes, should wear her shoes out with so much exercise!

For an evening party, Betty tended to wear thinner stockings and a darkish coloured dress. She always looked smart at hunt balls. She had a diamond pin and a sapphire wristlet. Her jewellery might be pearls (she had a long rope) or a bar brooch. From her mother Betty inherited a stomacher. This is an expanse of jewellery on stiff material as worn by Queen Elizabeth I. A stomacher is worn pinned across the breast like an enormous brooch.

'HORSE AND HOUND': *Her independent unconventional views and enquiring mind were formed by being educated at home within a family with strong Banffshire connections…*

Generations of young people from all walks of life have benefited from her knowledge and enthusiasm in country lore, especially hunting.

A unique character, with an encyclopaedic genealogical know-ledge of local people, a redoubtable raconteuse, a great personality and always interested in the young.

Betty's life took place to a large extent in five houses. Four in Kent and one in Scotland; Kemsdale – where she was born, and lived until she was three years old. Mount Ephraim – the Dawes family home, where Betty spent her childhood and portions of World War II. Swordanes – purchased by her parents – on the links in Banff. Berkeley was her mother's house, Betty lived there for 6 years in the '20s. The last is Waterham, Betty's home from 1931 and where she lived for the rest of her life.

Kemsdale lies about 2 miles and Mount Ephraim 3 miles away from Faversham. They are both situated in the Parish of Hernhill. Berkeley was half way up Boughton Hill, about a mile away, and Waterham, still in Hernhill – is the other side of the Coastal Road, a mile and a half away from the main village. So Betty's life was in Hernhill.

In Banff, Swordanes is on the sea coast and half a mile down the hill from her mother's childhood home of Colleonard, in a very close community.

Then there was her great last wish – to be chopped up, fed to her beagles and to have 'just one more day's hunting'. Which luckily for her relations, proved to be illegal! **'Seemed perfectly reasonable to me, but I'm told its against the law. It should be my decision.'**

One day Noel Watson, Betty's huntsman in the '60s, was driving home with her after beagling, when Betty suddenly exclaimed, **'What a lily livered bunch of milksops solicitors are!'** This remark stemmed not from some failed litigation, but from her wish for her solicitor to write into her will that she wanted her body to be fed to her hounds after she had died! Her solicitor (who was also an execu-tor of her will) had refused point-blank. *'How will I find anyone to cut* *you up Betty?'*, the poor man replied. Betty had told him that it was the least service he could have done for an old friend like her. **'After all,'** she said, **'I wouldn't hesitate to butcher your carcass, if you asked me!'**

Chapter Two
Father

William Charles Dawes was born on 20 September, 1865. He was baptized in Surbiton, at Christ Church. His parents lived in Surbiton at the time so he was probably born there.

He was the fourth child and eldest son of Edwyn Sandys Dawes and Lucy Emily Bagnall, who were first cousins. Six more children followed. Husband and wife shared a grandmother, in the Evangelist Victorian children's author, Mrs Sherwood. (Did the ability to tell a good story come down the family to Betty?)

By the time Willie was about 10, the Dawes family returned to their old family home of Mount Ephraim, in Kent.

Willie's father, Edwyn Dawes, was the family live wire. He had seen service in the Crimean War at the age of 16, from a P & O ship, the SS *Nubia*. Edwyn remained with the P & O until he became Chief Officer. He travelled in the Far East, once being shipwrecked off Sumatra and spending five days in an open boat, before being picked up and taken to Singapore. He was in China and India from 1856 to 1865.

Mount Ephraim from the air

A spectacular advance was made in this young officer's career at a time when he was on board a merchant vessel, in the port of Calcutta. The owners of the vessel were wanting to develop the port, but they were having difficulty in working out the volume of material that they would need to remove annually when dredging silt that had been brought down by the main river.

The owners were explaining this to their shore officers. One of the captains said that he had got a young officer who was clever with mathematics. Edwyn Dawes was duly sent ashore, and he managed to work out the amount of silt that was considered likely to be deposited, and the capacity and number of dredgers that would be required to keep the port open.

William Mackinnon, senior partner of 'Mackinnon and Mackenzie', Calcutta also met the young man on a voyage, and invited him to join the company ashore in Calcutta. After a year or so Edwyn Dawes became 'Willie' MacKinnon's personal representative in Bombay for a few years. He married his cousin, Lucy Bagnall on 21 March 1859 and their eldest daughters were born in India. Owing to Lucy's health they all returned to England in 1864. Willie Mackinnon sought Edwyn out and invited him to set up in London with his nephew, Archie Gray, as their agent. Thus was born 'Gray Dawes'.

Mackinnon said they could become London agents for British India. He could then throw some coaling charters and insurance business their way.

Edwyn was a Member of Lloyds and became a Victorian Shipping Magnate. He had a terrific business ability, was unusually energetic, both physically and mentally, sweeping people and furniture aside in his wake.

Edwyn Dawes became Chairman of the New Zealand Shipping Co., the Australasian United Steam Navigation Co., the South African & Australasian Supply Co. and a director of the Suez Canal Co., British India Steam Navigation Co., the Queensland National Bank., the Southern Mahratta Railway Co., the West of India Portuguese Guaranteed Railway Co., the North Queensland Mortgage & Investment Co. and J B Westray & Co. These showing his world-wide interests.

Edwyn Dawes headed a body of ship-owners to attend on the Income Tax Commissioners in the City of London in 1896.

He became a Magistrate and was awarded a knighthood (Knight Commander of the Order of St Michael and St George) in 1894, for providing employment in his village in the agricultural depression of the 1890s.

There was great unemployment in Hernhill, following the end of the Boer War. Sir Edwyn employed many locals in an estate gang of about 50, to build a cart road through Blean Woods. He also caused a 'folly' to be erected. The Tower was built in the middle of the woods, high up, which had a wonderful view out over the Thames Estuary. It is now called Tower Woods.

Sir Edwyn Dawes was said to be 'one of the outstanding figures in the English shipping world', and a man who 'coupled with keen intelligence an incredible capacity for work'.

The goat, the butler and the coffin

Sir Edwyn died of diabetes and pulmonary TB at the Grand Hotel, Puerto, Orotava, Tenerife on 21 December 1903. He was 65 and obviously expecting to die. Travelling on board ship going out to Tenerife, he was accompanied by a goat – as he didn't drink cows milk – and his butler, Jessup.

An old docker recalled, *'Dawes, I remember Dawes. I remember loading his coffin on as part of his luggage, and unloading it 6 months later with him in it!'* He was buried at Hernhill where there is a tablet erected to him by his workmen.

All this was a hard act to follow for his son Willie. There were ten children in his generation, five of each sex.

The Moravian missionary

Willie was sent to school at Winchester. He only lasted at this famous school for a term, after which he was returned home as 'ineducatable'. He was dyslexic, and his father, Edwyn was furious. *'Right, you may start at the bottom of the shipping industry,'* he told his son.

But a Moravian missionary friend, who knew how rough the docklands were, said to Edwyn, *'How long before the whores and opium dens get him?'* And he added, *'I'll educate your son'.* So Willie Dawes lived with the missionary in Limehouse for a year. Willie groomed the missionary's horse and dug his garden.

As the area was such a dangerous one to live in, once a day a Policeman called and escorted the missionary's wife, Willie and a large dog to the nearest shop for supplies, and afterwards returned them home again.

The missionary taught Willie how to read and write, in the course of that year. Edwyn thereafter sent Willie's younger brothers to Haileybury to be educated.

As a young man, Willie was sent to Calcutta, India to learn the family business, but came home within the year, suffering badly with sunstroke. Willie became dumb for some time as a result of having had too much sun.

He used a slate to write messages on, and ever afterwards, hated the sound of the schoolroom slate. One day, out with a sister, Willie noticed she was about to be bitten by a snake. He screamed and re-found his voice and thereafter was no longer dumb.

He followed his father in his many business activities, but with less drive and brilliance.

William C Dawes became Chairman of J B Westray & Co., the New Zealand Shipping Co., the Federal Steam Navigation Co. and also Commercial Union Assurance Co. He became head of the New Zealand Loan and Mercantile Agency Co.

In 1893 he married Jane Margaret Simpson on 19 January, at Hampstead. Willie and Jeannie were a devoted couple. They 'never slept a night away from each other'.

Their first child Sandys (Edwyn Sandys Dawes again) arrived on 15 January 1894 in Langley, Putney-Heath. Willie and Mopsie were living at No 5 The Hill, Putney. Their next house was Orchards, Hernhill – for a short time, then they took up their abode in Kemsdale, another house in Hernhill, two and a half miles from Faversham.

Betty was born next, on 26 February 1901 and their third child was Slotty (William Lancelot), born on 16 March, 1904. This completed the family. In 1904 following Sir Edwyn's death they moved into Mount Ephraim

Willie Dawes and his siblings were said to have all hated each other. The 'hatred' came when the others found out that the property had been entailed to Willie. And this ill-will suddenly burst open – because they were all expecting chunks of it.

Ownership of land was power. Whoever owned the land had the power to grant it in an entail. This ensured that land went on down the generations. The 'grantee' could entail the property to his first legitimate male heir, and so on downwards, so that the power and prestige of a family didn't get dispersed. If there was a wastrel son in one generation, he would not be able to flog off the family acres, but he could mortgage it.

Having got Mount Ephraim back into the family, and rebuilt it, it ended up a very nice property. Sir Edwyn understood only too well that it could not remain in the family, unless it was entailed, because nobody would be able to afford it. He had already settled money on his other nine children.

So nobody got any more, in that will. At the reading of the will, they were absolutely, outright, appalled. They couldn't believe what they were hearing! Willie got everything. The anger was so immense that Aunt Betty's story was that two brothers were seen walking round the gardens with a gun that night, to shoot Willie!

The result was, that that age-group didn't really speak to the Kent Daweses any more. They all went off to Surrey and places.

Apparently the grandmother, Lucy, was only allowed to move the furniture from her bedroom. She went off to live in Bath for the rest of her life – until she died on 23 April 1921 when feelings still ran high between the brothers.

Mount Ephraim is a large house in Kent which the Dawes family has owned for generations (since 1695). But the house had been let to the Vicar of Hernhill for a generation or two, because Sir Edwyn's father had been a vicar in the Midlands. Having made his fortune, Sir Edwyn recovered the house in the 1880s. It had previously been a Queen Anne black and white timber house which was then completely rebuilt when the family returned to it, owing to dry-rot.

Both Sir Edwyn and Willie extended the house of Mount Ephraim. Willie built the servants' wing in 1912. He also built the £500 ballroom and main bedroom above (which was cheaper than hiring a marquee). The Tickham Hunt Ball was held there in the season 1908/9. The brickwork was up to the first floor, with canvas sheets draped over the walls.

The re-building made Mount Ephraim, instead of a charming, medium-sized Queen Anne house, a huge imposing red-brick barracks. (Indeed, during World War II, half of it was used as an army barracks.) It has a fabulous central hall with a carved Italianate staircase.

Rieu, one of Nelson's captains, was born at the house. Also Henry Morton Stanley was sent off from Mount Ephraim to Africa in 1871, to find 'Dr Livingstone, I presume?'

Mount Ephraim is on the North Kent Downs, in the triangle between Canterbury, Faversham and Whitstable.

The area had been all woodland in the past, with fields painstakingly grubbed out from them. The locality has views of the Thames Estuary.

It is undulating hill country, going down through orchard-lands and 'Thanet beds', to flat marshland along Oare Creek between Faversham and the coast, opposite the Isle of Sheppey. Hops and fruit are grown extensively.

Some of the hills are quite high – 350 ft, and during the Second World War, fifteen radar pylons were grouped upon one hill to watch the enemy flights from France. One pylon is left now (minus the top 50 feet) and is still a considerable landmark for miles around.

Part of the higher hills are clay. One whole hilltop was dug up and taken off to make up the sea-wall following floods, after the sea came in in 1953. Clay Hill is now 50 foot lower.

The gardens of Mount Ephraim are 7 acres, with a slope down to a man-made lake. Willie especially enjoyed setting out the Edwardian gardens. There is a Japanese rock garden and bridge; yew hedges, enclosing and dividing the formal garden design, and a fountain on the front lawn.

A beautiful topiary of yew-tree shapes was planted in 1911, which has a layout of ships, aeroplanes, a chair, a tank, an elephant and many others shapes.

There are stone Palladian terraces which used to have Italianate stone and lead statues; classical figures, lions and greyhounds. There are terraced rose gardens, borders, special trees, such as the Waterloo tree, and an area called the Land of Beulah. A motto-gate leads into fields and orchards extending from the garden.

In those days, at the beginning of the century, Mount Ephraim was open to the public once a year. There were many tennis parties, played on the three grass and two hard courts.

Willie took to the management of his 2,000-acre estate, much more so than to his City life, as he had quite a nervous disposition.

Rhododendrons had been planted around the Tower in Blean Woods that Sir Edwyn had built. Part of the Sunday ritual was that the whole family had to go for a walk round it.

Mount Ephraim's estate workforce included thirty-three farmhands, fifteen gardeners, a team of lawnsmen, and two men just to tend the orchids. In the house there was a cook, housemaids, plus household staff, a valet, footmen and a butler. There were also nannies, governesses and tutors as needed.

Willie suffered from ill-health which limited his 'drive' in the City. His main achievements were in Kent. His greatest energy was put into his estate, his garden and into hunting. Hunting was a way of life.

He was Master of the Tickham Fox-hounds (Joint-Master with Lord Harris for many years). Blean Beagles and a pack of Harriers. Willie was an avid Liberal but Lord Harris was a Conservative. And so they couldn't talk to one another about the hunt during the Election Campaign, because it would be seen to be wrong. So Lady Harris and Mopsie ran the hunt whilst there was an election on!

The Dawes/Simpson family

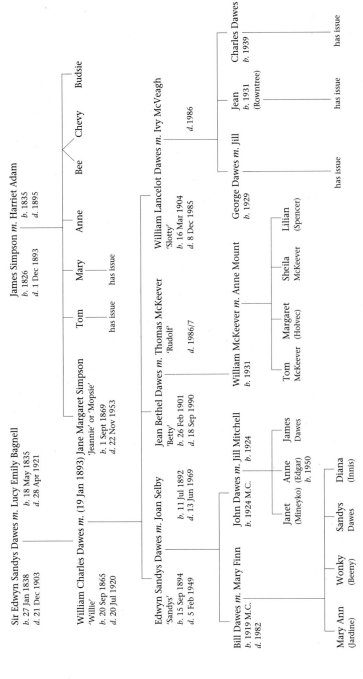

James Simpson *m.* Harriet Adam
b. 1826   *b.* 1835
d. 1 Dec 1893   *d.* 1895

Tom   Mary   Anne   Bee   Chevy   Budsie
has issue   has issue

Sir Edwyn Sandys Dawes *m.* Lucy Emily Bagnell
b. 27 Jan 1838   *b.* 18 May 1835
d. 21 Dec 1903   *d.* 28 Apr 1921

William Charles Dawes *m.* (19 Jan 1893) Jane Margaret Simpson
'Willie'   'Jeannie' or 'Mopsie'
b. 20 Sep 1865   *b.* 1 Sept 1869
d. 20 Jul 1920   *d.* 22 Nov 1953

William Lancelot Dawes *m.* Ivy McVeagh
'Slotty'
b. 16 Mar 1904
d. 8 Dec 1985   *d.* 1986

Jean Bethel Dawes *m.* Thomas McKeever
'Betty'   'Rudolf'
b. 26 Feb 1901
d. 18 Sep 1990   *d.* 1986/7

George Dawes *m.* Jill
b. 1929

Jean   Charles Dawes
b. 1931   *b.* 1939
(Rowntree)
has issue   has issue

has issue

William McKeever *m.* Anne Mount
b. 1931

Tom   Margaret   Sheila   Lilian
McKeever   (Holvec)   McKeever   (Spencer)

Edwyn Sandys Dawes *m.* Joan Selby
'Sandys'
b. 15 Sep 1894
d. 5 Feb 1949

John Dawes *m.* Jill Mitchell
b. 1924 M.C.   *b.* 1924

Janet   Anne   James
(Mineyko)   (Edgar)   Dawes
b. 1950

Bill Dawes *m.* Mary Finn
b. 1919 M.C.
d. 1982

Mary Ann   Wonky   Sandys   Diana
(Jardine)   (Beeny)   Dawes   (Innis)

16   Her Master's Voice

Chapter Three
Mother

Betty's mother was Jane Margaret Simpson. She was called Jeannie, and later Mopsie. She was a Scotswoman, born and bred in Banff – a small county on the east coast of Scotland (to the north of Aberdeen), and facing northwards on to the Moray Firth. Her father was a whisky distiller.

Jeannie Simpson was born on 1 September 1869. In Jeannie's generation there were three boys (but one died after a fortnight) and five girls.

Mary and Jeannie both got married. Harriet (known as Budsie), Anne and Caroline (nicknamed Bee) remained single, and maiden aunts to Betty.

Thomas Adam was Betty's great-grandfather.

He purchased the estate of Eden castle and [latterly] lived in Bowie Bank with his unmarried daughter, my great Aunt Jean. My mother, all her Family and all the cousins stayed with him in the holidays. No parents permitted to stay with them. How they all survived I don't know. I have grown up on stories of what they did that made them united all their lives.

Blackberrying

Jeannie caught whooping cough. This took a long while to recover from, so she was sent into the hills with her sister, Bee. They stayed up in Tomintoul.

She always remembered one day when they were all very naughty. She and her sister were out in the fields, and had been eating blackberries. Suddenly a little pony and trap came past. And the lady called them over and said, *'Now you lot. Why are you here?'*

And Jeannie said, *'We're the Distiller's children, Ma'am.'*

'Oh, are you. That's all right then. And you're eating all my blackberries, are you?'

Jeannie asked, *'How did you know that?'*

The lady said, 'Well, little girl, your face is black with the black-berries you're supposed to be picking, but you're eating them instead. Come here. Give me your handkerchief.'

Jeannie gave this lady her handkerchief. The lady looked at it, put her finger in and spat – very vigorously – like mother's do, and then she rubbed the girl's face all over with the handkerchief. Then she handed it to her and said 'Right, my darling, now don't forget; in your life, you'll always be able to say: "Ah, but who's had their face washed by the Queen's spittle?"'

And this was Queen Victoria – out in her pony trap with her man-servant, John Brown. Tomintoul is just north-east of Balmoral.

Jeannie was slim and elegant when young. Later on she became short and stout, but had had an 18-inch waist for her wedding dress. Her slim granddaughter Jean Dawes was surprised (when trying this garment on two generations later) that although the waistband was too big, she could not get into the bodice, owing to the fact that women were so tightly laced in Jeannie's day! All her life Jeannie had tremendous sex appeal, and a striking eye.

Jeannie married in Hampstead, London when she was 23 to Willie Dawes, a gentleman from Kent who was a City businessman.

How Willie and Jeannie met each other.

Jeannie had very good hands – for riding horses. Very fine hands so that when others couldn't make horses go – she could. She was a renowned horsewoman and had been to a finishing school in Paris. James Simpson had gone over to one of the exhibitions to sell his whisky.

They had relations or friends called Hassel – who lived at Green Street Green, near Dartford and Bromley. Jeannie was invited down there to stay and to hunt with the West Kent. That is where they met – at some hunt function, or dance in that particular area. There was a letter sent up from that side of the family to say that, 'One Willie Dawes was paying a great deal of attention to Jeannie Simpson!' A bit of inter-family gossip had come up – about 1890.

In 1916 R Jock painted a full-length portrait of Jeannie and charged £382 10s. 0d. on 14 October. It still hangs in the hall of Mount Ephraim opposite a portrait of Willie.

Jeannie regularly followed the West Kent pack, also the Eridge.

Some of the family, notably Willie's brothers and sisters, were inclined to look down their noses a bit at this down-to-earth Scots girl who was a Distiller's daughter. As a consequence of this, and later of Sir Edwyn's will, Betty, who was very family minded, knew very little of her uncles and aunts on her father's side. Some family rifts didn't get healed until a wedding in the 1920s or '30s, and some rifts took even longer.

Sir Edwyn kept wallabies at Mount Ephraim, also peacocks. One day, as the peacocks screamed at the crack of dawn, Jeannie was discovered outside shooting at them with a bow and arrow, in her nightdress! (Tradition is divided on whether this was Jeannie or her daughter Betty. One story says there were peacocks when Betty was a child. She hated the noise, so she took a bow and arrow and tried to shoot them. She wasn't successful and so was at loggerheads with the head gardener, who always wore black gloves.)

Sir Edwyn was very fond of his daughter-in-law and would ride with her continuously. He was believed to be in love with her.

Jeannie was at her carpentry one day and she accidentally hit a large whitlow on her thumb very hard with a hammer! This would have hurt considerably, but it was her father-in-law, Sir Edwyn who fainted, and Jeannie had to cope with him!

All her life Jeannie had more outward charm than her daughter, Betty.

Willie and Jeannie (or Popsie and Mopsie as they were called), bought and extended an extra home in Banff called Swordanes, about 1900 – to keep up the contact with Scotland and for sport.

To Mopsie sport was the business of life. She was a sportswoman – particularly hunting and fishing – and was a good shot. Mopsie's grandson, John Dawes remembered her through her sports activities:

Fishing

The Scattertie beat of the Deveron is about 10 miles from the sea at Banff. The beat is a mile with a quarter (the upper part of it) on both banks. The Deveron is famous for sea-trout with June/July the best time.

Mopsie rented it. Her daughter-in-law, Joan Dawes once caught a 10 lb salmon, just downstream from Moggie Mull. It had taken her well over an hour to land it. Mopsie also fished. When she was 80, she caught another 10 lb salmon. The Scattertie Pool close to the hut was her favourite place.

Scattertie was part of the Craigston Estate, belonging still to the Pollard-Urquharts. Bruce Pollard-Urquart was the Laird, before World War II and after. Mopsie leased the fishing and paid an annual rent of about £80. When she died in 1953, the Estate wished to 'up' the rent by 50% to £120. Slotty said this was much too high and let it go, without discussing it with the family. The price of £120 was extraordinarily cheap.

Mopsie's sons, Sandys and Slotty, were both much keener fishermen than her grandson, John Dawes.

Hunting

Mopsie rode 'Suffolk Punch', always with Leonard Whitehead her groom in attendance. Her two horses were always hacked to the meet by Leonard – having no horsebox. She rode perhaps one day per week with the Beagles and one with the Tickham.

Tennis

John Dawes gave her a new racquet for her 80th birthday. He enjoyed playing with her. She stood on the service line and if a ball was short or long it was 'YOURS'. She had an excellent eye and a difficult spin service.

Shooting

Mopsie went partridge shooting after the Second World War. She would drive her Land-Rover on the end of the line of guns with the windscreen down and shoot from the driver's seat.

Wheelwright

Mopsie was a fine carpenter and made the cartwheels for the ESD (Edwyn Sandys Dawes) pony cart.

Mopsie was great in the hunting field, rode on a VAST side-saddle and only gave up at the beginning of World War II. Her horses (old) were never sent to the kennels 'for one more day's hunting', but buried under roundels of trees on Mount Ephraim estate.

Mopsie rode on an uncured saddle at some stage. The rubbing caused by these rough pummels, gave her great lumps on her legs.

Later on Mr Capon was the village tailor in Boughton and Mopsie, her sister Bee and daughter Betty had been down, because they were needing 'adjustments' to be done to their clothes, etc. Usually needed letting out. *'The britches will learn to fit.'* Anyway, this duly happened. And they all left, and another customer arrived. Mr Capon observed, *'There go the three biggest bums in Kent!'*

Betty used to tell a story of being a Distiller's granddaughter. That the whisky was to cure all ills. They even poured it down the inside of their boots as they got wet when they were out shooting, because the duty on it wasn't high in those days – before the '14 War. It was used for medicinal purposes and goodness knows what. Basic whisky. Whether it did any good or not – but in Edwardian times, the biggest fear of that age-group was illness. Everything else in life – if you worked hard and had got the money – you could buy. But the only thing you couldn't buy was your health. Whereas today we take health for granted – the fuss that was made for the slightest little thing, had to be seen to be believed. If the kids fell over and scratched their legs, Mopsie always carried an iodine pencil – it might go septic – then you'd have to have your leg amputated. With infectious diseases – diphtheria, whooping cough, measles, mumps – all those sort of things – mad panics used to take place. Whereas today they are sort of treated with contempt.

On trips to London, the horses would slip over sometimes (on the slithery streets) and couldn't get up and were struggling. Mopsie would go and sit on the horses heads so others could then undo their traces and get them to their feet.

Betty remembered her father used to say, *'Jeannie, I don't buy expensive clothes for you to go and sit on horses heads.'*

Going out to dinner in a horse-drawn carriage in London one day, the horse slipped over. Mopsie jumped out of the carriage. She put a cloth over the horse's head and sat on it. She then helped the coachman get the horse upright. The next day she asked the driver to tea! Very unconventional.

Christmas was not a festival that was kept in Scotland. Betty remembered: **'Mother didn't bother about Christmas – being Scotch.'** And one year Betty overheard their house-guests say, *'Well, it wasn't much of a lunch. Hope we get a decent dinner.'* They had only had cold meat for lunch!

Chapter Four
We used to – an Edwardian childhood

Jean Bethel Dawes 'Betty', was born 26 February 1901. Her birth-place was Kemsdale House in Hernhill, where her parents lived at the time, which was not far from Mount Ephraim.

WILLIE MCKEEVER: *In his local (as opposed to his business) diary, Grandfather Willie mentions walking to Boughton to enter the birth of his daughter, Betty, in February 1901. He walked to Boughton from Kemsdale where they were living. In the 'Births, Marriages and Deaths' he registered it, and put down his occupation as Ship Owner.*

She just missed being a Victorian. Here is one view of Betty, from a friend.

HUGH CURLING: *I've known her all my life. I've always insisted she hung about waiting to be born, so that they could say, 'The Queen is dead. Long live the Queen! Betty McKeever's taken over from the Queen.' Because the Queen died in early January.*

One interesting vignette of Betty's long life; she said she could remember as a very young girl, being taken to visit a very old man who had been a drummerboy on the field of Waterloo (1815)!

Betty was the middle child, with two brothers. Sandys was seven years her senior and the adored elder brother. Slotty, the youngest by three years learned to be competitive.

The family moved to Mount Ephraim from Kemsdale in 1904, following Sir Edwyn's death, when Betty was 3 years old. She was a sturdy child with long, reddish, fair hair and a great zest for life.

There were tales of a long free childhood:

Very good, I thought. Long summer days when the pony walked up and down, and the mowing machine whirred, you know. The old gardeners gardened. The birds sang and we birds-nested, wild-flower gathered, caught butterflies...
[She had a good egg collection.]

**We went butterfly collecting and birds-nesting. To be
frowned on today, I suppose. And prizes were given for
your knowledge at school. All the local things like botany
and birds, butterflies and things. So everyone took a great
interest in the country.**

There was a pony trap with a lively Javanese stallion, also an old
Welsh cob. The children drove the hot-at-hand Javanese stallion
with the old coachman up behind, ready to heave on the reins of
the governess cart.

Everyone knew everybody else and Betty did not go to school.
She careered around the village of Hernhill in a gang. **'I've been a
villager all my life, because I was educated at home, so all my friends
were the children my age, either working for my father, or friends in
the village. You see, we were bounded by the trotting of a horse.'**

**We never knew anybody in Canterbury – because of the
hills, but in Sittingbourne, that area, and Milstead – nice
level trotting.**

A very long journey would be 15 miles, that meant 30 miles that
the poor horse would have to travel.

Betty's father insisted that the men were properly addressed by
the children, always as 'Mister'.

Betty had a hand in many local projects as a youngster. She
remembered an oak tree – the children helped with burning up after
it had been felled. The oak was wedged up on blocks for the winter.
The boughs were cut up. The right-angles were put on one side for
decks and rigging on barges. Cordwood was brought down to the
house for burning.

Mr Wood, the old woodman gave Betty a sharp adze. (He was
with her grandfather, father, brother and nephew.) The following
spring he made flooring and gateposts – then the bark went to the
Tannery at Canterbury for tanning. Mr Wood and Mr Oliver were
there. The children turned the posts into shape, in hot ashes – to
make a pointed end, until the posts were hard, harder than any
wooden posts you can get now. They roasted potatoes in the hot
ashes. There were rows about the state of their boots afterwards.

**The thing I always enjoyed doing, was, they used to burn the
ends of the poles instead of tarring poles. Old Pout would do**

that and all we kids used to get up there and mothers didn't like that. My mother didn't, anyway.

You burnt the tops and the lops off the oak trees. You had these chestnut poles, you see, and you twiddled them in the hot ashes. Well you can imagine, kids went too far, and we used to take potatoes and chestnuts; put them in to roast. Then we went to get them – and burnt our shoes. But it was quite an artistic job. We never could 'point' them. Mr Wood used to come round and give them a wallop, here and there. And there was a stake point.

You know, I dug some stakes up, that I knew were in the ground for over 40 years and they hadn't rotted at all.

The other thing was clay burning. Same fire, more or less. You chucked lumps of clay into the fire and old Pout used to go round with a hammer and we kids had old garden rakes. We used to keep raking this clay until it came down to the right size it was wanted to make gravel for paths. Red clay. So there was never a dull moment.

The clay gravel was wonderful on tennis courts, drives, etc. and was very pretty.

There was a wheelwrights at the back of the Red Lion pub in Hernhill. Edward Foreman's grandfather was the wheelwright, Mr Foreman. He was a churchwarden and talked to the youngsters about behaving themselves, and religion. The children gathered up the sawdust and shavings for their rabbits.

Betty was at the wheelwrights for two weeks. Eventually she and the others were each given a bit of wood, and allowed to turn their own piece into a top on Mr Foreman's lathe. All the tools were sharp. Then the children went to the forge and were each given a nail – which was burned through the top. They could then use waxed string or bootlaces, by preference, each to whip their own top with.

Other games

Window breakers: The children, with their tops, running from Staple Street to Orchards. Smaller members of the gang in front. The biggest one would yell 'stop', and someone usually got hurt.

Bowling Hoops: Great big metal ones. The flint roads had 4 inches of mud in the winter. By May, there was a swap over and in the summer, wooden hoops were used instead – and there was 4 inches of white dust on the roads.

They made and used stilts. They also made bows and arrows. It was rather frowned upon but they still did it. All the boys and girls played together.

The blacksmith was Mr Samuel Curling. He had a long horn and bellows at the forge. Betty shod her own pony on one occasion – under instruction. She has done so since, with the leather apron.

I blew the thing to keep the fire going for so long, that when his son Horace retired, he gave me the trough where I used to douse the iron. I've got it now with plants in it. A very great treasure.

Betty's father had a building gang. So the youngsters learned how to lay bricks, mix cement and how to plaster.

The children learned about the countryside. The names of plants, flowers, trees (Betty was never very good at trees) and birds. They all collected bird's eggs, but were only allowed to take one if there were at least four in the nest. It certainly taught them the different species.

At the Potteries, good flower-pots were made as the clay was very porous. There were two potters and it was quite an industry. They made money making drainpipes. The children dug out square holes. The clay was puddled up, water was added. They raked the mixture to get the weed out. The water was drained out. They dug out the clay and threw it into a mould hole inside a building. A horse walked around mixing it, in a type of thick iron board (like a steamroller on its side). The clay was thumped out on an iron table. A lever with three or four holes, pulled the clay into different sized moulds. These had a large square of wood with wires between it. The clay was pressed through the moulds, like a chaff cutter.

The clay was chopped into 1 or 2 foot lengths for drainpipes. Tiles were made, too. Then the pipes were dusted with sand and put into kilns to be fired. The coppice wood faggots were used for the fire. Pots were made by hand on a turntable. Small basins and jugs were made for the cottages, but the clay was not fine enough for ornamental work. The Potteries were worked until World War II, when you were not allowed to light fires, because of the blackout.

A pair of working horses were kept on the estate. They did as much work as a tractor. (Joe was still there until 1939.) The waggoner would get up at four in the morning to bait his horses, then he had his own breakfast. He would be working them at six, then he went away. After dinner the waggoner would groom his horses for two hours, so they were in the most magnificent condition, and be back at work at 2 o'clock.

They would deliver feed to the other departments on the farm, and the waggoner always stole handfuls of feed, here and there, for his horses.

He would block up the draughts in the stables; and sweat up the horses to make their coats shine, until they looked terrific. Their beautiful coats were the pride of his life.

Betty learned all these different trades from the people.

Sir Edwyn's Butler, Jessup, stayed on with the family after his master died. He would beat the children when they were bad, and then tell on them, which Betty thought was awfully unjust. Jessup, who always wore white gloves, was around until 1920. He went blind.

Betty was riding from the time she could sit on a pony. She always rode side-saddle. She was 'blooded' 'B B' at Lees Court with the Tickham, when she was about 3 or 4. (This was a tradition out hunting, to smear blood from the kill on a person's cheeks on their first occasion out.)

What upset Betty's mother was she'd hunt for a bit and then her father would let her go home. So she would come trotting home on her own on her pony, at about 3 years old.

One day she was riding home. She got a bit worried because she wanted to spend a penny and she couldn't get off – side-saddle – by herself. What was worrying her was she was going to make a mess of the saddle, that really was worrying her. She met one of the farm workers and he said, *'What's the matter?'*

'Could you lift me down? Can you hold my pony?' And she jumped off.

'Do you want...'

'No, course I don't want any help.' Betty interupted, and she slid by – 3 years old. She came back and was put back on the pony and so went home quite happily.

Rook's Parliament

A very young Betty was out with her father. Father looked over the hedge. **'Let me see'** she asked.

'Quiet,' Father cautioned.

'Let me see.' Betty insisted.

'I'll lift you up but you must be very, very quiet.' Father perched her on his shoulders. *'Here, Betty, let's watch this and you'll remember it for the rest of your life.'*

They saw a very large ring of rooks, 300 – cawing. Into this ring came three crows (or large rooks) and the company fell silent.

The trio stomped across the middle of the ring. Chattering started up again, but after a while another three 'rooks' came in. The middle one was all bedraggled.

The biggest rook questioned the bedraggled one. Then the whole company of rooks fell on their bedraggled prisoner and pecked it to death!

In Betty's childhood, they used to train in the girl's waists with a bodice – laced in tight. The hips and busts of the bodice were let out twice a year from the age of 6. However, the fashions changed from when she was 10 or 11 – so then everything just went out.

Once Betty scraped or stung herself, when aged 10. An old farm-hand decided that the best treatment would be for him to pee on the injury, which he did, in the stable.

Betty found her younger brother Slotty (Lancelot) very annoying. He was his mother's spoilt little favourite 'Benjamin'. Betty was her father's favourite. All three children were very competitive. One day Betty teased Slotty mercilessly. He always had trouble with her, because there was four years between them and she took full advantage. And her father loved her. Slotty was always rather sickly. Every time he was put in boarding school, Mopsie used to bring him home, if he had a cold or anything. So he never got educated properly. Slotty was physically not as strong as Betty was. She was a strong girl and he didn't stand an earthly!

Betty teased him so badly one day, that he picked up an axe and ran after her with it. She ran straight in to her father's study. So Slotty got himself beaten for that – never forgave her!

Sandys was sent to Street Court Prep School (where he was once beaten twice in one day). He then went to Loretto, Edinburgh for a short time. Sandys got diphtheria one summer, as a teenager. He nearly died. He was packed in ice at Mount Ephraim. His temperature went up to 106°. Sandys was brought back ill from Loretto aged about 16 with pleurisy and was never sent back again.

In 1910 he was tutored by 'Humf' – Douglas Humphrey. Humf was employed to teach Sandys, who was seven years older that Betty. She would have been about 9 or 10 at the time he came. Betty was very fond of Humf.

In due course Sandys went up to Magdalene College, Cambridge.

Betty was taught by her Aunty Bee (together with Slotty and Cousin Alan Simpson) through a correspondence course PNEU (Parents National Education Union). Aunty Bee taught her to draw. Professor Francis Eeles, Curator of Ceramics at the V & A Museum used to stay at Mount Ephraim. So Betty had a good introduction into the arts.

I've been brought up strictly by the Book and I believe what it says in the Book. I believe in Adam and Eve – which I'm told other people don't today.

Slotty, Sandys & Betty

Hounds leaving the van for a days sport

Chapter Five
The Blean Beagles [1]

Betty's father, William Dawes, first hunted as a boy of 14 in Kent with a trencher-fed pack of harriers based near Hernhill Church. There was a hare-hunting tradition in East Kent and this pack was founded in 1853 by a local farmer, Merton Mercer, of Church Farm in Hernhill, who gave up in 1883. *'He was one of the old type of Kentish Yeomen farmers who might have sate as a model for Jonathan Jobling.'* wrote William Fawcett. Lord Throwley continued hunting the country, first with beagles and later with harriers.

In 1894 William Dawes founded the Blean Beagles. He hunted for three years in that same area of Hernhill, then changed to Blean Harriers in 1897, which ran until 1903. He disbanded his hounds in 1907, partly because the country was getting over-planted with fruit, and partly because he went to New Zealand for a year.

From 1904 to 1910 the country was hunted by the Badlesmere Foot Harriers.

Beagles are the smallest of the hound breeds. They are 10–16 inches tall, harriers 18–20 inches tall and foxhounds 22–27 inches. Beagles hunt hares and have been around since Elizabeth I's time. Generally the beagles were hunted on foot but a few non-runners would follow on horseback. The 'Huntsman' is in charge of the pack with a horn to blow different instructions to the hounds. The Huntsman is usually on foot and there are a couple or more 'whips' or 'whippers-in' who assist in keeping order in the field and with finding stray hounds. They need to be good runners. Hounds are always counted in couples so a pack could be anything from two couple upwards, but would generally have between 12 and 25 couple.

William Dawes returned to England in 1908. At this time he preferred the Tickham Foxhounds and became Joint-Master with Lord Harris from 1909 to 1915.

In 1909 George Alcock, a Blackmore Vale Huntsman who joined the Tickham, made friends with the young Betty when he discovered she could really blow the hunting horn. He 'blooded' her at Lees Court Park (you weren't supposed to wash it off), then he persuaded Miss Guest – who was Master of the private Inwood Beagles pack – to send Betty Dawes a couple of beagles. There was a bitch, Welcome; and Scorcher – a 'whiskery gentleman' who probably had a terrier for a sire.

Betty started hunting on the farm with beagles and terriers and Labradors, rabbiting mainly and having lots of fun.

Then, at the end of Betty's first season, her father Willie discovered he had diabetes, which in those days was a very serious illness. A whole day's fox-hunting became too much for him, and was 'a bit annoying', but with Betty scampering through the orchards with her motley pack, and obviously having a great affinity with hounds, Willie decided to re-form the Blean Beagles and make the 8-year-old Betty their Master. She was the youngest Master in the country.

When I was eight, my father gave me a pack of decent beagles, which he always hunted himself. Before that I had two old beagles that the Huntsman of the Tickham gave me, and a bobbery pack of Fox Terriers when I was between seven and eight. Then in Nineteen Hundred and Nine, I was officially made Master. I was only allowed to hunt them on high days and holidays when Father wasn't there. But, on his death in 1920, of course, I took over properly.

Her father got together some more drafts of 14-inch stud-book beagles. Gordon Epps became professional Kennel-Huntsman until 1912 and Albert Butcher and Slotty were her first whippers-in. Betty hunted them in her holidays, riding side-saddle. In 1912 her pony was Greyfriar. But her father hunted them more often, from ll am till 1 pm, riding his cob; after which his huntsman took over.

Beagles came from Halstead Place, Stoke Place, Leigh Park, Spring Hill and St Bees Kennels.

Miss Katherine Camp (who was a governess of Betty's at this time, in addition to Aunty Bee) was invaluable to the whole enterprise, acting in liaison duties, having both height and prowess as a runner. Lessons were made flexible to fit in with hunting.

Noel Watson remembers seeing a photograph of Betty sitting side-saddle on her pony, with her governess at its head and her beagles held up by a young boy, one of the gardener's sons, who whipped-in for her. All three people were dressed in matching hunt livery with the famous white collars of the Blean.

Betty learned early to take responsibility for the welfare of her hounds. She learned to stitch up her beagles when cut and had also to learn about mucking out and what to feed them.

She told a tale to Stuart Newsham of *Horse and Hound*, about William Selby-Lowndes, 'Old Selby', visiting Mount Ephraim during the summer of 1910, to judge the Tickham Puppy Show. He was the well-known eccentric Master of the East Kent Foxhounds:

STUART NEWSHAM: *On the morning of the puppy show, he shocked her nurse by stomping into Betty's room before breakfast, clad only in a bath towel.*

'Can you make a puddin' girl?'

'No, Mr Lowndes.'

'Disgraceful, call yourself a master of Hounds and you can't make a puddin'.' 'With that he stomped out past the speechless nurse, leaving a trail of drips behind him.

After breakfast the pair of them disappeared into the kennels and he gave her a practical demonstration of the mysteries of boiling up pinhead oatmeal. 'You should be able to jump on it when it's cooler. If you take a spade it must be able to stand upright in the puddin'.'

Making a pudding is a lengthy process and the pair were quite absorbed all morning, blissfully unaware that the household was searching high and low for them. Eventually they were marked to ground, Selby Lowndes was whisked off to the puppy show, but Betty had first to change her frock – it was stiff with oatmeal!

He taught me to whip-in to his hounds and improved my horn blowing. At the end of one day he said: 'if you blow a really decent 'going home' now, girl' – he always called me that – 'I'll give you my favourite horn…' I've still got it.
{1980s}

Arthur Finn's grandfather, William Colthrup, when he was young, used to go down on hunting days to look at his land at Seasalter, and on the way back home from his day's work he'd drop in with Mr Dawes's beagles or harriers – latterly of course, Betty's beagles – somewhere round Hernhill.

Ninety-four year-old Madge recently remembered that she had known some people in Hernhill in the old days – Betty's father and mother! Madge Simmons had actually been out with the beagles in the 1900s and had almost frozen to death. In true form, Betty had said, **'Oh, you'd better whip-in then,'** and told her to get on with it.

The Huntsman and whips had their own 'orders' which are set out below in an abridged form. Their whole tone ensures good hunting pracrice. Betty was acutely aware that being allowed to beagle and hunt requires good manners from the hunt. Permission from landowners and goodwill from the community were not to be taken for granted but worked on. So this is how it is done.

Blean Beagles – Code of Practice

Instructions

The huntsman and whips duties are the same in that they must avoid all damage, see that the field does no damage and if damage takes place, stop and put it right. They must ring up and apologise. They must greet their field at the meet by the removal of their hats and they must say goodnight to their field in the same manner. At all times they must greet farmers, workmen and others on the land. They must not hunt a hare if they have had occasion to handle her. They may only hunt in a garden that they know they are welcome in, or if they have been invited into same. Do not hunt in towns or villages.

Remember – you are only allowed on the land and have no right to be there.

Huntsman Is responsible for the hounds in the field. Where they go and when they whip off, etc: Since, in our case, the Master pays the damage, he must only go where he and she have agreed.

He should be alone at all times in the field. His whips should be on either side of him. He should arrange a special call on his horn for each whip to come to him if desired. He should cover his ground closely in drawing.

Nothing annoys farmers more that to have their land drawn blank when they keep hares. If he zig-zags, it enables old and very young to keep up and they all pay to hunt. If his hounds are at his heels, he should walk round behind them – at the same time encouraging them to hunt. Instruct the whips and field to whistle or call to him if a hare is found. Nothing spoils hounds more than holloaing. He should call his hounds by doubling his horn, his whips should rate hounds to him. He should lay them on and on the first sign of a whimper he should cheer, on getting a cry he should blow 'gone away' and 'forrard'.

His whips should rate hounds on or 'forrard on', according to their position. The huntsman should rate on his slack hounds. The whips should continue to run wide on either side. When hounds check, the huntsman should stand still and he should insist that everyone else does the same. The only people who should ever move at a check, are the whips, who might if wide, go forward to try and view, or to protect hounds from running into danger on a railway or road. The huntsman should leave hounds alone, in the hope of them recovering the line. By the time he is ready to cast, the hounds will have spread out and forward. If there is no indication of which way to cast, I think the best cast is back, least likely way first – and wider and slower the more probable way.

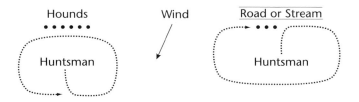

There is always a reason why hounds check – and these are a few. A good huntsman thinks them out before he moves hounds.

A change from upwind to down. Hares nearly always run to the upwind when started, to enable them to change to a safer wind if pressed. New sown manure, sheep or people over the line. Running on roads or tracks, or swimming down streams and coming out lower down.

If you think it is the latter reason you have lost, you cast forward and then round, or up and down the road. The huntsman should gather the hounds quietly for casting, and the whips should assist by turning the outside hounds.

When a hare breaks cover or is done, it is usual for the whips, or any member of the field, to 'forrard' hounds on with cap and voice, and to run on with the leaders. The huntsman doubles and cheers later rating on all hounds to the leaders. At all times, the huntsman should keep his hounds up to the leaders and if hounds divide, a whip should be sent to either continue that hunt, or whip off. Never let your leaders down, but get main pack to them or they will lose drive. Instruct whips to count hounds – at meet, during day, and at end.

Homework had to be done. Betty had to spend many hours writing letters – planning the meets, thanking the local farmers – but for whose courtesy her hounds would never have been able to hunt.

Betty was given a pack of beagles when she was young, when Aunty Bee was her governess.

How do you educate a daughter? It was decided the proper way to educate a daughter was to give her a pack of beagles. That may sound silly, but it wasn't. You see, I had to first of all, I had to have a hunt servant and see that he was properly dressed. Take him to the tailor's and have his uniform made. I then had to pay him and get the money from the estate. Then I had to see that the beagles were fed. And I had to buy the food. Do all that sort of thing. Then I had to write to all the farmers, to ask them if it was all right if I brought the beagles on to their land. And then afterwards I had to write and thank them very much for letting me come there. 'And we had a lovely day, thank you very much for having…' So you see, really, for a little girl in a hunting family, it was the most wonderful education you could give.

In the 1912 edition of *Bailey's Hunting Directory*, it was mentioned that 'Miss Betty Dawes is still Master of the Blean Beagles'!

Chapter Six
Hernhill – the old days

Betty was foremost a local person. One day, in the 1970s or 1980s, she gave a talk to the Hernhill Womens' Institute about the old days in her village. These stories are taken from the tape-recording.

Individuals

The powerful figures in the village that I remember: Mr and Mrs Adam – He was the schoolteacher. Miss Jacobs – infant teacher. Most kind but we were all scared of her. Mr Wilson Wesleyan schoolmaster in Boughton, taking Hernhill scholars. Mr Burgess Dunkirk schoolmaster. They all loomed very large, for I played with all the people in the village. So we were frightened of them.

Other powerful people were: Samuel Curling in the forge. Edward Foreman over at the wheelwrights, where we were taught to make tops and we played. Mrs Clarke's father [Mr Vinson, who lived at Kemsdale]. We moved to Mount Ephraim in 1904 to make way for Mrs Clarke.

My father and Mr Vinson took a very prominent part in the life of the village. They were both Liberals. So they didn't always get on with some of their neighbours.

Skating

Mr Vinson was a marvellous shot. I remember him teaching me on the pond at Kemsdale to skate. My father took no trouble. He put some skates on me and said, *'There's a kitchen chair. Learn to skate.'* He skated along competently and said I would never learn. I think you all skated well, didn't you, Daisy?

DAISY CLARKE: 'I didn't. My sister did.'

Yes, I think Mr Vinson taught us all. Mr Vinson took a great deal of time teaching me to skate. That was the only time I ever had a skating lesson and was very grateful for it. Not that I was ever much good.

Travel to Whitstable

But the village life was, I think, easier to run, because you had this collection of people who... couldn't get very far at all, if they didn't have a horse and cart. If they had children, the children had to walk. Old Mrs Pay took her family from the back of the forge to Seasalter, so that they could see the sea. Some of them were my age and they'd never been down to the sea. She walked the whole lot down to Seasalter [3 miles away] and back.

Other people used to take the wagonette and carry a lot of us down to Whitstable.

When Father was flush, he took us to the 'Bear and Key'. When he wasn't flush, we went to Lucy Kent's Tearooms. It's still there, along the front. It's a wooden thing. Henry Irving and Ellen Terry's signatures along the wall can be seen to this day – [the great Edwardian actor-manager and actress]. We'd have shrimp teas there. I actually rather preferred them. We used to go to Seasalter, but roughly, as children, we didn't go out of the Parish at all.

Blowing up trees

Mr Pud, lived on the right if you come up from the Dargate pub [The Dove] to the Red Road, on the right

Very often they'd grub trees – cut the tops of trees first. At the first experiment I nearly 'went West'... They had got Curtis Harvey from Faversham to blow the roots up, they charged so much an acre for blowing up the big trees. They were blowing up trees along the empty Thread Lane. There was my father, Mr David Smith and Mr Watson Smith, who were standing there by the road, as it goes down to the Potteries. They had a huge dial [Root plate]. It was up in the air. Everyone was watching the trunk and Mr Pud grabbed me up (I can feel it now) by the arms, and he threw me over his head – very brave thing to do 'cos he never stepped back; and saved me. The tree had gone about a couple of feet into the ground.

About a fortnight afterwards Mr Pud got pneumonia and he died. I always reckoned I'd never be here if it wasn't for Mr Pud. He was buried in Hernhill.

Communications in the village

I always think, looking back on it, when you hadn't got any telephones at all, it's simply extraordinary that nobody ever seemed to panic. The system worked.

So, when anything happened, you depended on local communications. I always thought it was something marvellous if somebody fell down at Waterham and broke a leg, a boy on a bicycle would appear panting with us [at Mount Ephraim] probably, and ask for what was known as a 'hospital ticket'.

Most people had a hospital box, and before that, two out-patients tickets. So the boy was sent skipping up, and old mid-wife Coombes would have been involved with this. They might have asked for the dog-cart or something, to take the person into Canterbury. But usually somebody else had organized that and it worked.

There were very few telephones. I don't know how many there would have been in the village when I was a child. We had one. Mrs Clarke, You had one at Kemsdale which was (1) or (2)?

MRS CLARKE: '(4) I think.'

We were (4) at the Mount. You had it before. You were (2), because Mother was asked to write the letter when Miss Eves [the last known telephonist] retired. It was from Kemsdale she was asked to write it. Then, at Kemsdale we were (2).

Theatre

Mr Clark, the Vicar, was always a very powerful figure – he used to run a toy symphony orchestra. The Vicar also used to run very good theatricals which were put on in the winter. But they used to put on three plays over Christmas, in there.

They used to have the village plays down in the Oast. How they made any money, I can't think. The kids paid nothing or a ha'penny if they had it. They were in a gallery along each side and there was one ladder serving two galleries. They climbed up in there and moved sideways, all the seats were in there. Of course there were those wide doors, but imagine if you'd opened them [in the event of a fire], they'd have just fanned the flames.

You went in at a narrow door – you had footlights with real candles surrounded by a little bit of tin, made on the farm. All those candles – I can never understand how they got away with that.

And that wasn't pulled down – the stage and everything – the Army commandeered it in the Second World War.

So we weren't that dull.

Holidays

Christmas was a Holy Day, not a holiday, and Boxing Day – somehow or other – didn't make any impression. We went hunting and we always went hunting, so it was just normal.

Whit-Monday was a real holiday. It certainly was a holiday for the people on the land. We used to have walking races from Mount Ephraim, right around the village past Sluts Hole (you probably call it something different now!) [Oakwell] and up the back drive.

We had a greasy pole over the lake. Father had a young pig. My mother wouldn't have that, and there was an awful row. She said they could have something but they weren't to have the pig. It sat in the basket. The first [contenders] tried to swim, and went along the greasy pole to try to get the pig.

And the fighting on parallel bars, all very bucolic. Much more rough than it is now. They sat hitting each other with cornsacks filled with pretty heavy stuff. There were generally a few casualties on the whip round.

I seem to remember one occasion when the whole village had a feed in Mountfield which was empty. It was certainly a great time with singing. At about 9 o'clock, the old gardener at the Mount, who was Scottish, got up to sing in a quaverous voice: *'Scotland that ne'er was conquered.'*

That went on about an hour! That wasn't a great success. I don't think it was ever repeated! But certainly, the idea that the village was dull is all wrong.'

Trades and industry

I think that there was more amusement – and industry – in the village then, than there is now.

It's very sad when you think we had a forge at Dargate, a forge in Hernhill. We had a forge at Graveney. I think there were two if not three forges at Boughton.

We had a wheelwrights up here. We had one in Boughton. We had three or four builders in Boughton.

There were two potters: My father's – Boughton Marsh, and there was Hounds Pottery. The Potteries weren't given up until the Second World War. We couldn't black-out the furnace things – the drying furnaces.

We had two brickfields beyond Waterham, employing quite a lot of people, down on the road to Graveney – just over the railway bridge. They made bricks there when I first went to Waterham in 1930. There were two active brickfields...

We also had a beautiful tailor at the end of the Second World War in Boughton, Mr Capon. I don't think anybody went with their clothes anywhere else.

We had a bootmaker, Mr Davies. We had wonderful shops. Mr Fierer's Empororim.

There were at least three butchers in Boughton. One was Mr Gamblon. When he used to come and run the dances in the Oast, I always felt exactly as if I were going to be slaughtered. Because he always started 'March and Lancers' with me as his partner. He walked up to you, just as if he were going to the Abattoir, until he collected eight people. The dances were terrific. Other local butchers were Mr Colegate, Mr Miles, the Staplestreet butcher and Mr Wise – quite recently.

Cricket

Now, you have a lot of rubbish talked about village life. Anybody who could play cricket well enough for the Dawes Institute,* used to get off from their work.

Remember, working on the land (most people were employed on the land, in those days) they worked 12 hours a day. Sometime in my late teens, it came down to 10 hours [a day] in winter, 12 in summer and that included Saturdays.

A Saturday-half-holidays didn't come in till 1920, though I think Mrs Clarke's father, Mr Vinson, and mine were both extremely unpopular, because they gave a Saturday half-holiday from 1 o'clock. They were taboo by the Conservative members. Something to do with their Liberalism. Oh, there was some hot feeling about that.

If a man was working on quite a small farm the farmer might let that man off, if the man was wicket-keeping, or a good fielder; or a good bat for the village – for village matches. And they used to play.

After my people left Kemsdale, they never really had a good ground. It was up at the front of the Mount and it was never very good, but never-the-less, it used to take place.

There used to be luncheons for the visiting teams and themselves, put on by Mrs Miles from the Mill in Boughton. Jolly good they were, too. I used to eat the crust off the game pies and things, at the back with the other children.

But everybody congregated to tea there. Then the following Saturday they all went orf with waggonettes and dog-carts – the men of the party – to wherever they were playing. There was tremendous interest in that. It was probably Belmont or up at Sittingbourne. They didn't go very far, you see.

* The Dawes Institute is a working man's club started by Betty's father at the Manor House, Hernhill, at the turn of the century.

Chapter Seven
Migration to Scotland

England got too hot in the summer, so for several months every year (possibly from as much as July to October) the Dawes family migrated to Scotland. To Swordanes, the house Willie and Mopsie had bought, situated on the links near Banff.

They were able to hire a family railway carriage. This would be joined on to the end of the scheduled trains. The whole family, with all their servants, dogs and plenty of chattels as well, would proceed north in it.

First, the coach would be attached to the train at Faversham for the journey to London. It would then be uncoupled and shunted round the sidings and pulled by horse through a tunnel under the Thames towards Holborn – to King's Cross. An old horse used to pull the coach across London to Euston or Kings Cross. But it was such a nice old horse, it all took rather a long time, and it was all very exciting. They always took a basket of cherries, to feed the horse on the way across. Betty once went on the horse-drawn trek, but usually the family enjoyed a sojourn in London for the day, at Queen Anne's Mansions and so her father and everybody else would get in. And the dogs were put underneath the coach – in a purpose-built kennel.

The next attachment on the journey north, was to the Scottish train.

Mopsie used to go up with her old dog, her shooting dog, whom she adored. The train used to stop at Crewe – for half an hour, or something like that. Mopsie had woken up, and it was a nice Autumn evening, and so, she was strolling along by the Scots train there, when: *'Suddenly'*, she said, *'I saw the Guard come swinging along, he stopped and whistled and said, "Come on, you"*. Mopsie stopped and looked around and said *'I know that dog,'* and it was her own!

'All this business of 'Must be on leads – muzzled and everything'. There was the Guard, walking up the train with my dog, off the lead, and he just turned around and whistled.'

She said, *'Who's dog's that?'*

'OOOh! This dog's an old friend. Been travelling up to Scotland at this time of year for years and years and years.' He said *'I can't bear it to be on its lead. I have half an hour. So we go for a walk together – down to the pub, or one of the houses. We spend half an hour there, having supper and things. The old dog sits, stays with me. Then we walks back together. Hmm, very nice old dog. I just whistle and it comes to me.'*

'Don't you realize,' Mopsie said, *'that is a very, very highly trained and very expensive shooting dog?'*

He said *'I didn't. Jest a friend of mine.'* With a wag of the tail from the dog, back the Guard went. Mopsie was so shocked! All this business of insurance and everything.

On arrival in Aberdeen, the family usually had breakfast in the Aberdeen Tea-room. Whilst this was going on, the family coach was transferred on to the end of the coastal train for Inverness. This went as far as Tillynaught where it was detached. And then on to the small line from Tillynaught to Banff, where it was put behind the train always known as the 'Coffee Pot'.

On arrival at the Brig Foot Halt beside the Boyndie Distillery – the family dismounted and walked the hundred yards to Swordanes. The coach was then towed the same distance again, until it halted and was uncoupled from the 'Coffee Pot' on the track, which was exactly between the house and the garden at Swordanes. Then an intense period of unloading occurred, with luggage being slid down the bank on a shute into the garden.

Meanwhile, the train completed its journey to Banff and by the time of its return, three or four hours later, the coach was unloaded and the charter was over.

One year Mopsie lost all her rings on the train. They were assumed to have been stolen and the Insurance replaced them.

The following year, travelling in the same family coach; before she slept at night, Mopsie put her rings on to the ring holder, which was velvet covered and finger-shaped. The next morning she put on her new rings, then more. The old rings were on her fingers as well as the new ones! They had sat there the whole year, despite intensive searching at the time of the loss!

Chapter Eight
Shooting

Betty was a first-class shot. Shooting has always been part of the fabric of her life. The Edwardian heyday into which she was born had the enjoyment of sport as the business of life.

> **Started shooting 1914. With a single barrel 28. 1 don't know if I'd have got started if the war hadn't been on. My father thought – better start. I was always walking along with the beaters and shooting, rather than sitting in butts and having the birds driven over.**

Betty shot with ferrets after rabbits. **'Shot pigeon here and in Scotland.'**

She remembers shooting a pheasant 6 foot above a keeper's head and was not, afterwards, allowed near a gun for the next year – aged about 12. She had shot much too dangerously close. Her father said she had to beat instead. Betty had a smock for beating in. It was very thick and suitable for tramping through undergrowth and brambles.

> **1915 I was 14. I was shooting partridges and pheasants 'cos all the men were away for the war. So I got a lot of grouse driving in Scotland, which suited me very well because it took place at a time when I was free. 12th August to, say, about the end of September. Then I came home to beagle. I never shot many pheasants, because I was always hunting. Shot a few partridges in my time, but most of my shooting was grouse – and snipe in Ireland.**

When she was being taught to shoot, the youngsters were never allowed to leave a wounded bird. **'It stopped children shooting too far.'** If you wounded a bird, you would have to stop shooting, spend half the day searching for the bird, then put it out of it's misery. Otherwise it would infect the stock. This stopped bad habits developing.

Record Day 1917

My brother-in-law, Andrew Mineyko had read in a sporting book that two national records were established in 1917 at Gordon Castle on Speyside.

1 One gun – spaniels chasing rabbits – 127 shot.
2 Lady Amy Coats – Largest salmon ever caught on line – 74 lbs.

So Aunt Betty told us this story one day in 1978 at her kitchen table in Waterham, as she was eating her breakfast of porridge at 12.30.

In 1917 when Betty was 16 she was staying at Swordanes, Banff. A day's shooting was planned some miles to the west, where the old bed of the River Spey was infested with rabbits, just over the bridge from Gordon Castle.

Betty's father was not keen to go, so Betty went with her friend Joan Sayer, Slotty, then 13 and a cousin, Alan Simpson, 16. They used the sort of cartridges you reload with powder and cap, 16 bore and 12 bore. Another gun turned up, the Hon John Cubitt, bringing his spaniel.

Isaac Sharp, the dog dealer at Keith came with dogs and ferrets to get the rabbits up. There were now thirteen spaniels, some of which were Betty's. Then two keepers came up with eight more dogs, then one more keeper.

All the guns shot. Alan got a bloody nose from the gun and Slotty was silent, having hurt his finger on the trigger-guard, so they retired. The Hon John shot his spaniel. He also 'carried on' with Miss Sharp. At 12.30 they stopped for lunch.

Over the bridge came a man in a bath chair. It was the old Duke of Richmond and Gordon. He exclaimed *'Only the quean* [Scots word for girl] *still shooting! Girl shooting – boys not! How many?'* They counted 114 rabbits. (The Duke knew of Betty's left-handed descent from the 4th Duke of Gordon and his gamekeepers's daughter!)

The Duke asked if they had ferrets there?

'They're in their holes,' answered the keeper, and Betty continued shooting.

So there was the keeper assembled with the spaniels, ferrets, Joan Sayer and Betty. Betty had shot 127 rabbits! The gun was wafer-thin afterwards.

The Duke's granddaughter, Lady Amy Coats, a young girl recently married, appeared in a boat with an old keeper who was unable to use the oars as his hands were occupied with bailing, and he was busy shouting instructions to Lady Amy who had hooked a salmon.

The keeper climbed into the water in a hurry to land the salmon, but he started coughing and wheezing as he had been gassed in France during the war. He was 6 foot 2 inches tall, like all the Gordons. Joan Sayer pulled him out backwards not forwards – to keep his lungs from further damage.

'Take the rope,' gasped the keeper. 'Tell her – get below the fish.'

The salmon towed Lady Amy's boat half a mile down river, with Betty and Joan dashing down the river bank to stay level. Betty got hold of the gaff, ready for action.

Lady Amy. 'What do I do?'

The keeper came up after them, wheezing hard. 'Don't gaffe it yet.'

So Betty made two half hitches of rope. She was still in the water, and she roped the salmon as it was too heavy for the keeper to manage.

Lady Amy suggested they should cut some off to lighten it.

'No,' said the keeper. 'It's a record.' Between them all they managed to land the salmon without cutting it. The keeper was right as the salmon weighed 74 lbs.

Lady Amy asked the girls to come and change at Gordon Castle, but Betty said, **'Better get the ferrets'**. Sharp, the dog dealer was furious, as he had been kept waiting, but he caught the ferrets and they went home.

Humf 'after eight days in the trenches'

Chapter Nine
The Humf letters

After Betty had died as a very old lady, a packet of 35 letters was discovered in her bedroom, kept in an old brown leather wallet. They were all from 'Humf'. Betty had spoken of Humf occasionally. His photograph lived on a table beside the fireplace in her sitting room but no one knew about the letters.

In these letters, we first meet Humf in 1910, aged 22. He tutored Sandys after his illness at Loretto and before he went to Magdalene, Cambridge and also did some bear-leading of Sandys in Paris later. Humf had joined his county regiment, the Oxfordshire and Buckinghamshire Light Infantry in 1912. There was a training commitment of one month a year – with plenty of polo.

Over the winter of 1912–13, Humf was tutor to young Prince Vladimir Galitsin at Gotchina, in Russia. In 1914 he tutored the son of Count de Salis KCMG, in Switzerland, until the outbreak of war, then was called up to serve as a Special Reserve Officer as the Germans invaded Belgium.

Douglas Herbert Washington Humfrey, nicknamed 'Humf', was born in April 1888 a younger son of the Rector of a Northamptonshire village called Thorpe Mandeville, near Banbury. Humf had his degree and was tutoring before entering the Church and following his father's footsteps.

Humf moved amongst the gentry, having the education, skills, interests and manners to make him acceptable to people from Clonmell in Ireland to St Petersburg; from the stables of Mount Ephraim to those of the Czar of Russia. And as with all his generation he was an assiduous letter-writer. Humf wrote as easily from his sickbed at the Sitwell's as from his billet on the Western Front. Betty wrote well too, so there emerged a considerable corre- spondence between the young girl and her brother's former tutor. She was 9 years old at the start of the correspondence and only 14 at the end.

This selection from Betty's leather wallet comprises the first and last letters, with a sample letter or postcard from each era of Humf's dramatically changing circumstances.

England

24.XII.10 from Thorpe Mandeville, Banbury.

Dear Betty

Ladies first! But I forget, do suffragettes count? Anyway I will write to you first to thank you very very much for the nicest of presents – just the one thing I was sadly wanting. I am going to christen it on Monday.

I expect we shall have great jokes to-night. I have got that ink bottle & false blot trick to play on one brother especially who thinks he is good at scoring off us. I bet I have him. Well, give my best wishes to everybody – don't forget Katharine. Again many thanks for the crop. Best love to yourself and the beagles

Yours affectionately
Douglas Humph

P.S. Don't give 'Miss Milligan' too bad a time.

This letter is addressed to Miss Betty Dawes, Swordanes, Banff, N.B. (North Britain, with nice George V Penny Red stamp). It was written from Renishaw Hall in Derbyshire, the country home of the Sitwell family. Sacheverell Sitwell (Dame Edith's brother) was fifteen years old and Humf's pupil.

August 12th 1912

My dear Betty

Like the Conservative win at Manchester yesterday your letter came as rare and refreshing fruit. That's rather a good beginning of mine but don't let Dad see it. As I have plenty of time I will try and write you a long letter. I am in bed, having been ordered by the doctor to stay in bed for two days. I was out riding on Wednesday, and what we think was a gad-fly stung me just below the right eye. As I did not get home for an hour I suppose the poison circulated. my eye got bunged up and my right cheek & glands swelled.

I have seen two doctors & they've put me on bread & milk (and no beer).

The worst of it is that I feel fit as a fiddle with an appetite almost as large as Baba used to have at Sunday afternoon tea time. The swelling has almost gone down and I hope to be about

& play cricket here tomorrow. You ask me if I got your last letter.
(Lady Ida Sitwell has just been in to see me and interrupted me.)
Are you having any of the Kent young ladies to stay up in
Banff this time. Anyway, they won't have me as chaperone going
South as Woggie had – lucky girl! Now I will tell you a few things
about myself, what I have been doing and what I am hoping to do.
I finished my training at Aldershot at the end of June. (At the same
time I shaved off my moustachis [sic]) I was very sorry to leave &
I made a lot of new friends there. In July I passed my exam on the
work. I now have to do one month every year which will always
be very pleasant for it means three things (i) work (ii) good pay
(iii) 3 days polo a week, as I have the luck to be in Earl
Fitzwilliam's company.

After training I went home and practically did nothing but
play cricket for a month. I then went and stayed in Shropshire for
a week with Edward Rouse-Boughton and I saw his beagles for the
first time. He has 11 couple – mostly 13 inch. He got first prize
at Peterborough for the best couple in a novice class. He has got
together quite a good pack considering the short time.

From Shropshire I came here a week ago to act as companion
for a month and perhaps more during his holidays to Sir George
Sitwells's son [Sacheverell] who is at Eton. Baronets, like flies,
seem rather fond of me.

The same day as I left one, Sir William Boughton, to come to
this one I received two wires – one from Sir Miles Stapleton asking
me for cricket and a ball at Henley, the other from Sir Offley
Wakeman asking me to two dances in Shropshire. Stapleton is
younger than myself and an officer in the Oxfords. I came here
through Mr Halford Dawes. Mrs Halford being a great friend of
Lady Ida.

This is an enormous place. They have also a castle in Italy
and another home in Scarborough. They do not go in for sport at
all. I am very glad I accepted as a lady staying here thinks she can
for certain get me a tutorship in St Petersburg to the son of Prince
Golitzine: the Prince is Master of the Czar's Hunt and a great big-
wig at Court. I do hope I get it. If I do I will go there in October &
not return till about June so I will try & come & see you once more
at the Mount, if I may before I go. It is nearly post-time and I
expect you are getting 'bored stiff' with my rambling letter. I think
this is pretty good writing considering I am only sitting up in bed.

I wish I had my old banjo in bed with me. Do you remember Jessie Marsh playing in my bedroom at the Mount? Mary used to come in and could not speak for giggling.

Tell uncle Chivvy that the cleek which I never paid him for is a topper. Have you had a golf competition yet. I played with you last year and you would not do a single thing I told you to.

Well, give my love to everyone I know, Uncle Tom, Cousin Lilian, Angus, Geordie, Jacko, Katharine, Alick, Auntie Bee, Mrs Tom, Aunt Ann, Mr & Mrs Dawes – Everybody

Best love to yourself
from your old friend

Douglas H W Humf

Russia

It was 100 years after Napoleon's invasion and all was serene on the surface.

Humf became tutor to Prince Vladimir, the son of HH Prince Galitzen, for minimally six months. His address was c/o HH Prince Galitzen. Imperial Hunt (La Chasse Imperiale), Gotchina, St Petersburg. He visited Moscow and saw an exhibition of relics of Napoleon's invasion of 1812.

Postcard to *'Miss Dawes M.B.B', Mount Ephraim'.*

25 October 1912

I bought this card in Moscow on Sunday at an exhibition of relics of Napoleon's invasion in 1812. You would have liked to see it. I expect you will frame this portrait. The above is my address now for 6 months. We started here on Sunday and it took 24 hours. We drive about in sledges with 3 horses. Troika – I have almost persuaded the Prince to let me bring back some beagles next year for him to start a pack near Moscow. There are 100 horses in the stables here & packs of foxhounds, borzois (wolfhounds) for wolves, & bear hounds. Five of us went out fox shooting on Monday, we saw three & got one. Going St Petersburg on Sunday.

Love from Humf.

Switzerland

Humf finished his six-month job at Gotchina. He took up his next post in Switzerland, tutoring for the son of the Count de Salis, British Minister to Montenegro.

1 March 1914: Postcard to Betty at Mt Ephraim, from Hotel Julierhof, St Moritz, Camfer, Switzerland. Title: Ski kjoring (horse tows you along on skis).

We are up here at St Moritz for a short time to do & try to do the silly things the best people do at these sort of places. To-day is Sunday so this afternoon we are going to do a little quiet skijoring as shown on this card. We had a glorious 18 mi. drive here right over the mountains. I have got some stamps for you & will soon have some Montenegrin ones from the Count for you. I might go out there myself sometime. Humf.

The start of The Great War

The Germans invaded Belgium and so Britain declared war on Germany on 4th August, 1914. This letter, written from Switzerland, was postmarked 3rd and 11th August.

Letter from c/o Count de Salis KCMG, Bondo, Promontogno, Grisons, Switzerland. 3 August 1914. Postmarks – 3 August and 11 August 1914.

My dear young Betty
Why do you always call me old Humf?
It is awfully kind of you to write from time to time and tell me all the news which always interests me so much. You must however have forgotten the photo of Mrs Dawes & my old pupil 'Earl's Hill'. I think thats a much more aristocratic name than 'Bracken' for such a noble beast. Please send me the photo later. If it is true Mrs Dawes has been offered £200 then my mind's at rest because even if for any reason he proved unsatisfactory I will not have been the cause of Mrs Dawes losing money over him. he first day I saw him, I suggested to Mr Armitage he was just the stamp to make £300 some day. Over Tipperary country he never did wrong and I pushed him hard my last few hunts. Nobody ever

rode him but myself. Has Mrs Dawes ever thought of showing him. He took a Second at Clonmel, entered at the last minute in dirty bad condition. Bracken is 5 yrs 3 mths now. When he arrived I felt a little anxious as to whether she was quite quite hopeful.

Horsedealing is a very dangerous pastime but I quite purpose to do a little of it when settled at Thorpe Mandeville but I shall never be like one of my future parishioners, a sporting farmer, who doesn't mind sticking his greatest friend.

I should like to have been at your puppy show again. I suppose Sandys chose Boney as his mount because the great Boney was the best character of modern days at raising the wind. If I come to England at all before the 22nd it will not be to shoot pheasants but to pot fat Germans. I am expecting to receive a wire every moment, if not to join the regiment, to get away from this dangerous area. Things are a little more quiet today since Italy has declared she will be neutral.[1 August 1914] *We are on the frontier. Switzerland has called up all her soldiers. The village is almost empty of men. The last go away to-morrow. It's a very sad state of things. All food has gone up 25%. The harvest is almost ready to gather. Mills are shut down. From the mill here the father and three sons have had to go. Two daughters are left to manage every thing. Their two draught-horses have been commandeered by the government. Every family in the village is practically robbed of its wage earners because they all have to serve. Some of the older chaps do look like brigands in their uniforms. Of course Switzerland only has to defend her frontiers against foreign intru-sion otherwise she is neutral. Every horse in the countryside has been taken up and how on earth I shall get 18 mis [miles] to St Moritz station if called away I do not know. I quite expect to footslog it.*

The Count who is in Montenegro as British Minister is in the middle of the conflagration out there. I am as hard as nails & fit for anything in the fighting line. Hope you have a nice time in Banff. Remember me to all my old acquaintances. I would love to play yours and Slottie's best balls. [cricket].

Best love to you all from old Humf.

Within a month Humf had re-joined the Oxfordshire &
Buckinghamshire Light Infantry and was in Belgium. His
father told Betty he was at St Nazare, France on 6 September.
He reached the front via Antwerp and Brussels. Humf was
wounded at Langemark near Ypres on 23 October 1914 and
came ashore at Plymouth, to recuperate at Portsmouth. He
stayed in England for three months.

Postcard to 'Miss Betty Dawes, Mount Ephraim, Faversham, Kent.'

Royal Naval Hospital
Plymouth 31.X.14

Dear Betty

*Don't be alarmed if you see my name in Monday's casualty list.
I only got a bullet thro' my leg & the wound has almost healed but
the muscle won't let me put my leg down yet. I rather hope to leave
this place on Monday either for home or for some private hospital
or home in London where I can get massage. We had some awful
hard fighting in Belgium last week & lost a lot of officers. I lost
all the things I was carrying such as sword, overcoat, burbery,
revolver etc. I only got myself & men out of a trench just a few
seconds before a huge shell fell in it & smothered the whole trench
& I expect my things are now reposing under 10 ft of soil & a tree.
When I got my wound we were going at the Deutchers with the
bayonet but they turned back as they always do when we **** at
them. It is nice and quiet here which is good for my nerves. Queen
Amelie of Portugal shook hands with me in Boulogne on Monday.
I am wearing a pair of Queen Alexandra's pyjamas given me by
the hospital.*

Love to all Humf.

Letter 2.I.15. 3/Oxf & Bucks LI, Cambridge Barracks, Portsmouth

My dear Betty

I received your very useful and most sensible present last Tuesday when I returned from home after my four days leave. I lost my last pair of wire cutters as you know & had not yet got another pair. I had no nice case for my last ones & used to tie them to my belt with a spare bootlace. They are awfully useful things in a country like Belgium which is very enclosed and every hedge is barbed. One afternoon I managed to cut through a hedge with mine & pushed my men through instead of having to send them round through an exposed gap on which the Germans had trained a machine gun. And that night I cut out a lot of wire and had it placed as entanglement in front of our trench to stop any surprise charges.

Did I ever tell you that the French who took over that trench from us the night I was hit said they picked up 640 corpses in front of it next morning. The Germans luckily did not attack my company that night more than that once but went right across our front to attack the regiment on our right.

We could only just see them & hear them in the darkness & I made my men fire into them by volleys as they crossed a road but we never thought we did such good work as we did.

I must congratulate you on downing a snipe. I would like to take you out as a sniper to pick off their officers. I hope Hodder & Stoughton sent you a book all right which I ordered from them in town for you.

I have also spent most of to-day in bed as my chest is still sore from the inoculation. I am going to be all right tomorrow in order to go over the 'Queen Elizabeth' in the afternoon. Most of the 'Audacious' crew are on here.

We have our noses kept pretty close to the grindstone here. I & another officer are going to be bold enough to ask the colonel whether we cannot occasionally have a hunt when the hounds are near by. One or two of our transport horses are quite good class. It is very hard indeed to get away for a night but if perchance I can get away first thing on a Saturday morning till Sunday night I will send you a wire as you say you would like to come down again before I go out. We send about sixty men out from here to the front every Sunday. We have 200 standing by for the next draft.

Sometimes a regiment wants men and not officers & sometimes vice versa. So it happens that officers from another regiment take our men out occasionally. I expect by now you and Slottie speak French awfully well.

Love from Humf

Humf returned to his regiment in France at the end of January 1915. He served with the 2nd Battalion (52nd of Foot) at Neuve Chapelle in the aftermath of the British Expeditionary Force's first planned attack on the Germans. The dangers of war and the steady exchange of letters made them very close.

In another letter he wrote, *'I believe if you can hunt beagles success-fully, you can lead men'.* Proving that he and Betty were very much soulmates.

May 1915. Last letter in packet.

15.V.15

My dear Betty

I will write you a few lines not knowing when the next opportu-nity may occur because as you gather we are in the midst of rapid times just now.

Many thanks for your letter. You come about next to my Mother in the matter of keeping me well supplied with correspon-dence & interesting details from England. I expect by now you have seen my letter to Slotty. I have no extra news to tell you excepting bits that I must not tell you as they would make you dream at night most horribly.

We are in a nasty quarter just now. We came out of the most uninviting trenches on Wednesday and have since lived in the only house in this village that we can find with a roof. It has no doors or windows.

Excuse bad writing but Mother is making an awful noise & makes me jump out of my skin every two minutes. She is just outside the garden, 9.2 round the waist and 100 lbs. in weight.

I have come to the conclusion I don't like war. We all attended an open air communion service this morning in an orchard. The Bishop of Khartoum took it. You could hardly hear his voice for the

noise of ours and the enemies guns. It was like being in a snow
storm as the blossom was all shaken down by the shocks.

I was very amused to hear about Hubert & his expanding ser-
vices. What an old pig Bracken must be. I am afraid I shall get no
tennis this year & do not expect to see England again till next year
unless the Germans give me a passport.

Did old Madam get rhumatics again when you went to dinner
or did you manage to retain your hot bottle this time.

I find a tot of rhum is much better than hot bottles but don't
you try it unless in the open at midnight.

I must now end. I may have a lot to tell you next time I write.

Best love to all

From Humf

Humf was doing his duty but could admit, in the close confidence
of the correspondence, that he was beginning not to like war.

The family story was that Humf had been killed in 1917, but it
is not too difficult to discover when an officer was killed. The War
Graves Commission lists that Humf was posted as 'missing, believed
killed in action, on 16 May 1915'. Possibly he was killed the very
same night that he wrote this last letter. Humf was 27. His name
is inscribed on the Monument to the Missing at Le Touret, not far
from Neuve Chapelle, Northern France. With the snowstorm of
blossom shaking down on him by 'Mother' firing outside his billet,
and the reply of the enemy guns, this was the end.

Chapter ten
The Great War – and after

Sandys went up to Magdalene College, Cambridge in the Autumn of 1912. He got a half-blue for hockey and a half-blue for long jump, his best jump being 19 foot 7 inches. Humf, at one stage, had been quite keen on Joan Selby, the doctor's daughter. But her mother said, *'Don't take any notice of the tutor, it's the pupil you want to watch!'*

By the age of 12, Betty could fish trout, blow a hunting horn and was a game shot. Having had an exciting childhood, roaring around the village, she probably had somewhat lonely teenage years. Of course, with all the chaps away, she did get more shooting and sport. But Slotty and Alan Simpson were both several years younger than her and Sandys was away. Her mother hunted a great deal. The local families Betty could mix with, would have been the Sondes family at Lees Court and Lord and Lady Harris's at Belmont. Both, old sporting families, but a few miles away.

During the war, on one occasion, Betty had incurred her father's wrath. She was being punished by being left behind on a shooting day. But she and Joan Sayer went out on their own and came back weighted down with game!

When the scoutmaster was called up, Betty took over the local Scout Troop. She was not adverse to girls being included. Today this is normal, but in those days it was unheard of.

Aunty Bee Simpson lost an admirer in the war. So, like many other women of that time, she remained unmarried for life.

Sandys went to fight in Egypt with the East Kent Yeomanry. He was present at the first Battle of Gaza – the one that didn't work. Then he got covered in boils and suffered with a carbuncle on his forehead. He got leave to come home and get married. The carbuncle burst, leaving a star-shaped scar, but he got better straight away.

Sandys married Joan Selby, on l August 1917. She came from Teynham, just beyond Faversham. The 16-year-old Betty was brides-maid. Joan and Betty got on well, with field-sports as a common interest. They remained good friends all their lives.

After being re-graded medically as 'C', Sandys spent the rest of the war in this country, as a re-mount officer at Sandwich.

Sandwich

During World War I, after Sandys had been invalided home after
Egypt, he and the other officers had to appear with their horses on
parade near Dover. And because he was just about to go hunting,
his horse was all got up and ready for that. So someone said, *'Don't
worry, I've got a couple of mules!'* So he and his particular friend, Frank
Playford, each had a mule to go on parade with.

The Commanding Officer, Colonel Lushington looked at this
and said, *'Um, we're going to have an Exercise today,'* – which involved
jumping. The officers all set off with their beautiful thoroughbreds.
Anyway, one or two of these mettlesome horses refused the jump.
But the mules both managed to jump it – cat fashion – and made
some of the thoroughbred horses look none too good.

Bill's christening

At the age of 18, Betty became godmother to her nephew Bill, son of
Sandys and Joan. Her fellow godparents were two very distinguished
American Generals.

Some twenty years earlier, Sir Edwyn had got in touch with an
American branch of the Dawes family. The two branches had not
actually met on the family tree since 1620, so the cousinship was
slight. The American and English families did not actually meet
up until the end of the Great War, when Sandys and Joan asked
General Charles Gates Dawes to be one of Bill's godfathers. The
other was General John Joseph Pershing, Commander-in-Chief
of the American forces in Europe.

The date was Thursday, 26 June 1919 and Bill was christened
Charles Ambrose William Dawes – (the 'Ambrose' was for the Dawes
who had emigrated to America in 1620) in St Michael's Church,
Hernhill.

General Pershing had brought his 6-year-old son Warren
with him. The General's wife and three daughters had been killed
in a fire in San Francisco, but the Dawes family believed they had
been killed in an Indian raid (could this be the version Warren told
Betty?) The little boy went everywhere with his father (who could
not bear parting from him) so Warren was present at the christening, and at the lunch afterwards.

Mopsie always thought Betty unintelligent, apparently because Betty had a high pain threshold. So when the talk turned to politics Betty was asked to keep Warren occupied which she did by playing trains with him under the lunch table. She therefore heard the seeds of the Dawes Plan being hammered out over her head. The Dawes Plan was the scheme which was designed to enable Germany to meet its post-war reparations bill and was introduced in 1924.

General Dawes* presented Bill with a gold cup weighing 1 lb. *'Is that really gold?'* he was asked.

'It better be gold,' he replied, *'I've paid for $2000 worth of gold.'* He had collected *'all the gold in Paris'* and had it melted down.

Visiting America

This was to be the one venture in Betty's life beyond the confines of the British Isles. She didn't hold with going abroad. America was all right though – they were our Colonies!

She went to America in 1919, when her father was still alive. She was there for nine months – and one of the reasons was that there was great talk that she might marry one of the Americans.

Betty had travelled to America on her own. She sailed from Liverpool, in some sort of ocean – passenger-carrying vessel (of some 200 or 300 passengers and freight) the RMS *Megantic*. There were icebergs off Newfoundland. She saw the Heights of Abraham and St Peter's Isle in the St Lawrence on her way and got off at Quebec. And then caught the train from there.

She stayed mainly in Chicago and told wonderful stories about her stay, because she was passed round the various cousins – American Dawes cousins. But the ones she had most affinity with were Uncle Beman Dawes (the General's brother, who had been present at Bill's christening) and Aunt Bertha. Now Aunt Bertha was very matronly and did not like opera. Beman was in the American Pure Oil Co and he owned quite a bit of it. He made his money in railways and planted the Dawes Arboretum. Of course, every businessman in those days, travelled the various States by railway car. Beman wasn't supposed to drink too much, because he was very

* General Dawes was Vice-President of the USA 1928–29

handy at lifting his elbow. He also liked playing cards. He used to play poker, in the saloons in these railway trains, with other businessmen. And Aunt Bertha said that, *'Betty should go with Beman and ride and learn the history of the States as they go through.'* Betty said that the reason Bertha sent her with him, was that it kept Beman on the wagon. They went to Florida, St Augustine, various parts of Ohio and Illinois and they were based about 16 or 18 miles out of the city centre of Chicago. She met her extremely distant cousins Carlos, Gates and Curtis Dawes.

On her travels Betty visited Columbus and Dayton, Ohio. She went to Pike Lake, Fiffield, where they were shooting deer in the snow. She also went to Evanston, Lake Michigan, St Augustine and the Mantangas River with an inlet to the Atlantic.

Betty met an elderly woman who removed her wig to show that she had been scalped by Indians.

Then Betty proceeded on to Miami and went shooting 'gaters in the Everglades of Florida.

Betty sailed from New York on her return. She was sent for, because her father was very ill. She was only in America for 8 or 9 months. Whilst in New York she bought a wedding present (a little late) for Sandys and Joan. Twelve teaspoons from Tiffanys – a different English wild flower shaped each handle. Betty came back in time. She was definitely 'the favourite' daughter.

Willie Dawes's health had been deteriorating but he refused to see a doctor. Mopsie had to use a subterfuge. She left him, as if by chance, in the same room with a certain Lord Dawson of Penn who was King George V's doctor. Lord Dawson diagnosed diabetes, which Willie's father Sir Edwyn had suffered from too.

Willie continued designing and planting his gardens even during the World War I.

When his illness worsened, Betty curtailed her trip and hurried home before her father expired. The Mount Ephraim Flower Show happened biennially. One year at Nash Court then one at Mount Ephraim. In 1920 it was held at the Mount on 15 July with a Pastoral Play. William Charles Dawes died on 20 July.

WILLIE MCKEEVER: *Diabetes, in the days before insulin, had to be well regulated, and Willie had to watch what he did. He got a stomach upset for some reason or other, in June or July, which turned to peritonitis and he was dead in a week.*

Chapter eleven
Sharing out the Mount Ephraim Estate – 1920

Willie Dawes's death was fairly unexpected and sudden. He was aged 55.

Financial planning from the tax point of view, was not something that had been thought of in those days.

Slotty was a minor, then aged 16, and Betty at 19 was under-age too. In the Dawes family, the girls didn't inherit their capital until they were 35 (to ward off any money-grabbing young men).

The boys inherited their capital aged 25, so Sandys, who was now 26 was just old enough to inherit.

Half the Mount Ephraim estate had been 'entailed' by Sir Edwyn, and went directly to Sandys: Mount Ephraim, Mount Farm, Orchards, Crockham Farm, Denstroude Farm and The Bounds – (bought from auction by Bryants in the 1930s)

Also Tower Wood, Thread Wood, Pottery Bank Wood, Dargate Plantation, Clay Hill (250–300 acres) and Mountfield where Sandys lived from his marriage in 1917 until 1925. There was a house, a walled garden and a pony paddock.

Sir Edwyn had set up an entail. (Later, in the 1940s, Sandys and his son Bill broke the entail, much to the fury of Grannie Mopsie and Betty.)

The unentailed portion of the Mount Ephraim estate and the 'London business' were both eligible for death duties.

At this black moment, Lord Inchcape (who sat firmly in the power seat of Gray Dawes now, and had a big say in Westrays) was going to *'walk all over the Dawes family'*.

After the death of Willie Dawes, his widow Mopsie took Sandys by the scruff of the neck, went up to the office of Lord Inchcape and said, *'You will employ my son. He is fatherless.'* And he did. The story is that they had a rare old ding-dong-doo.

MOPSIE: *You needn't pull the wool over my eyes because your grandfather came out of the gutter, out of the back streets of Glasgow,* [he was from Arbroath] *and my grandfather was a Distiller to the Duke of Fife.*

There was a rare old battle – and he gave in.

Very wisely the executor had said, *'We must preserve the London business* [Westrays] *at all costs.'* This would continue to provide employment for Betty's two brothers and their sons, in time to come. Sandys and Slotty both had jobs as shipbrokers to the New Zealand Shipping Co. London was where the family money was made.

The executor continued, *'Therefore, in order to settle the Death Duty bill, we ought to sell the unentailed portion of the estate.'*

A very nice glossy catalogue was drawn up by Ivo Neame, the local land agent and one of the Mayfair agents, like 'Knight Frank & Rutley'. Rather a good, full-sized catalogue, listing a number of lots.

For sale were Church Farm, Monkshill Farm, Brookhill Farm, Brook Farm, Waterham Farm, Parsonage Farm (including Klondike). There were numerous cottages and other bits of property.

At the auction – very few things sold. Only Church Farm, Parsonage Farm, Brook Farm and some cottages.

Then the auctioneers sent a tidy bill for running the auction and preparing the catalogue.

Drawn out of a hat

Mopsie, by now widowed, and being very Scots, stomped with her walking stick, and said that she *'was being taken for a ride by a lot of bloody estate agents!'* Then she added, *'We will sort out the children's inheritance.'* Mopsie proceeded to cut up all the unsold lots out of the catalogue, and put all the chopped up lots into a bowler hat, and set it on the billiard table at Mount Ephraim.

A visitor who was there at that time, assisted with this 'share out' – rather like a game of rummy.

The estate was parcelled out into farms, houses, farming land, woods, marshland.

The visitor who oversaw the 'share-out', didn't really realize the great significance of this event, this game of chance; that this action would shape the future pattern of the Dawes's lives, and decide the fate of the land.

Mopsie, Betty and Slotty were allowed two pulls out of the hat to Sandys's one, as he had the entailed estate already.

Slotty had 30 or 40 acre of marsh at Graveney, Seasalter and the Black Dairy, some cash (not in auction) and 24½% Westray shares. (not in auction). He later bought Malmains in 1929.

Mopsie had Thread Cottage; which was left to her (Mopsie later left it to grandson John). Thread Orchard and woodland, also Scab's Acre. A bit of Pudding Lane, some marshes at Seasalter, Bridge Wood (which she left to Betty in 1953), Dargate Common, Holly Hill (which she farmed – then left it to grandson George Dawes who sold it to his cousin John Dawes in 1961).

Sandys had Monks Hill, some 'Pylons' bits of Courtenay and 24½% of the Westray shares.

Betty had Waterham, 30 or 40 of acres marsh at Graveney, Chestnuts and another piece of 'Pylon' fields. Betty's land at Waterham was let to a tenant, Albert Butcher, for the next 10 years, but it was a big incentive for her to remain in Hernhill.

Chapter Twelve
The twenties

Lucy Dawes's funeral

In April 1921, Sandys and Betty went to their grandmother's funeral, accompanied also by Joan.

Lucy Dawes, née Bagnall was buried in Bath, where she had retired to for the last 17 years of her life as Sir Edwyn's widow. The Bagnall family hadn't been terribly happy about the fact that old Lady Dawes had been left only her bedroom furniture by Sir Edwyn.

Sandys and Joan were in a different vehicle from Betty in the funeral procession. Betty, in a strange town, was left stranded and alone on the pavement, as a frightened 20-year-old girl, by the angry Bagnall family.

This occasion had other angry vibes too. Feelings still ran high between Willie Dawes's brothers and the Mount Ephraim Daweses. Betty didn't know a lot about her father's brothers and sisters.

They had all gone to the funeral in Bath and Betty said it was very fraught, because it was the first time that the two halves of the Dawes family had really met up (apart from Bethel), since the alleged horse-whipping episode, over the house that never was – on the Courtenay Road. (See Betty's Early Stories.)

Betty's parents had a flat in Queen Anne Mansions in London. They kept it until about 1930. It had a warm-air grating in the courtyard. Betty would stay up there and was 'finished' with the famous dance teacher, Mme Vacani, who taught in Victoria Street and who used to admonish her student teacher. *'Miss Smith! You have a ladder in your stocking. It's no good having a ladder in your stocking. There's nobody going to climb up it!'*

Betty would come up to London with Sandys, after a day's hunting, and as there was a hairdresser down in the basement of Queen Anne Mansions, she would go to be 'frizzed' (as she put it) and primped, and then go dancing.

Betty had brought back from America the latest in modern flapper dresses which had no sleeves. This was considered very shocking and not the done thing at all!

She was quite a gay young thing – by all accounts – at the equivalent of raves nowadays. She spoke of the flappers and said that everyone was banting or slimming, but Betty herself wasn't.

Friends of that period were Geoffrey Slazenger and Golly Gardner (female), who went to South Africa later.

Betty remembered dancing on the frozen lake of Chilston Park, near Maidstone – by the light of car headlights.

The social strata was very, very clearly defined in those days. You knew your place in it. Betty struck up an acquaintance with a woman from a different class whilst exercising a dog. She was invited around for tea. Betty went to tea with her fairly often, until it was discovered that the woman was a high-class courtesan!

Geoffrey Gilpin used to partner Betty at London parties. Returning to the Bath Club (where Sandys stayed), the doorkeeper would fall asleep. So Betty would lift the flap of the letterbox, and Geoffrey Gilpin would wake the porter up, using a pea-shooter – to hit him on the nose! Another escort, Arthur Dalgety, was not such a good shot.

Geoffrey Gilpin

WILLIE MCKEEVER: *Geoffrey Gilpin was one of Mother's old flames – and would have married her. I often talked to Geoffrey. He said, 'I would have loved to, really loved to have married your dear Mother, and I proposed to her frequently, but Sandys wouldn't have it.' Neither would Mopsie, because he was Catholic.*

He was a great friend of Father's, who knew him well and was one of his cronies. Father introduced him to me after the War.

Geoffrey's father was Roman Catholic and a trainer at Newmarket. All the boys were brought up Catholic and the girls as Protestants [like their mother].

Geoffrey went to sea – at the age of twelve, in a Windjammer. Took his 1st Mate's Ticket in Sail. He had no fear of the sea because he was born with a caul on his head as a baby. Which means – there's a superstition – that if you're born with a caul and you keep it then you'll never drown. And he had it round his neck on a piece of string for his whole life, I gather. And that's how he managed to get through all his sea-faring days.

Stopped off in Australia in about 1908 or '10. He jumped ship and went up into Queensland. He and another chap. And they took a tract of Queensland – you rented Queensland in those days. The tract was 5 miles by 4. They got a string of horses and went up to their claim. Just a tract of open bush, or closed forest. And the first thing you did, according to Geoffrey, was you felled the trees of the open forest, to make a post-and-rail fence around the property. And you lived on kangaroo skins. Because they shot kangaroos. Then you'd go down to the city with probably a dozen or so of horses, one behind the other, every three or six months. You'd have a month and you would paint the place red and remove all the tiles, and also sell your kangaroo skins. You would come back with enough provisions, after a good old binge. And then, about six months later, your partner would do the same thing. Play high jinks at the coast.

When the '14 War was declared, they took their string of horses, 25 between them. Went down and joined the Australian Light Horse; taking their horses with them for the government. They kept the best horses to ride themselves.

They were shipped off to Egypt. Now the Aussies, I gather, were no respecters of persons. And he was with English Aussies – Protestant.

His descriptions of the Australian Light Horse in Cairo; I gather they got on to the rice wine (or whatever they have in Egypt); and they took Cairo to pieces and got into the hareem of the Khedive.

The [authorities] had to sent one of the English line regiments, the Dorset Regiment or something, to restore law and order and get the Australians out! Whole battalions of them got in the hareem! Shots were fired. There was a hell of a job getting them out! And they thought they'd better get them out of the way, quick.

So the Australians were all moved out when the Gallipoli Campaign started, and promptly shipped off through Cairo to Gallipoli, in very smart order, because they'd caused such havoc in Cairo. Geoffrey was a trooper – one of the ones taking Cairo to pieces. He said it was great fun. Oh dear me, yes!

Now, there was problems with mines, in the Dardenelles at that time. And Geoffrey had got a 1st Mate's Ticket in Steam (he'd passed all the exams before he had jumped ship). So they took him out of the Australian Light Horse and put him in command of a minesweeper.

While all his friends were getting their throats cut by the Turks, Geoffrey was puffing up and down the Dardenelles opposite – clearing the mines for the supply ships – 1915/16. That's what saved his life. Stayed in the Navy until he got demobbed. He was brought back this way [through Kent] *as a sailor rather than as a soldier. So that was his '14 War.*

Came back, never [at that stage] *went back to Australia. He went up to Newmarket to his family. They also lived at Dunstable. He was a bit of a playboy I think. Gambling on the horses.*

He was a'courting with Mother, I gather, quite strongly in the mid '20s. He told us he was definitely going to marry Mother, but Mopsie wouldn't have it.

I can remember him coming to stay at Waterham in the mid '30s. He was a friend of Father's. [Betty gave the crucifix Geoffrey had given her to Kate Mineyko, her Catholic great-great-niece, in 1985 as a Christening present.]

In the end, he married a Canadian girl and they had two daughters. He later lived in Ireland, after she died. He wasn't Irish, he was English. His father trained Pretty Polly, the well-known filly that won The Oaks – in 1922 or '23. And Geoffrey had a bronze model statue of Pretty Polly, standing in the hall of his flat in Dublin. He was latterly fairly blind having put his eyes out chopping sticks, and died 1972/73. The McKeevers were buried in Mount Jerome not far from Geoffrey Gilpin.

I met him several times. I was very fond of Geoffrey – a great character. Mind you, swear like a trooper. Every other word was a b. or an f.

Betty hunted in the 1920s as much as six days a week, sometimes. She went out with her beagles, also with the staghounds, foxhounds and harriers.

A great feat of hers was being able to pee from the side-saddle! To remount her horse after getting off was much more difficult.

Sandys was Master of the Tickham Foxhounds for the 1921/22 season. Then in 1927 he became Master of the Mid-Kent Staghounds, hunting carted deer. Betty would follow John Dalgety's line, often in the opposite direction to the rest of the field, but always ending up with the hounds. All her hunting experiences had been in Kent, except for half a season in Yorkshire with her father.

Originally the Mid-Kent hunted horned stags but because they kept getting the antlers snagged in the bines of the Kentish hop-gardens, the stags were polled. More latterly they hunted hinds which gave a better run but were always called 'stags'. All the stags had names. One of the most famous of these was called 'Kale Hill' after the place where a historic hunt started.

Betty rode in Ladies' Races at the local Point-to-Points – side-saddle of course. She also later, rode in some in Ireland.

In one Point-to-Point Betty was in a photo-finish for second place. She was taught by a doctor to 'lean forward' and then 'lean back' whilst jumping.

One day at the Mid-Kent Staghounds Point-to-Point (in the days before Ladies' Races) there was one race when Sandys finished first, Slotty second, Knowles third and Betty fourth.

Knowles said, *'I didn't know I was breaking up the family. I would have slowed up!'*

There was a Point-to-Point picture of three lady riders which Betty produced one day to explain her 'forward' riding seat: the photograph showed Betty in the middle, Ivy Dawes (a wonderful horsewoman) and Daisy Walker. There they were, going over one of the steeper jumps. A photographer was sitting under the jump, taking pictures of them as they came down. So the horses were landing steeply, and there is Ivy, leaning well back, there is Daisy, leaning well back. But there is Betty, riding side-saddle – right forward!

Yes, you see. The whole point is, the first footage a horse takes, after a jump, it jumps down like that. And as it lands on it's feet, it brings its hind legs down, and the first movement after going over the jump – is up!

BARBARA AMOS: *His Honour was a young horse. Betty entered him for the Mid-Kent. Because Daisy Walker was also riding in it and riding side-saddle, they made us carry a terrific weight. I agreed to ride the horse if somebody agreed to carry my weight cloth* [from the horse's back to be 'weighed in' after the race].

*Betty said, '**No problem**'. So I rode this horse. A very very nice horse but very very green. Somehow we won it and Daisy was second. Betty was absolutely thrilled because it put the value of the horse up immensely.*

Sandys also became Deputy Master and Deputy Huntsman of the Ashford Valley Foxhounds. Later on he was Master to the Romney Marsh Harriers..

Hunting with the Mid-Kent Staghounds – sometimes the field consisted of Sandys and Betty alone, at the end of a long day. *'So there's only you and me, Betsy-Jane,'* he would say.

Sandys and his wife Joan lived at Mountfield – just across the road from the front gate of Mount Ephraim. They had two sons: Bill, whose christening in 1919 had been so memorable, and John my father, born in 1924.

Mopsie, with Betty and Slotty, stayed on at Mount Ephraim until 1925. Mopsie then purchased Berkeley, which was half-way up the steep Boughton Hill on the Canterbury road.

Berkeley was a rambling house in 30 acres, with two pairs of cottages and a single Coachman's cottage for Bill Friend, also some grottoes. Mopsie and Betty moved in. During her six years there, Betty described it as the only time in her life that she didn't live in Hernhill Parish, they were in Dunkirk! The house was built on unstable clay. It stayed in the family until the 1950s. (Later, after it was sold – when one could shake hands through the wall between the library and the dining-room – the decision was made to demolish Berkeley.)

Sandys, Joan, and their two boys Bill and John, left Mountfield and moved into Mount Ephraim.

Berkeley gazed down on Mount Ephraim, from three-quarters of a mile away. Mopsie kept a telescope – just outside her bedroom on the landing – which was trained on the Mount.

One day, Mopsie saw heavy saddlery or some such thing, being loaded into a box which belonged to her – probably plywood – strapped on to the luggage carrier, on the boot of her son Sandys car.

Mopsie complained to Sandys, that the saddles were too heavy to be put into 'her' box. The atmosphere became ferocious! And the front door of Mount Ephraim was closed, and never used again in Sandys's lifetime! This happened in about 1930. To this day, the front door is used but rarely.

While living at Berkeley, Betty once drove down Detling Hill and discovered she had no brakes. She made it to the bottom and took the car to Rootes Garage. They said to her mother, *'Well, you know what young girls are.'* They sent the car back saying that it was perfectly all right. So Betty drove out again. She went down Detling Hill and again discovered she still had no brakes. Someone else investigated and concluded that, yes, she had no brakes, and that Rootes had completely failed to sort out the braking system on the car. Betty had been driving around with no brakes, and, as she put it, **'only by the Grace of God.'**

Slotty went to Cambridge and thought the time wasting and drinking there was dreadful. He was horrified and said no child of his would ever go there. (At Slotty's funeral it was said that he went to Loretto for only a fortnight and to Cambridge also, just for a fortnight!)

Sandys was a terrible example of how not to work and enjoy your life – at Cambridge. He did absolutely Sweet Fanny Adams – but he did get a half-blue at hockey.

Sandys and Slotty worked in the City between the wars.

JOHN DAWES: *They went into 'Westrays'. Sandys, after he got out of the Army. I think it was a little bit of a shaky start when my grandfather, Willie died in 1920, but my father, Sandys kept it going.*

He'd manage to hunt 4 or 5 days a week, his regime was: He hunted Monday. Left the hunting field at 4 o'clock and arrived in the office just in time to sign the odd cheque. Was in the office all day Tuesday. Put in an appearance Wednesday morning – before going down to hunt with the Staghounds, meeting at 12 o'clock. So that he had an hour in the office, first. Stayed down that night [in Kent]. *Hunted Thursday. Did the same act of going up Thursday night. Was in the office Friday, and came back Friday night. And he hunted the Staghounds on Saturday.*

He was Chairman of Westrays, but a Director of The New Zealand Shipping Co. and never active in it, other than as a Board Member.

A great deal of Sandys's business, was done with business colleagues from the back of a horse or in the Bath Club.

Slotty was more active. He had been privately educated, and joined the firm in 1925 or '27.

Slotty had more of the Adam ancestry in his make-up. He was more of a businessman. But if he invested his money in something, Betty and Sandys put their money into something else.

St Michael's Church, Hernhill

In the 1920s, there was a blazing row with Hernhill Church and the powers-that-be about the Dawes Chapel. The Dawes brass memorial plate is still on the wall. It is now used as a little Vestry.

The Chapel had a set of six chairs, which came from Netherdale on the Deveron in Banff. They are made of birchwood with wicker-work backs and seats. The six chairs came out of the Chapel because the Archbishop, or one of the Vicars, didn't consider that the Chapel had been properly consecrated. So it wasn't to be a Family Chapel any more. Mopsie determined (Willie McKeever remembers her as being very determined) – that she would clear everything out of the Chapel! The chairs went up to Berkeley and Betty inherited them on Mopsie's death. The chairs are still in the dining-room at Waterham.

Mopsie and Betty moved church. Willie was christened and his mother and father were married in Dunkirk Church.

One of the big advantages of having land in Dunkirk parish, was that there was no tithe. This was because the parish was created by Queen Victoria, after the Courtenay* riots in 1838. She was horrified to think that there were heathens in this part of Kent. They created Dunkirk parish, exempted it from tithes and so the church was built, a Victorian church. (It has since been sold and is a private residence now.)

There being no tithe in Dunkirk, it was therefore a good place to farm, although the land was diabolical. (The tithe was as much a burden in those days as business rates would be today.)

---

* Courtenay was a fellow named John Thoms who claimed he was the Messiah and styled himself Sir William Courtenay. He was a Cornishman who caused havoc and rebellion amongst the locals of East Kent, especially up in the Blean. On 31 May 1838, he, plus eight followers were shot under the Crooked Oak, during the Battle of Bossenden Woods. Our last English Civil War. Queen Victoria built the church to tame the Blean Savages.

Chapter Thirteen
Blean Beagles [2]

During the Great War, Willie Dawes had decided to have a dog-hound pack only. In 1915 he disposed of nearly all the bitches.

After his death in 1920, there were doubts in the family as to whether they could still keep the Blean Beagles going. **'A private pack. Mother couldn't afford to keep it on.'** The Mayor of Faversham came to the rescue and said the beagles must be kept going. He was Mr Evan Jenkins, a keen beagle-follower and the local chemist at Market Place, Faversham. He said that the hounds were a local amenity, and begged the grieving Betty to keep the pack going. Councillor Jenkins became Chairman of the new Subscription Pack – in the 1921/22 season.

The two remaining brood-bitches were sent to highly accredited sires, and these formed a level 14-inch high pack.

Betty early learned the importance of good public relations with the farmers and landowners whose land she hunted over.

The Blean Beagles now hunted twice a week in the hunting season, and did so for the next 70 years (except during wartime) as is described in the Blean Beagle's Code of Practice in chapter five.

Betty took her pack out, riding side-saddle and carrying the horn. The Hunt staff and followers were mostly on foot. If the hounds checked, she would not cast until the first runners came up.

Hugh Curling, who still beagles, remembers being blooded with the Blean on Boxing Day in 1923.

ELIZABETH CURLING [Hugh's sister]: *Perry Court, where I lived. There was a field up there near the Waterworks called the Pug Hole. Pug means clay – very heavy. We used to beagle as children. My memory was always of seeing Mrs Dawes [Mopsie] in full hunting gear. Top hat, veil, side-saddle and habit. Very well mounted. Going across those hills – and Betty, far less well mounted, and certainly less well-dressed – a couple of paces behind.*

She was always good with the young. Hugh Curling walked from Perry Court by Faversham to Selling for one Beagle Meet. **'I must get**

you a lift home', Betty told him. Sure enough, when the time came, Hugh found himself perched behind Hugh Filmer, who was driving back to Faversham in his horse-drawn cart. Hugh Filmer was the local undertaker and young Hugh Curling was sitting on a coffin!

Hugh's cousin, Barbara Amos also remembered her kindness.

BARBARA: *My first meeting with Betty was when the beagles were heard on Gosmere – where my father farmed. I was about ten and I'd got my first pony. My father said, 'Go and join them. ' I didn't want to go at all. I was much too nervous about the whole thing. However, he said, 'Go on.' So I got my pony and rode across the fields. Half way towards where Betty was, the pony decided to roll. I thought it was dying! But it got up and I scraped the mud off and got on, and, feeling terribly ashamed of my condition, I met Betty, who of course, couldn't have been kinder or more helpful. And from then on I was a regular follower of the beagles.*

She taught me so much about hunting. I used to feel very important, because I used to open gates for her. She would say **'Go and turn those hounds, Barbara.'** *And I'd tear off on my pony. I really had a very happy relationship with her.*

I stayed close to Betty. She was remarkably good with children and young people, even then. Totally without any 'side'.

To get to a meet, Betty's hunter would be harnessed up to pull the dog cart full of beagles. The Tapir, harnessed to the beagle cart, went like a rocket. He would then have the side-saddle put on, do a day's hunting with Betty riding him, then return home the same way, pulling the cart.

Harry Butler, who had whipped-in for the Tickham, became Kennel Huntsman for the Blean Beagles in 1926. Effective blowing on the hunting horn eluded him, but he had a beautiful voice.

Breeding beagles had always interested Betty. She tried for fairly big-boned beasts with sloping shoulders, and her 'type' continued right through her lifetime. Her beagles had short backs, powerful quarters and a more 'flexy' pastern. The later hounds looked very similar to pictures of the early ones. **'If they haven't the quarters to push themselves along they tire quickly – it's difficult to find the type.'**

'The type always suited the country, so there's little point in changing it.' She built up her pack to 17½ couple.

Harry Butler's keenness to show the hounds, led to success on the flags at the Peterborough Harrier and Beagle Show, between the wars. (Nowadays Peterborough is run in conjuction with The East of England Show.)

In 1987 Betty told *Country Life* of her long series of successes with Harry Butler at Peterborough – as early as 1921. 'That was with Romulus in the Unentered Doghound Class. His litter brother was named Remus; their foster-mother was a cat.'

Blean Ballyboy won the Unentered Class at Peterborough in 1928 and 1930. Later he won the Doghound Championship. In 1928 the cup was presented by the Prince of Wales, whose brother, Prince Henry had on occasions followed the Blean Beagles with some of his soldiers from the Cavalry Depot at Canterbury.

WILLIE MCKEEVER: *They also did very well breeding hounds. Won the Prince of Wales Cup [EdwardVIII] in 1929/30 at Peterborough, a perpetual cup for a year, and had a wonderful party with Aunty Bee's old Trojan Hound Van.*

Sandys, her and Harry Butler – coming back from Peterborough. They parked the old Trojan at the Savoy Hotel, the hounds at the back. Carted out the Prince of Wales Cup, had dinner at the Savoy, with a bottle of Champagne provided by Sandys. There was umpteen others turned up as well – his London friends – to drink to the health of the beagles, out of the Prince of Wales Cup. Because they'd won it at Peterborough.

Other dog winners there in those days, were Conqueror, Rollicker, Schoolboy, and the brood-bitch Speedy. Other beagles mentioned by name. The dogs: Carnival, Ganymede, Gladiator, Gazer, Javelin, Radical and Juggler. The bitches: Dahlia, Gratitude, Goodness, Welcome, Goddess, Countess, Saucy, Ruddock and Speedy.

Her sideboard and shelves groaned with the weight of numerous silver trophies won on the flags of Ardingly and Peterborough etc. Her beagles became so popular that they commanded very high prices and being a good businessman, Betty took full advantage of this fact and regularly sold her puppies extremely well. This upset the 1930s Pundits of the 'Master of Beagles & Harriers Association' and the Blean Beagles were struck off the regular Register. (It's against the MBHA and the MFHA to sell hounds, they can only be drafted to other packs.) This didn't worry Betty in the least, the Blean Beagles were her private pack and she carried on as normal.

'Pasture, plough, hop-gardens and woodland go to make up the [Blean] country, while there is much grass marshland near the sea' wrote William Fawcett, in a booklet published by The Hunts Association in 1939. 'Here are found the strong marshland hares which give so many good runs. It was [with] two of these hares that the Blean made hunting history in 1914 and 1932. Both hares were killed in the sea after long and famous hunts. The marshland hares are strong and hardy customers.'

Betty became an expert in the welfare of hounds and was always consulted by other Hunts.

When Betty moved to Waterham on marriage in 1931, her kennels were opposite her house, and very much part of life.

A good friend of the Dawes family was Joan Sayer, who was born in 1899, the last of five sisters. Her parents wanted a son so much, that she almost fitted the bill. Unfortunately not quite, as Pett Place, their estate in Kent, was entailed to the nearest male relative, her cousin Gerald Sayer. After her father died, the family moved to Claremount, Charing Hill.

Joan was keen on running and very fleet of foot, winning many races, and never being beaten at Foot Point-to-Points around the South of England. She was very attached to horses and other animals – cats and dogs. She hunted with the Mid-Kent and beagled. Joan was the greatest beagler. She whipped-in from 1922 to 1940, and was the first proper whipper-in. She and Helen Bouch were honorary Joint-Secretaries also. Joan stayed on as Joint-Secretary until 1980, and followed the beagles every week until her death in 1993. She never married and later on lived in a Nissen hut in the village of Egerton, called Brisenden Bungalow.

The very first Blean Beagles' Point-to-Point Betty organized on horseback in 1925.

> BARBARA AMOS: *I was then aged seventeen and found it an extremely stiff course. The first obstacle was a spar-fence which your horse had to clamber over, you couldn't get through. It was a very tall spar-wood fence. Then we were across farmland and right out into the marshes. It was three miles and at the end I was absolutely dead. I couldn't possibly jump the dyke, so I just went*

into it, climbed out and it finished up-hill on plough. It was very very gruelling. I won it! But a cousin of mine went in. He was exactly my age and he went in to the men's race. At the end of it he said, 'This course is totally unsuitable for any woman!' But it was a great success.

Mignon Allan is shown in a photograph on foot at this period, jumping a huge dyke on the marshes in a beagling race.

Roy Carr whipped-in in 1926. Peter Goodwin was whipper-in after 1936. Peter beagled for the seasons of 1937, 1938 and the first half of 1939.

PETER: *A day spent with Betty in the hunting field was always full of interest. If hounds were hunting then Betty's knowledge of hares, where and how they would run, was phenomenal. Betty knew hares and knew her countryside. If, on the other hand, a hare was not put up, Betty would walk her mount quietly along the hedgerow, pointing out things of interest. She had a very good and wide knowledge of nature, especially local, as well as many other subjects. At the same time, Betty was always interested to know what you thought.*

Betty knew every field, hedgerow, gate and farm track for miles around, for she had spent a lifetime covering them. She knew just where she could take her horse or need to leave hunting to the whips. Betty also knew every farmer and farm-worker. Miles from home, she would stop and speak with someone who was perhaps, repairing a hedge. She would know his name and most probably the names of his family, would remember that when talking to him perhaps some year or two back, that his mother had not been very well and so would ask after her present health. Betty's memory was excellent.

When Betty first invited me to carry whip: Harry Butler was the 'first whip' with Joan Sayer, Helen Bouch and myself supporting. When he could find the time, Stuart Boult would also be in the field with us.

The Butler family lived first at The Lodge, Mount Ephraim. Harry's younger son, Joe Butler was born there (Betty always claimed to have been present at his birth.) The family then moved to the cottage opposite Waterham.

JOE BUTLER: *Hunting was a way of life, with horses as well. My father used to look after the horses – the hunting horses. Paddy next door was with them and they brought* [the horses] *up.*

A hard old life for m' father, 'cos he used to have to come back, after they'd finished hunting; do the horses, probably feed the pigs and so on (took 2 or 3 hours). He'd come indoors and he'd be on his knees. I remember Mum used to say at times, that she thought Mrs McKeever saw more of my father than what she did, herself. Times were hard then – a different sort of world.

Sadly, Harry Butler died in 1938, after twelve marvellous years with the Blean Beagles. Joe started working on the farm in 1942, but he didn't look after the beagles much.

JOE: *See, my father used to look after 'em. Mrs McKeever did try at times to get me interested in the beagles but I never was. I would feed 'em and went out with them once or twice, and done things with 'em, but I never took it up. She kept trying to get me to, but it never appealed to me.*

Joe's elder brother, Jim, who was born in 1919, became Betty's next kennelman.

Betty surrounded by hounds

Boulty

Stuart Boult who was born in 1912, was a good runner and remembers hunting between the wars.

BOULTY: *I whipped for the Blean Beagles for about 5 years. I first started whipping for them when I came down here, which was before the War when I was just on 20,* [about 1932] *Betty said,* **'Nice to see you young man, who are you?'** *So I introduced myself. Of course, being her, she gave me my own name, rather than some fancy name, like Bill or Billy. She, with respect, called me* **'Boulty'**, *in the Scots way.*

Luckily, I had a job with a haulage company down in Ramsgate. The man who ran it, actually did it to use his money, because he was very well off, and he had a yacht. So he used me all the summer, to help him with his yacht, and as it was a haulage company, the summer was our busiest time. In the winter, we did the builders, things like that, but it wasn't essential. So when he said to me some time about having a holiday, I said, 'Well, you know, it would be silly of me to go and leave a holiday area, to go somewhere else. I'd much rather take a holiday of one day or two days a week going beagling.

And I did, for the best part of 5 or 6 years, twice a week, Wednesdays and Saturdays. It was lovely, you see.

Quite formal – beagling before the war. I ran, but if it was a nasty long ploughed field or something, Betty would give me her stirrup, or if it was up-hills and things like that, she used to give me a hand and put me up behind on Lucky, an absolute pet of a horse. Then we'd all go back, wherever we were hunting from, and have tea at some very nice house.

One was tired after running from 12 o'clock in the morning, and Betty would just expect me to stay. **'I've put you in the Little Hell'** *the room opposite the piggery – just automatically.*

I used to write up to the 'Horse and Hounds' with a report, and I would sign it 'White Boots' a Nom de plume.

I was amateur – like my father. My father whipped to the West Norfolk. Of course, in those days, we hadn't got motorcars. We lived at Herne Bay. Betty would come and have supper with us.

Betty used to shake hands with everybody. And she said **'No, this is. I'm the servant. All these people come to watch my beagles. I'm having to show them the sport. I'm having to**

ask them to come. I'm having to ask them to pay, you see.
So everybody has to be treated with respect.'

*I used to have to dress properly, but Betty always turned herself
out like a member of the gentry.*

*The Meets were very much local ones. We never went very
far. The marshes at Graveney were great favourites. You could go
which ever way you liked from the top of the hill there. And the
old people would stand on top of the hill and watch, all round the
marsh. So we did a lot of meets up at Graveney. And then there
were the social meets. Went as far as Chilham, down there. Two
farms on that road. One was a lovely farmhouse and the other
was in Chilham valley. We used to meet down there and have
tea about twice a year.*

*On the Faversham Road towards Ashford, there were lots of
mostly roadside meets – very seldom Pub meets. Sometimes we
went up as far as Wingham, but it was nearly always the marshes.
And the lovely land from there to Ashford to the top, to the hill
by the Canterbury road. In those days people didn't worry about
horse-boxes much. As it was walkers and motorcars, it was the
side of the road, or a farm, and park the cars all round the farm.
We had the hound-van.*

*I remember Betty rescuing a horse from a bog and having to get
into the bog alongside the horse to get the ropes underneath!*

Harry Butler

BOULTY: *At Hernhill Church, I'll always remember burying Harry
Butler. We were all very sad about that. His sons were nice lads.
My brother was at New College as an undergraduate and as a
graduate, at Oxford. Soon after he had taken over as secretary of
their Beagles my brother said that their huntsman asked and said,
'You know anything about beagling, Mr Boult?'*

*'Oh yes', my brother said, 'I know a lot about beagling. I used
to hunt down in Kent with the Blean Beagles.'*

'Oh yes, their huntsman was a man called Harry Butler.'

*My brother used to say to me. 'It was awful. I stood there
whilst the most awful leer came over the face of this huntsman.'*

*'Ah ha!' he said, 'I know Harry!' But my brother could never
get out of him what he knew about Harry. But obviously Harry was*

*a character! But all these old huntsmen, who used to be there,
knew very well. Harry Butler was a lovely man.*

*I remember Harry's funeral, when the Tickham turned up, and
the Stag turned up and they blew him away.*

Harry Butler with Betty

Chapter Fourteen
Early Betty stories

The Edgar's dining-room chairs

Betty told this family story to show the history of a set of six dining-room chairs which we – Colin and Anne Edgar – had inherited. They are beautiful balloon-backed nineteenth-century chairs and have been handed down the family, through the generations:

Mopsie's parents, who both came from Banff, were James Simpson, a whisky distiller and a farmer, and Harriet Adam.

Harriet's father was Thomas Adam who was the son of a shoemaker of 34 Bridge Street, Banff. He left school at 11, and went straight into the Bank – the North of Scotland Bank. At the age of 28 he came back to Banff.

He entered the North of Scotland & Clydesdale as a messenger boy – was back in County Town of Banff as manager of Bank. He became chairman of the Bank, and was first chairman of North of Scotland Railway and Provost of Banff.

Thomas Adam lived at Bowie Bank (pronounced Boy) which was three or four miles to the south of Banff. He lived until 1893 and never drove. Thomas Adam married a wife 4 years older, a 'Miss Birnie'.

The old boy her father was called Richard Birnie. He was a saddler, also a good actor. He was sent to London on subscription, then he joined the firm Macintosh & Story – saddlers in the Strand.

Birnie designed the 'pelisse uniform' for hussars, used before World War I.

He became a card-playing pal of George IV (Prinny), when he was the Prince of Wales. Birnie was a good revolver shot, too.

Richard Birnie became the first private detective for a Royal. When Prinny became King, he knighted his pal as Sir Richard Birnie.

The Knights of England

'Knight's Bachelors – 1821 Sept 17
Richard BIRNIE, chief magistrate at Bow Street.'
[At Carlton House.]

Sir Richard became Recorder of Bow Street. When elderly Sir Richard Birnie married Miss Story, she was the age of Betty's grandmother. They had two daughters, the Miss Birnies – who used to stay at Colleonard, the Simpson's house. In 1878 the two Miss Birnies went on a walking tour, from John O'Groats to Inverness.

Pre his London days, Birnie 'got' a daughter. She was also called Miss Birnie. The girl was kept by her mother, Ella Gordon. (Ella was a natural daughter of the 4th Duke of Gordon by Maggie Wishart, his Gamekeeper's daughter.)

Ella Gordon had a cottage at Gaveney Brae, which is now Banff Golf Course. Richard Birnie visited her one day – and found a child with no shoes and stockings and the mother 'carrying on' with sailors. Birnie picked up his child and walked back to Banff, where the girl was put to live with the Hon Mrs Abercrombie – who had lost her husband at Trafalgar. Her son Harry, was the same age as the 'littlie's' age, no more. Birnie paid the Hon Mrs Abercrombie to have Mary brought up. Mary (or Mary Anne) Birnie did 'the Season' but there was the problem of whom could she marry? An illegitimate girl whose mother was illegitimate also, but who was brought up as a lady. So she was married to Thomas Adam when he returned to Banff as the Bank Manager in 1832.

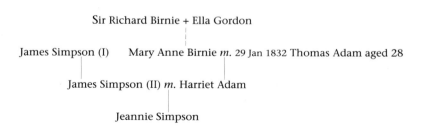

Sir Richard Birnie + Ella Gordon

James Simpson (I)   Mary Anne Birnie *m.* 29 Jan 1832 Thomas Adam aged 28

James Simpson (II) *m.* Harriet Adam

Jeannie Simpson

Thomas and Mary Anne Adam had five children, one of whom was named Harriet.

Harriet Adam married James Simpson of Gillymill and later of Colleonard. Colleonard was a tenanted farm of the Duke of Fife.

James Simpson II's grandfather Alexander Simpson had owned three ships – and he had died aged 44 and was buried in London.

Alexander's son, the first James Simpson was a calligrapher, i.e. a letter writer.

The first James (called 'Fisheye') had a horse and cart and carted stones and helped build the arches of Banff Bridge – to span the Deveron. He married the Convenor of Roads' sister. James (I) 'thought of' a Distillery with Major James MacGilligan. It was then simple for James to take the tenancy of the Mains of Colleonard. They put up a Distillery by the Duke of Fife's wall, within smoking distance of Duff House and smoked out the Duke's seat.

James Simpson I came out of the Distillery when it burnt down – 1878 or so – Betty's mother was 8 or 9. He then got back into ships. One ship got wrecked on Gashouse Rock by Banff Harbour.

James Simpson II was son of the chap who came out of the Distillery. He married Harriet Adam – second time around. He was asked into the whisky business by the Distillery firm and he rebuilt it at Boyndie.

The chairs – Colin and Anne Edgar's dining-room chairs – started out with:

Thomas Adam of Bowie Bank – on his marriage in 1832.

Then to his daughter Harriet Adam and James Simpson.

Then to Caroline Simpson (Aunt Bee) her youngest daughter.

They were then left to her great nephew John Dawes as a wedding present.

Then given to his daughter Anne and Colin Edgar on their marriage in 1972.

The chairs were always at the schoolroom at Colleonard (which was bought by the Simpson family in the 1960s and then subsequently sold by them in the 1990s.)

Told in the late 1970s, this is a great example of 'a Betty story'. She would wind in many other stories on the way and then return to the original one, when the hearer had almost forgotten it and this gave us not only the history of our chairs, but laid out the Banff family history.

She told these stories her grandparents had told her about their grandparents. This gave Betty an aural memory back to the time of George IV (1820)!

Godfrey the highwayman

There was one 'gentleman', Mr Godfrey, who was hanged at Godfrey's Grave. My father used to tell me that he was a Highwayman and that he lived on the other side of Forstall Road, going down towards those marshes, at the back of Snowdown, where Mr Bones used to live. Going down the back there.

That Godfrey kept his horse down there. Of course, all Highwaymen had to keep in with the people about. Otherwise they told on him, you see. It was a good place to go, because he could go up into the woods, and preyed on the people going along the A2 – the coaches. So Godfrey rewarded everybody.

He had lots of ways of coming back home. He could come back via the Potteries or come back way back through the marshes, and round there. He was finally caught and hanged.

Well, my father couldn't resist letting him ride Black Bess to York! And do other things which as I grew older and read, I realized was a lot of lies, and Father had been 'romancing'. (Amy Robsart was supposed to have fallen out of the Tower!) Father told very good stories – a little of no good.

But what was interesting, was when I went to Waterham, we built on a sitting-room [and so had a building site].

Old Dr Selby, my sister-in-law's father, was Medical Officer of Health for the Swale. There were some boards outside, and he and Mrs Selby arrived to pay a call. Old Dr Selby was about 6 foot 1". He had his black suit on and he had mud up to his knees.

I said, 'Good gracious! Did you fall into the foundations?'

And Mrs Selby said, 'No, trust Prideaux to get in a mess!' I can hear her now.

He'd been called in because when they got the water done [waterpipes, so that the corner could be widened for the bus] **and they'd got to** [the bit now called] **Godfrey's Grave, a body** [thought to have been a child's], **had been dug up.**

Father had always said that Godfrey was a dwarf and a hunchback, and that didn't hold true to Dick Turpin, so I was rather doubtful about that.

Anyway, Dr Selby said, 'It wasn't a baby or a child at all. It was a man with a hunchback and I think he'd been hanged.' So that was something true.

I always thought Godfrey should have been re-buried, but he wasn't. They dug him up in 1932. He was the only celebrity I really know of here in Hernhill.

Horsewhipping?

Willie Dawes's younger brother Edwy had been promised a house by his father, Sir Edwyn. In those days the estate baked the brick in the Pottery. Folklore said that Edwy was one of those people who could never make a decision. The bricks were amassed, and put on the site adjacent to where the house would be built, which was between Courtenay and Bossenden, in Church Woods but nothing was ever done. Edwy hummed and hawed and puffed and blew hot and cold, and the house never got started. He was waiting to get some more cash out of his father, to make a start, but Sir Edwyn Dawes died in December 1902.

That bit of the estate was of the entailed part. When Sir Edwyn died, Willie inherited, who at that time was living at Kemsdale. He said to his brother, Edwy, *'No, no! this is all gone now. You've mucked about too long. You're not doing one thing or the other. If you don't get the bricks cleared up, I shall clear 'em up! You've had it.'* Willie would remove the bricks.

Edwy hummed and hawed and Willie simply pinched the bricks!

Willie used to commute up to London and live there during the week. So Edwy and some men, plus the other younger brothers Darcy and Halford, arrived one Saturday, on to the forecourt at Kemsdale, allegedly, to get reparation for the terrible way he, Edwy, had been treated over this house. Edwy was going to horsewhip his elder brother! Anyway, it didn't take place, as Willie was a stronger character than his two brothers. He saw them off the place. How? Who can say, but Willie and Mopsie were a formidable pair! And it was she that was the more formidable because Willie had quite a nervous disposition.

Hares

There was a story of Betty's about hares. For some reason they were trying to bring down hares from Scotland, to repopulate Kent stock. The hares would be caught and put into a box, about the size of a shoebox, with their back-legs completely trussed up in front of them.

They travelled south by train and when they arrived in Kent, the hares would be undone, then taken out of their boxes, and set free. They would hop off quite happily.

The awful part of the story is that someone on the train complained and said it was cruel packing the hares so tight. So on the next journey south, the hares were given a much larger box and, of course, the hares had bashed themselves to bits – the eyes got ashed out – in the spacious boxes. They all had to be destroyed. They were wild animals and if you were transporting them, the answer was to pack them tight. Betty herself wasn't involved.

Savoy

Betty went one day into the Savoy and said, **'I want Bed and Breakfast.'**

'We don't do that, Madam.' So she said, **'Oh well fine, I'll go somewhere else.'** So she went to Claridge's.

Another time in the '30s, Betty went to the Savoy and she saw what looked like an elderly waiter, wearing his white tie and things. So she went and tugged at his coat-tails, and it turned out to be her younger brother, Slotty.

Spontaneous combustion

Betty told this story about Celine, Mopsie's hairdresser, who drank absinthe frequently, and got drunk at a country house. Celine had the door shut and there was a huge fire burning. She drank liberally, then a coal sparked out of the fireplace, on to her dress and so Celine exploded! Spontaneous combustion. All that was left of her was a black deposit round the walls and her black buttoned boots – with her feet still in them.

Christabel, Lady Ampthill

Christabel was a contemporary of Betty's. She was very attractive and was out to shock. She was Mrs Pemberton's niece and in Debrett's is listed as Christabel Hulme, daughter of Lt-Col John Hart. She married Lord Ampthill in 1918 – on the assumption that she *'would not go the whole way'*. She got pregnant but was a virgin! There was a famous court-case on the virgin birth of the next Lord Ampthill (4th Baron – he was born in 1921). Christabel won, but she was divorced from the 3rd Lord Ampthill in 1937 and he married again. Johnnie Russell was the eldest son by Lord Ampthill's second marriage and tried (in about 1976 and because the uncles suggested it) to challenge the title. The day before the vital blood-test, Christabel died of old age!

Sandys had contracted ringworm. Christabel caught it from him. She had slept in his bed one night, as he was absent.

The next morning out hunting, they met. *'Hello, Sandys. I borrowed your breeches for hunting.'*

'Good morning, Christabel,' he replied, *'I've got ringworm!'* She then rushed to a cottage and scrubbed herself!

To date this episode there is a letter on 19 February, 1915 from Humf who asks: *'I hope Sandys's ringworm is better?'*

Christabel and her husband visited around the Continent, and, as one does on holiday, asked people to visit – never expecting to be taken up.

A Hungarian Count Shellmetzie and his Countess took them up. They were very strange, and wanted to know if a person was an aristocrat or a peasant. Gordon Mitchell was a bit of both. But – King Richard II had once said that he would ennoble all the Yeomen of Kent! Although this didn't happen, it was enough for the Count. He was able to talk to people after that! Jean Fraser was OK as she was second cousin to Lord Lovat.

Paddy Cassels, Betty's stableman looked aristocratic to Count Shellmetzie, as he had nice, narrow feet; but he wasn't. *'Us Daweses were just riding peasantry!'*

In her 60s, Christabel drove with a friend either to or from Burma to England. She had no green card or driving licence. Just talked her way through.

Christabel retired to an Irish castle on an island with a moat. A young girl went to visit her. Some stories say this was Betty, some say not, but she rang the bell, then rowed over the moat to the castle on the island. There was no supper. As there was nothing to eat the next day, the girl, having followed a hen, found an egg to eat for breakfast. The only one on the island.

Back on the mainland they went to the races and there was lots to eat and drink. Christabel was happily asking everybody back for tea or drinks. And Betty (or whoever), being quite young, was saying **'Christabel, there isn't any food.'**

'Oh yes, there is. Don't worry. Everyone, come back to eat.'
'There isn't any food'.

They went back to the village. They had to keep the horses on the mainland. *'Betty, you go round and get the bread. Bring as many loaves as you can get.'* So Betty did, and she rowed herself across to the house, to find Christabel in the dungeon kitchens, opening tins of Kittycat. Tins and tins of catfood. *'No its delicious. Absolutely delicious!'* She filled her guests with catfood.

JEAN ROWNTREE: *In '48 when I was 17, I did something quite out of character, or amazingly brave. As a secretary from London, I hired a horse with the Beaufort and I went out hunting. I must have done it because Aunt Betty told me Christabel Ampthill was going to be there. Anyway, somebody gave me the courage to go and do it. I stayed two nights in the 'Hare & Hounds' pub, and my horse was brought round, because the Meet was going to be there. So it was all frightfully cosy. The only one who talked to me was Lady Ampthill, looking absolutely gorgeous. Elegant, beautiful, side-saddle. Everything totally perfect and a great big flower. She was sweet to me. She was really, really kind and I had a lovely day out. It was huge fun – all on my own. Thanks to Aunt Betty's friendship.*

She had a very smart dress-shop in Park Street, just off Park Lane.

The stag that went to France

Betty's brother Sandys, was Master of the Mid-Kent Staghounds for many years. They used to hunt 'carted stags', that is, captive park red deer, one of which would be transported to the Meet on a day's hunting. and turned out. Since World War II, the Mid-Kent only hunted hinds. The 'stag' would be given 10 or 20 minutes or so 'law', whilst the hunt enjoyed a stirrup cup or two, before the pack was laid on. The stags were all corn fed (unlike their wild brethren) and not knowing the country, they tended to run straight; so it was not uncommon to have prodigious long hunts. Sometimes the stag made good its escape and became an 'outlier', at other times it was taken and motored home again after being lassoed. (The story is that hounds had their canine teeth drawn so they couldn't damage the stag.) The 'stag' would generally go down in water at the end of a day's hunting. The system then would be for the whip to wade into the lake or stream and put their arms round the beast's neck.

On this particular day the stag was turned out in Marden and ran to the coast near Folkestone! Here it turned at bay in the surf. Sandys Dawes and the redoubtable Betty McKeever were in at the end. Betty said that her brother held the hounds back and, as there were no other competent men present at the end of this phenomenally long chase, he threw her the deer rope with the cry, *'Save the stag, Betty!'* She said, **'I threw off my habit and waded out into the sea'** (although some felt it unlikely that Betty, as a female, would have ever done this).

The sight of the formidable Betty plunging through the briny, waving a lariat obviously must have unnerved this stag, for he turned and swam for dear life into the English Channel where, as no boat was available the tired hunters had to leave him.

When they regained the clifftop they, and other survivors of the hunt, could still see the stag swimming manfully out to sea, when a passing trawler, sporting a French Tricolour hove-to and pulled the stag aboard before sailing south.

It was not until a long time later that it was reported that the crew of the trawler had put up the stag (still alive) for sale with the rest of their catch. The stag was apparently purchased by a French nobleman who had a silver collar made for it with the inscription of how it had been rescued by gallant French fishermen (who had witnessed the closing stages of the hunt through their telescopes) from the perfidious English hunters. Thus adorned, the stag spent a peaceful retirement in the nobleman's park.

A newspaper article on this stag said approximately: 'French trawlermen had found the stag off the coast of France. There was an argument between the French and the English. The Department of the Environment said that the English could not take the stag back, owing to the quarantine law of not being allowed to bring in cloven-hooved animals. And the French could not kill it as they could not import venison into France. The disagreement went on for months.' A terrible problem as there was no birth certificate. Another story said that Edward VII when visiting France, was taken to see it!

There was a similar courtcase in about 1928, when the RSPCA got involved. The men involved were acquitted of cruelty, but the whole story could be two separate incidences amalgamated. The answers have got lost in the mists of time!

Dormouse

Betty told versions of this story to practically everyone.

She was out hunting one day when she met a Woodman, who had just chopped down a tree which had a dormouse nest in it. The nest had got dislodged and there was one small occupant hopping about.

The Woodman asked Betty what he should do.

So Betty put the dormouse in its little woven nest, under her top hat. **'It will be quite all right, because I have my veil on.'** She continued hunting all day.

When she returned home, the dormouse skipped out and was fine. Betty kept it in an old tin kettle at the warm end of the kitchen, until it had finished hibernating. She kept it as a pet for a long time.

Possibly the same dormouse lived in a cage with a little wheel at Berkeley, which it used to exercise itself on.

The radar pylons at Dunkirk (in the same parish) were secret. A strange and intermittent noise appeared on the radar. Was it enemy signals? The direction of the signal was found, and it was discovered to be Mickey on his wheel! The dormouse had activated the radar or something and caused a major scare and the radar warnings had been scrambled.

Chapter Fifteen
Visiting Ireland

In the late '20s Betty went for some hunting seasons in Ireland, because there was Foot and Mouth in Kent so therefore hunting had to be stopped. She hunted with the Meath, Ballymead, Carlow, Queens Country and the Kildare packs.

Betty went to Ireland from about 1926 to 1928. She was a paying guest at Leopardstown, of the family of Ivy Flora Eva McVeagh. She brought Ivy back, who met Slotty and they got married. And then Betty went over another year staying with the McVeaghs and met Rudolf McKeever and they got married. He was a cattle and horse dealer from Co. Meath and Betty married him – having been refused permission to marry Geoffrey Gilpin – who was the love of her life, because he was a Roman Catholic.

Rudolf McKeever was Protestant Irish from County Meath. He went to school at Campbell College in Belfast. His brother, Eric McKeever had been the Irish champion steeplechase jockey.

Betty always enjoyed her time in the Emerald Isle greatly.

MIKE FIELD: *She had a reputation as a fearless rider, was one of the first women to take up Point-to-Point riding. One of her fondest memories is taking on 15 gentlemen riders in Ireland – and beating them.*

Betty was once talking about what was and what wasn't a luxury.

I will tell you what is luxury. It's if you've had a day's hunting in Ireland. And then you come back at the end of the day, and there's somebody to do your horse, there's a steaming bath in your bedroom with a fire lit. You drop your riding clothes on the floor. Somebody else takes them away, and you dress for dinner. That is luxury.

She did have some wonderful times in Ireland.

JEAN ROWNTREE: *My [Irish] Grandfather died, unexpectedly. He had a weak heart, always had. And therefore my Grandmother ran the estate, because my grandfather was supposed to be too weak to*

run it. He could ride a pony and hunted about four days a week.
Had a pack of hounds and goodness-knows-what. A good life. And
anyway, one morning, he sat up in bed and said, 'Maud, I don't
feel very well. I don't think I will have a swim before breakfast,
in the lake.' Fell back as good as dead.

They found there was virtually no money in the bank account.
They had thirteen servants in the house, a pack of hounds, a stable
full of horses. Regrettably, the older brother, who had been rather
shell-shocked in the war, sold the farm off. The farm wasn't near
by, but it was a major income. He went and sold it, which was
ridiculous. Ma and Aunt Muriel decided the only thing they knew
anything about were horses, so they started gathering horses into
the park and trading them. Then my mother or someone had the
brains to put an advert in the Sunday Observer. 'Come and hunt in
Ireland, and we'll look after you as a guest.' Aunt Betty answered.
I think she brought her horses over, which was crazy. Would have
been pretty stupid [facing English hunters] *over those Irish banks.*

It was Aunt Betty who brought my Mother [Ivy} *back to*
England. Pa [Slotty} *met her, then went to Ireland and bought a*
horse off her. He decided the only way to get his money back was
to marry the girl!

They moved to Malmains a year after marriage after renting
a house called [Harewell], *on the Ashford road into Faversham.*
Found Malmains at last and they felt that was it.

On 1 June 1928, Slotty and Ivy married. Their honeymoon was
in New Zealand. They lived in the old house, Malmains near the
village of Pluckley, about 16 miles away from Hernhill, where they
had a long and happy marriage together, celebrating their Golden
Wedding in 1978. They and their family were very much part of
Betty's family and there were continuous close contacts and visits,
all their lives.

Chapter Sixteen
Marriage

On 17 June 1931, Betty married Thomas Henry Wright McKeever, who was always called Rudolf. Betty's wedding was a very small affair. She was married at Dunkirk Church so all she did was walk across the road from Berkeley.

Apparently Slotty had said to her and their mother. *'Look here. What are you going to do about this wedding? You've got to invite half the County – because of who you are.'* Betty was Master of Hounds and everything. Everybody would expect to come. *'You've either got to keep it literally to the family only, or have everybody.'*

So they kept it to the family – a very small affair. Anyway, Dunkirk Church was very small and they were married there owing to the family disagreements with Hernhill Church.

Sandys and Slotty tied a garden roller behind the bridal car. The couple set off from Berkeley, at the top of the long steep Boughton Hill. Bill Friend was very slow. He had been the coachman and then became the chauffeur, and he drove very very slowly as he had difficulty changing gear, so the garden roller overtook them!

Betty told a friend that she had run off with Rudolf on the rebound. Because it didn't work out with him, although she never complained. She said **'Rudolf had no idea about farming. He did the daftest things. We had no money at the time – it was the time of the Depression.'** Betty said the ancestors of the McKeevers had made their money out of donkeys. Rudolf was a horse-dealer, mixed up with trading horses.

WILLIE McKEEVER: *My Irish Grandfather bred horses and had brood mares, and I've got photographs, before the '14 War, of mares and foals, which had been shown at Balls Bridge and which were out there and he had a couple of well-known stallions.*

Now, he was running that stud, up until the end of the '14 War, and he took it on himself, for this Count Stalberg. That was where the money-bags was. To fund all this, Count Stalberg won the Cunningham Cup in 1911, on one of my grandfather's horses [there is a set of six prints showing the field]. *Basically the*

The McKeever Family

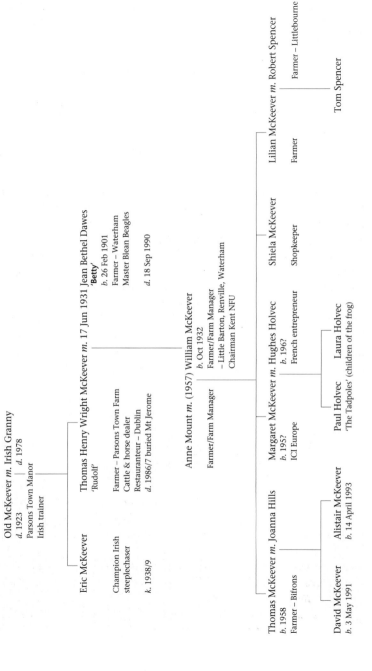

McKeever family's business, based in Meath, was supplying cattle from the West of Ireland, over into England. They were cattle dealers and they used to send an awful lot of finished cattle, both from the North Wall at Dublin, and from the Port of Dun Laoghaire, to Liverpool, to the Vestey slaughter-houses in Liverpool. Several boat-loads every month. They were all cattle that McKeevers had amalgamated and gone around markets buying, and sending over there. Because I can remember Father telling me the state that those city slaughter-houses were in. He'd been over there as a boy, before the '14 War. He said it was absolutely disgusting, the way that things were done, the cattle coming off the boats.

On marriage Rudolf and Betty moved into Waterham. This had been the main farm that Betty had inherited from her father's estate. It is a lovely old house, the other side of the coastal road from the rest of Hernhill. The beagle kennels were situated opposite, across a quiet lane. The house is attached to an extensive rambling farmyard and the farm.

Waterham is an old, old house, of about the 1400s. It has a king beam truss in one bedroom, steep old winding stairs with a rope handrail, an ancient kitchen and beams everywhere. It is a very liveable-in house and most attractive. It sits in its garden with a pond at the back. Betty and Rudolf built on an extension – a large airy sitting-room and main bedroom above.

Waterham

They asked for estimates from several local builders. One of these estimates was much lower than the others. Very curious, so Betty asked the builder to call, and then asked him straight out. **'Mr Jones. Your estimate is much less than the others. Why?'** He said he expected the other builders had included the cost of foundations in their quotes. This turned out to be true.

Challenged as to why he had not included foundations for the new construction, he said they were not necessary. Waterham had been built several hundred years previously and was a 'Listed Building'. Mr Jones explained that there were no buried foundations under the walls; the reason being that the original builders understood how the Seasalter marsh ground moved under the walls, and that if the walls were on the soil, they would also be moved and so not be damaged – but that this had since been forgotten.

To prove his statement, they went outside and at a point where the ground was soft, he took a long, steel rule and plunged it straight under the wall, horizontally. *'The marshland moves. With foundations – the walls crack!'* Mr Jones then went on to point out where the walls of the nearby cottages – which had been built at a later date, and with foundations – had required to be strengthened with iron tie-bars.

Betty accepted his estimate and the new extension of Waterham has no foundations.

She became pregnant. Two weeks before her child was born Betty climbed up a ladder to pick her fruit. She fell and the baby didn't move for a fortnight, and then was born with a bruise on his head.

Rudolf's and Betty's son was born in October 1932. He was named William McKeever, but always called Willie, after his grandfather. He was christened at Dunkirk.

Betty always used to tell a story to Geoffrey Neame about his great grandfather, Frederick Neame. In the '30s, Frederick Neame owned a car but really only used it on special occasions, otherwise, he used to ride everywhere on horseback. He once, very near the end of his life, bought a horse, which was extremely frisky, and it eventually threw him – and killed him. But literally about ten days before he was thrown from that horse (a gelding), he had been riding along, and Betty McKeever and Rudolf were walking along a lane about a mile or two from Boughton and came up to him. The horse reared, and Rudolf grabbed it by the reins, by the bridle and so pulled it down.

Geoffrey's great grandfather Frederick actually raised his whip and shouted at him, *'Un-hand me, Sir! or I'll have you for assault!'* Being a rather old man, he was so hurt that someone felt they had to bridle his horse, and that he couldn't ride, because he was a brilliant horseman. Rudolf was not very popular after that.

Frederick Neame got extremely upset with Rudolf and practically whacked him. Then he got killed himself two weeks later by the horse, in 1934.

Rudolf and Betty farmed, but there were difficulties. The farm did support her and when her shares didn't pay, life was very difficult, and they had to get rid of a lot of people who were dependent upon them. (The '30s recession lasted from about 1931 to 1936.)

And farming was not doing at all well then, either. It was a very difficult time, financially, for everybody. And Betty still kept her beagles going, and she still kept her farming breeding going. But anything that is thoroughbred, does take a bit more money than just growing potatoes. The times were pretty difficult.

Bankruptcy

WILLIE MCKEEVER: *Father and Mother were married in '31, and he had a share in his Father's business (who had died in 1923), which was a farm in Parson's Town, Battersdown in County Meath. He had his younger brother Eric and his mother there still. The farm was considerably mortgaged to the Irish subsidiary of the National Provincial Bank. All was going reasonably well, but suddenly in 1935 or '36, the National Provincial Bank withdrew the facility, and wanted the mortgage paid off.*

The bank decided – to get this order enforced – to take my Father, who was the eldest son (rather than his mother or his younger brother), to court for bankruptcy. But they wouldn't do it in Drogheda, where the loan was taken out, they decided to do it in Canterbury.

And the object of the exercise, according to Mother, was that [the bank] *thought they were on to a jolly good thing. That if this came up in Canterbury, they thought that Daweses would fund it, to keep it out of the Courts, and that the McKeevers would get their money* [and pay-back the bank]. *It was a 'fishing expedition' according to Mother and Sandys. Of course, the Dawes family* said it was a bloody try on. 'To hell with them. Saluté, thank you very much) cuss du [curse you]!'

Plus the old lady my Grandmother, being very Scots, said, 'We can play them at their own game. Let them go bust. To hell with it!' It didn't help the future. It didn't help, I don't think, the future of my Mother's and Father's marriage. But there were other complications – as I will come to in a moment.

The case came up at Canterbury Civil Court, and my Father was made Bankrupt. His mother and younger brother, were kept on by the bank, to continue to run the farm in Ireland, which they did.

The bank was wanting its money back, so it sued and won. Well, it didn't get its money back, because there was no money available. Because 'Daweses wouldn't pay up', to bail the McKeevers out to keep it out of the paper. My Irish grandmother, never forgave the Dawes family over this. Because I gather, bankruptcy, in those days was a terrible disgrace.

Mother & Father married in 1931 and P & O hadn't paid a dividend because everything was slumped so there was no private money coming in.

Most of the Dawes family money was involved in P & O because of the tie-up with Willie Dawes's Death Duty Settlement.

WILLIE MCKEEVER: *Father and Mother went bankrupt. And I can remember vividly here, we had no car. We didn't have a cheque-book and everything was bought with cash. They were running this business here, and on a Friday, we used to go in to get the groceries. Lewis Finn from Lorenden, gave Mother and Father a horse called The Tapir, which was a van-er, and we used to trot in with a sort of four-wheeled, big old dog-cart. Used to trot in and out of Faversham with The Tapir once a week. And that went on until – a car was acquired in about the Spring of '39. 1 don't remember a car before then.*

Now in the '30s, to keep the family afloat, of course, we still had a staff here, in spite of the farm being bankrupt, surprisingly. What made the money, was the sale each Spring, in May of two horses at Tattersalls. I can remember going up as a kid to Knightsbridge Green – where they had the horseboxes and everything else. These horses had to stay in the yards, where they were trotted up and down, which was Tattersall. It was bombed in the

War and after that it was moved to Newmarket. Now the horses that were sold were four year olds. And we did two a year. Now they came over from Ireland as yearlings, and were wintered. They were then 'broken in', because we had a nagsman called Paddy. And he trained and broke two horses every winter. They went hunting, and hopefully they would be out for the Point-to-Point season, to be sold the following May at Tattersalls, as guaranteed to go in all gears. They were very popular with Shire hunts, for people who hunted. And the sale of those two horses, virtually, is what the family lived on. From about 1935 till – the last pair were sold in '38, the year before the war. I don't think there was a pair sold in '39.

My Father came out of the business here at Waterham, and left it pretty well for Mother to run. And Sandys got Father a job, in London, with a firm he had something to do with, with the Playfords, called Pressure-Tight, which were involved with plumbing fittings. And Father lived in London in a bed-sit, during the week, and occasionally came down here at weekends. I vaguely remember him before the war, coming down at weekends.

I remember various occasions like Easter time, when we would hunt for Easter eggs, those sort of things. And I can remember walking cattle from the station – with the dog cart, where they'd come into Faversham station. Some of them were driven down out of the pens where you unload them, down into Faversham Cattle market. We used to drive them down, because not only did we have cattle for ourselves, but he bought cattle for other people.

About 1938 the marriage began to break up. Betty was away for long periods running Aultmore as a commercial grouse moor, and she left a young woman to run Waterham. Willie says *'Now, there was a falling out. I understand the young woman and Father got together and there was a bastard child.'* (There is no record of what happened to the child.) *'There was a hell of a stink.'*

Then the Irish family went bust. Rudolf's brother Eric was killed in a car crash. He had just become a professional jockey and was coming back from the races one day, fell asleep at the wheel and was killed. This left Rudolf's mother at Parson's Town Manor on her own.

Rudolf gave up his job at Pressure Tight and went back to Ireland in the Spring of 1938 to sort out his family affairs. The marriage, by the Spring of '39 was somewhat shaky.

He was still in Ireland when war was declared in September 1939 – and he did not come back.

Betty said that she and Rudolf **'parted for financial reasons'**.

I came down here with my husband in 1931, and then he went off – following a job in London. Times weren't very good, and his things in Ireland went wrong. It was complicated and things there...

Betty and her brothers considered him 'bloody yellow' not to come back and fight for his country.

Betty and Rudolf never met again.

Chapter Seventeen
Farming [1]

The farmhouse of Waterham is set between orchards and flatlands, heading towards the marsh.

There are 39 acres of land at Waterham, partly fruit and partly grass, with two pairs of cottages for the farm staff to live in.

It was a fragmented farm, of rather mixed acreage. Betty had her 28 or 30 acres of marsh at Graveney, which had also come to her out of the 'share-out' in 1920.

Furthermore, she rented from Sandys a fair acreage of rough pasture back across the coastal road, up in the Blean.

There was 'New Zealand' and the adjoining fields. The story goes that Sir Edwyn Dawes once met Dr Selby (Joan's father), who was out in his pony trap. The doctor had been travelling past the high sloping field when it was being grubbed out from Blean Woods at the turn of the century.

'That looks like New Zealand,' the doctor said. 'I was born there.'

Sir Edwyn was doing a lot of business out there at that time, so he said, 'I shall call this field New Zealand.'

Betty farmed other fields in the Blean. 'Little Joy' was one, and she owned a 'pylon' field, a bit further away (where the fifteen radar pylons were put up on the top at Dunkirk, from 1936 onwards and during World War II).

So there was a compact farm with farm buildings and orchards at Waterham, also flat marshland and high rolling pasture.

WILLIE: *Waterham and the tenanted lands, came to something under 200 acres. Monk's Hill added about another 200 acres, which was taken on by us in the Autumn of '42, sold to us at Michaelmas* [it had been Mount Ephraim Estate unentailed land]. *I remember coming back in March '43 and the previous tenants were thrashing out their stacks from the previous harvest – the '42 harvest – and the stacks belonged to the ex-tenant. Uncle Sandys was able to get vacant possession on the death of the ex-tenant Alfred Bones. It stayed in the family until 1965/'66.*

We always did rent a lot of land from Lord Sondes at Seasalter and that just stayed on.

Betty was farming possibly as much as 300 acres at that time. Waterham had probably three or four permanent workers on the farm. Others would come and go temporarily, and fruit pickers came in seasonally.

Betty and Rudolf had their profitable horse-breeding trade which was in the stud-book. They also kept sheep and pigs.

The Irish nagsman, Paddy Cassels, helped with the sheep. When drunk he would gallop up to 'New Zealand' and 'look' the sheep.

Pigs had been kept by the beagle kennels at Mount Ephraim up until the beagles moved to Waterham in 1931. They started breeding the pigs pure, in mid to late '20s. Pigs were kept at Waterham until Monk's Hill was sold up in the mid '60s.

At Waterham Betty farmed Large Whites – pedigree stock. As at Mount Ephraim, the pigs were put by the beagles kennels because the pigs were good grubbers.

Willie McKeever spoke of his mother.

WILLIE: *My mother got a fine piece of advice when she started farming – from an old farmer, who said: 'If you want to have an easy life, you should never go too far away from the indigenous breeds of the region.' In other words, Kents will survive on the North Kent marshes better than most other breeds of sheep, because they had been bred to do it for years and years and years. And Sussex cattle will do the same thing. I think that advice still holds good today, although the farmer spoke in the days before animal medicines were in the fore as they are now.*

Betty was a livestock breeder, she sold hunters at Tattersalls, also beagles. In '38/'39 the nagsman broke his leg so Betty broke-in a couple of horses, herself. She exported some to Sweden and Holland. She also showed Large White pigs and Sussex cattle.

In 1936 or '37 they advertised for a person to come and manage poultry. Jean Fraser answered the advert. She was a girl fresh from the West of Scotland College of Auchincruive, just south-east of Ayr which is still functioning today. Betty wrote and offered her a job. Originally she came as temporary chicken woman for around about a fortnight. She was to become Betty's companion and remain at Waterham (except for the war years) for the rest of her life. She lived with Betty for nearly 50 years.

'Miss Fraser' (as she was called by everyone for the next 10 years or so), had a National Diploma in Poultry and Dairying and became an expert in poultry. She was a tall upright Scots girl of 5 foot 8 or 9 inches, who held herself well. She had brown hair and blue eyes.

Jean Fraser was born in Inverness in 1915. She attended Auchincruive straight from school. Her father was a stalker on the Lovat Estate. He was in the Lovat Scouts and was killed during World War I. Her mother was also a Fraser, and her grandmother a MacDonald.

At Waterham, they became involved in poultry in a big way. An expensive incubator unit was built.

Around the farmyard they had Rhode Island Reds, Light Sussex and White Leghorns.

They also raised Runner Ducks and Khaki Campbells.

The chickens did very well. Joe Butler remembers: 'They got prizes and one thing and another. There used to be a lot of those '1st Prize', '2nd Prize' – pinned up in the Oast.'

Jean Fraser boarded in one of the Waterham cottages to start off, with Paddy and Mrs Cassels. After about 6 months she moved across the road to Waterham, which was to become her permanent home. Betty did lots of small amounts of business with all sorts of people who had accounts with her. She sold trays of fruit, she sold lots of eggs. Also potatoes, honey and chicken.

There were turkeys sold at Christmas 1936 at 2/3d a lb. A 22 lb turkey was £2 9s. 6d.

Eggs @ 1s. 6d. a dozen.

Chicken (dressed) @ between 1s. 2d. and 1s. 6d. a lb. Two would cost a customer something between 8s. and 10s.

There was her livestock too:

Kent lamb @   £1   5   0   in August.
A teg   @   £1   18   0   in May.
2 pigs   @   £2   10   0   = £5 0 0 in June.

She would sell to grocers and greengrocers; Whitstable, Herne Bay and even Banff – charging carriage.

Family were her customers. They had running accounts which were paid now and then. Mount Ephraim must have bought all their eggs from her as they were charged by the 30 dozen – £4 2s. 6d. or the 60 dozen – £9. These large quantities of eggs would be kept in a preservative called 'water glass', inside a crock. They also bought butter, cream and manure.

30 Bushel Grains 17s. 1d.
50 tomatoes 10s. March.

Her mother Mopsie, at Berkeley, bought broom-heads from her daughter and fruit. Also oil, got saddlery repaired, and had loads of logs delivered.

The fruit was a great part of the farm. Betty had several orchards with lots of different varieties of fruit trees. Here is a running account from Waterham to 'Messrs Graham & Co', Banff who would buy from Waterham in the 1930s and have it sent by train (or have it driven up overnight by lorry) to the grocer's store in Banff:

Aug 22					
20 x 14	N/R Boxes 'Belle de Louvain'	5/6	£5	10	–
12 x ½	N/R/H/S Boxes 'Worcesters'	6/–	3	12	–
15 x 1	N/R/S Boxes 'Bramleys'	10/–	7	10	–
Aug 30					
25 x 28	Clapps Favourate	6/–	7	10	–
20 x 14	Marmarchs	5/–	5	–	–
5 x 14	H Guages	5/–	1	5	–
	PAID 7/9/35		£30	7	–
Sept 10					
20	Bushel Bramleys	10/–	10	–	–
10 H	Bushel Fertility	6/–	3	–	–
Sept 24					
8 x 1	Newtons 4 x 1 Lanes	7/–	4	4	–
	PAID 25th				
10 x ½	Conference	8/–	4	–	–
10 x ½	Fertility	6/–	3	–	–
10 x ½	Worcesters	8/–	4	–	–
	PAID	28/–	4	–	–
Aug 18					
3 x ½	Worcesters	–	–	–	–
26 x ¼	Belle de Louvain @ 4/–				
	carriage 1/11/8	–	6	11	8

			£	s	d
Aug 19					
3 x Worcesters		5/–	–	15	–
10 x ½	Dr Jules lst	10/–	5	–	–
10 x ½	Dr Jules 2nd	8/–	4	–	–
Aug 26					
9 x ½	Harvest Mages	7/–	3	3	–
4 x ½	Belle de Louvain	7/–	1	8	–
			20	17	8
Sept 30					
5 x ½	Conference Pears EF	6/–	1	10	–
1 x ½	Cox Orange E F	12/–	–	12	–
1 x ½	" " Blemished	5/–	–	5	–
2 x 2	Worcester F	3/6	–	7	–
1 x 1	Blenheim F	8/6	–	8	6
3 x 1	Blenheim E F	10/–	1	10	–
1 x 1	Brambley F	8/–	–	8	–
5 x 1	Brambley E F	9/6	2	7	6
1 x 1	Derby E F	7/6	1	17	6
4 x 1	Worcesters E F	8/6	1	14	–
		11/5/6			

Apples: Cox Orange, Worcesters, Blenheims, (Lord) Derbys, Newton Wonder.

Pears: Conference, Citron des Carmes, Dr Jules Guyot, Clapp's Favourite, Fertility. There were several varieties of cherries, greengages and soft fruit, too.

In 1941 Sandys's younger son, John Dawes came to work for Betty at Waterham as a 17 year old. He worked in his summer holiday (20 July to 20 September – approx) then he worked for her again after leaving his school, Stowe in December, until he joined the Army in August 1942 aged 18.

At this stage Bill Foster was Foreman at Waterham and his sister Dorothy worked in the house. The workers included Peter Boorman, Henry Brooks and Jim Butler (Harry Butler's elder son). There was a Fordson tractor and horses to work the farm.

JOHN DAWES: *My rate of pay was 6d per hour (2½p). My First Task was to take 70 cartloads of dung out of Waterham yard in the trailer!*

Harvest. There were 7 acres – next to Pudding Lane. Bill Foster, the Grieve or Farm foreman cut the headland with scythe plus cradle (to avoid wheel machine loss). I bonded up after him. No string allowed so I made bonds which were, I think, 8 wheat stalks each way and tucked in.

Cutting. A paraffin Fordson tractor towed a reaper and binder. The sheaf knotter was sometimes troublesome and re-threading the needle was complicated. Carrying to the stack was by horse and cart plus ladders. One man or two loading with pitch-forks, plus one stowing. At the stack, Bill Foster was the stacker (most skilled), one person on cart plus one on the stack. As the stack rose then one person was in the LUBBERHOLE (a space left in stack, half way up, for standing in).

Threshing. The same fields with 3 or 4 stacks. The steam traction engine was used plus the threshing machine.

Best wheat was put into sacks. (There was also tail wheat – for hens – and chaff.)

8 Pints = 1 Gallon
8 Gallons = 1 Bushel
8 Bushels = 1 Quarter
2¼ cwt = half a Quarter

I could carry a 2¼ sack but not lift it off the ground. Sacks got taken to 1st floor in 'Oast' and then shot on to the floor in a mouse-proof room (I lost my 'Swain & Adeney' hunting knife in the wheat).

Haymaking. This was either by tractor or horse – on a hay-knife. The hay was left for 2 or 3 days then turned by pitchfork. When it was dry – a pusher fork, taking 2 rows, was put on to the front of the car or tractor and pushed to the stack. A tall pole plus a pulley-and-grab was operated by a car and swung to the stacker and released.

Bird Scaring. At the longest – from 5.0 a.m. to 9.0 p.m.

I was not there during the fruit-picking, which took place from October to November.

How I left. Henry Brooks and I were put on 'Piece Work' (an agreed sum for the whole field) in the North Field of Dargate Common. We went into a major thistle area – and dealt with it.

When we had done the worst part first, old Bill Foster put us on 'Time Work.' We had slogged our guts out to do the hardest bit first! I left!

John joined the Army on 20 August 1942.

Steam-Ploughing

The sloping permanent pasture of 'New Zealand' was steam-ploughed during World War II – as part of the effort to grow more food in this country, during the period when ships carrying imports were being torpedoed.

Steam-ploughing involved having two traction engines, each of which was worked by a man. One of these engines pulled the plough from the top of the hill, and the other traction engine pulled it back down again from the bottom. A third man worked the plough, which was pulled on a hawser between the two engines. The plough was cocked up one way, pulled by the hawser to do a seven-furrow plough up the hill. It was then cocked up the other way and returned, to plough seven more furrows downwards. The two traction engines then moved along and continued the process until the whole field was ploughed.

Out hunting. John Dawes, his governess 'Scottie', Betty & Mopsie

Chapter Eighteen
The thirties

The old governess from Mount Ephraim, Miss Cotteral, known as Scottie, came as companion to Betty when Rudolf was around less frequently. Then after that, of course, Jean Fraser was about in the house. Waterham's telephone number at this period was Boughton 27.

There was a cook at Waterham before World War II. Then later on there was Mrs Grinter.

JOE BUTLER: *A marvellous cook. The reason I say that is because she used to make these lovely chocolate cakes. Well, I was only a child, and I remember we used to go over there and I used to see that. Lovely.*

Betty had blood-pressure problems, caused by falling down from a barn.

A certain rivalry showed between the brothers Slotty and Sandys. Sandys was Chairman of Westrays and was the live wire. Slotty was much quieter. Slotty used to complain that Sandys was never in the office, always hunting and riding around with his friends from the Bath Club.

Mopsie answered Slotty, '*Don't be silly, he does twice as much business on his horse than you do sitting in the office, and answering the telephone.*'

JEAN ROWNTREE: *Before the war, they had a wide circle of what I call 'County Families'. And I think Pa had a very big ego trip in the war. Because having always been sat on by Aunty Betty and Uncle Sandys, mentally, Pa was rather strict and responsible and serious. Though he could be frightfully funny, he could throw big sponges with the best of them. But he was never as outlandishly naughty as Uncle Sandys.*

Uncle Sandys was outlandish. He tried to shut me in the silver cupboard at Mount Ephraim – terrified the life out of me! Thank God Mama let me out. Uncle Sandys could be cruel. Pa could hurt as well. They all could hurt mentally. They all had tremendous charm. *Pa never had the charm that Sandys had. Pa never had the friends. But in the County classes, you see, Pa was just a second son, of a nice place, and they were moving in their own circle of wealth.*

Sandys had a phenomenal memory. If a road-sweeper opened the gate for him out hunting, Sandys would ask, *'Who's that?'*

'Mr Smith,' would come the answer. Sandys would always remember the man's name, if he came across him again.

Golden Miller

At Cheltenham Racecourse there is a statue of that most special horse, Golden Miller. He won the Cheltenham Gold Cup five times – each year from 1932 to 1936. He won the Grand National in 1934.

Family tradition has it that the McKeevers had had something to do with his foaling. The McKeevers could never have afforded to put it into training like Dorothy Paget – who acquired the horse. She could afford the best trainers.

Dorothy Paget had hunted sometimes with the Mid-Kent. It was Sandys who put her on to buying Golden Miller (and another famous racehorse Insurance) which started a very famous partnership, between the lady owner and her racehorse.

Both brothers continued racing at Point-to-Points and Slotty went further. He was a bruising rider and a very fine steeplechaser In 1938, he competed in the Grand National on Hopeful Hero the only grey horse running. Slotty completed the course and finished 8th. A great achievement. (Battleship won at 40-1.)

> WILLIE: *Slotty used to own Hopeful Hero (previously) but he'd sold the horse to Jack Siley* [who was in ship repairing]. *Slotty continued to train him, so Hopeful Hero won under Siley's name. Slotty was only the jockey and trainer. He had to justify his expenses to Sigwell the Steward because otherwise he was compromising his amateur status.*

Betty travelled up to Liverpool to watch the Grand National – on spec. She had nowhere to stay because the area was full of Irishmen.

In the same year, Slotty also won the amateur National Hunt Chase at Cheltenham on Hopeful Hero.

At this stage, Sandys was the sailing person in the family. He sailed *Nighthawk*, a Thames barge built by Charlie Cooper and *Rainbow*, an Essex 'I' design.

Sandys changed to sailing Sharpies (12 square metre class) in the '30s from the Corinthian Yacht Club at Burnham-on-Crouch. John Hacking was his (smart) crew or a member of the family. Joan Sayer also crewed for him. He twice sailed for England in the Thirties, as did his brother in the Fifties.

Sandys hunted in the winter and played squash at Alfred House, Faversham, or at the Bath Club. In the summer he played tennis and sailed. He had one week's fishing in Banff each year.

Haycock

One year, Sandys and Betty drove to Scotland from Mount Ephraim, and on the first night they were to stop, Betty wished to stop at the 'Haycock', a famous seventeeth-century coaching inn on the A1 at Wansford, near Peterborough. Sandys wished to have dinner at the Haycock and then motor on further, so they could get further north. Unfortunately for Sandys – he'd been stung by a hornet under his moustache, on the journey up. And his face, being fair skinned and all that, he swelled and he swelled and he swelled. They went in to the Haycock, and they ordered their dinner. Betty ordered a couple of rooms, and Sandys tried to say something to the receptionist.

'Take no notice of my brother, he's an idiot,' said Betty, because the receptionist couldn't understand a word that this very swollen face, *'Phraw, phraw, phraw'* said!

So they had to stay the night in the Haycock! Betty drove on the next morning – because Sandys really was in a dreadful mess.

To get to a hunt meet, which could be a fair distance away, Betty would hack – ride slowly – on Lucky Day. She would hunt all day, then hack home. Other horses of hers included Golden Patriot, Dunduckady and Whisky. (John Dawes hunted as a boy on Fizzer.) She would hack for miles to get to the Stag Hunt at Bethersden. But there were other ways to travel.

There were sidings at different stations, and cattle trucks were converted to take hounds and horses. Betty would load up at Faversham Station and then go to Canterbury or Maidstone, and get shunted on a branch line to go down to the Stag Hounds – to some of the Meets of the Mid-Kent. That was how you sent horses to anywhere else from the local area. They used to tack on to the train as many cattle-floats (or horse-floats) as they wanted – between the wars.

Nora Bearsby remembered Betty coming back to tea with them after hunting. They got off their horses and Betty was wet through, completely and utterly wet through. She stood in front of the fire-place to dry herself, and she said to Nora's mother, '**Have you got any methylated spirits?**'

Nora thought she wanted to drink it, but Betty wanted to pour methylated spirits down into her riding boots. She said, '**You won't catch a cold or anything if you just use methylated spirits.**'

Nora went into their shop and got a bottle of meths. She poured it – in front of a roaring fire! She didn't catch on fire though.

JOE BUTLER: *I always remember Mrs McKeever trying to get Willie interested in riding. Paddy, next door, I remember him having Willie with this harness on him, with a little pony and a handle sticking out the back of it, that Paddy used to hold on to. Honestly, Willie was dead scared, he cried at times. I remember that, and I'm almost sure that that put him off. I don't think he's ever ridden, has Willie.*

Betty was a great help to the Finn family who were hunting friends. Mary Finn's younger brother Lewis had died young. Betty helped by taking the girls to Point-to-Points and generally transporting them around. She made sure Mary and her sisters got out and about at this sad time.

Mount Ephraim was divided up, in 1935, to save on the rates. Which meant no furniture was allowed in the south end, so Sandys and Joan moved to the north end.

Willie remembered coming to stay for Christmas at Mount Ephraim in 1938 with Geoffrey Cuttle, who was his age.

WILLIE: *This was before the war had started, and that end of the house was not furnished. I can remember there was a clockwork train set that John had had out, and it ran all the way round where the billiard table is now, and it was a wind up one. We*

*used to play with it. It was a Gauge 0 that you wound up. It was
quite a magnificent lay-out that had been left there by the two
older boys, after they had gone back to school after their holidays.*
Geoffrey Cuttle [whose gradfather had been Willie Dawes's
clerk] *and I aged about seven or eight used to play with it.*

*Mopsie had taken a lot of stuff to Berkeley. That end of the
house was virtually never furnished until after the war, but the
dining-room was furnished.*

Betty was always left of centre politically. She voted for Percy
Wells, the Labour candidate, but generally she was a Liberal.

Willie on a pony, being led by Paddy Cassels

Chapter Nineteen
Banff

The 'Banff' existence was of great importance in Betty's life. It was home from home. Mopsie was a Banff woman and there were aunts, uncles and cousins who made up a full community, especially in the summer.

Banff is a self-contained old town. It is not very big and built upwards from its own small harbour. Duff House, the seat of the Dukes of Fife, is an eighteenth-century Adam-style palace on the east side of the town situated on the River Deveron, along Gaveney Brae.

There was a quartet of Simpson/Dawes houses, on the west side of Banff. The Simpsons had lived at Colleonard for generations. The house was stone rendered with harling (cement mortar) and was built in a T-shape to catch the sun. There was a long picture window above the fireplace in the ante-room on the first floor. The house had an old-fashioned air and sat under the brow of a hill.

Colleonard, which means wood-on-the-height, was rented from the estate of the Dukes of Fife. The Simpsons ran a Meal Mill until the World War I. They had put in a whisky distillery at Boyndie. Mopsie's brother Tom Simpson lived at Colleonard with his family.

WILLIE: *One reason that my Great Uncle Tom refused to use the dining-room at Colleonard during the war, was that it brought back too many bad memories, because he lost his own wife in '36 or '37, and he lost his younger brother, Aunty Bee's twin brother, Chevy. They were both buried immediately before the war out of that dining-room, so it was very very rarely used – and a lovely room it was. It was on the ground floor and the drawing-room above it had been built by their father on whisky money, after his success at the Paris Exhibition that they put up the Eiffel Tower in the 1890s.*

There were quantities of Simpson and Henderson cousins. Betty was always family minded and knew them all. There were plenty more cousins from Grandfather James Simpson's first family and also a collection of maiden aunts.

Aunty Bee made her home with her sister Mopsie from before First World War. She educated the younger generation and later, helped to run Mount Ephraim Estate (with G W Finn & Sons) for her nephew Sandys, paying the wages, etc. She remained a companion to Mopsie and lived wherever she did, all her life.

Aunt Budsie painted beautifully and was a brilliant pianist. She was highly strung, but went over-the-top, and ended up in a 'home'. She died there in 1955.

Aunt Anne, or Great-Grand Aunt Anne as she was known to later generations, resided at Colleonard Cottage, the farm end of Colleonard (with Willie McCatty in the other half). She was a bit of a dragon and became deaf at an early age. Tom Simpson's children Orrock, Lilian and Alan, all learned to speak with practically closed lips, because Aunt Anne could lip-read!

When Betty's Simpson uncle and aunts were children, one day they were playing at the old distillery at Banff.

They had all climbed inside the distillery chimney, which had been felled and was lying on the ground. Aunty Bee got stuck half way up the chimney! Eventually, they had to attach a rope around her ankles and haul her out backwards. After that she became claustrophobic and when indoors, she always had to have the window open.

A lane called Josie Allan's Brae led directly from Colleonard's gate, over the hill, straight down towards the other two houses a mile away on the links, near the mouth of the Boyndie Burn.

Mopsie's elder sister Mary had married Tom Henderson and with their family of six, they would descend on Links Cottage on the shore for the summer months. No one resided there, as they were otherwise in Kenya.

Then there was Swordanes, the house bought at the turn of the century by Willie and Mopsie for summer holidays. It was a comfortable, gabled house on the Banff links, the foreshore of the North Sea, slightly to the west of the town. Originally, Swordanes had been three fishermen's cottages converted, with bits added later, such as a gunroom, a larder and bachelor servant's rooms, opposite the drive. (Female servant's rooms were the other side of the cloth – green baize door.) The house was completed by 1910. It had a sea-view over to Morven.

Willie Dawes built a concrete bridge across the Boyndie Burn (which was washed away in floods in the 1950s).

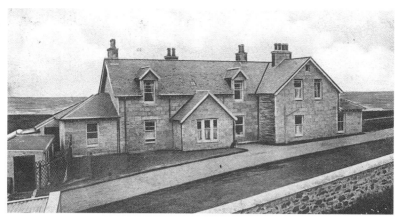

Swordanes

Mopsie also owned Linksfield Farm and a block of cottages up the road which included a laundry cottage.

Every summer all the Dawes family went north from Kent. They did this right from the beginning of the century until the late 1950s.

So what was the attraction of this remote east-coast Scottish retreat?

The answer was 'Sport'. There were two partridge shoots. One in the vicinity of Colleonard, with two or three thousand acres. Angus was the Keeper. He might have put down a few pheasants for stock as well; but not to make it a very serious pheasant shoot. There were plenty of rabbits also, and pigeons.

There was another shoot on the Craigston Estate at Scattertie, which lies a few miles up the River Deveron. This was rented from Bruce Pollard-Urquhart and he had a Keeper called Drummond. Scattertie was two or three thousand acres also. Enough for four separate partridge shoots. This shooting became available after 1 September.

The Aultmore Shoot was quite separate, and lay about 15 miles away. Aultmore could produce shooting for three separate days per season. The Lodge was fairly primitive with seaweed mattresses. Much later Betty remarked, on seeing bog cotton at West Tempar in the highlands, **'I am sure the sheets at Aultmore were made from that'**. Sometimes she lived there, and other times would come over from Swordanes.

WILLIE: *Her father had the shooting at Aultmore, rented from the Countess of Seafield – the Seafield Estate at Cullen, before the '14 War, then after he died they kept it on. They ran it in the '20s then it was given up. Mother* [Betty] *had it again in the '30s, when she took it on again under her own wing, with paying guests for grouse-shootings in about 1925/26/28, up until about '35 or '36 when it was given up after Father* [Rudolf] *went bust and they were officially bankrupt.*

At the end of her life Betty came back and visited old haunts with Willie, and described old times:

On the way to Aultmore Lodge – where we had the shooting from 1917 to 1941. My father built 2 Bathrooms, a drying room, new Dog Kennels etc. He died in 1920 & never saw these additions. My mother let the shooting for 1920, '21 and '22. She took over [until] I came of age in 1926 at 25. It was a lovely moor belonging to Lady Seafield & Keeper left in Cottage. I was never happier in my life than at Aultmore. We went up to the Lodge and found the Keeper's grand-daughter, who said if we could fight our way through the forest, we could walk from Cottage to Lodge – approx. 100 yds. We got through Forest trees within 2 ft of windows. No view left & Ledge falling down & pheasants reared in same.

The more [moor] all forest trees. Shooting – Roe deer and pheasants. I wish I had not gone to see it.

She often referred to a 20-stone ghillie, who used to delicately pick and eat a blaeberry and announce, *'So refreshing!'* Betty always wondered what power a blaeberry had upon so stout a man.

Mopsie's 'Scattertie beat' on the Deveron was half an hour's driving from the house, and gave them all good fishing sport for many years – until her death. Betty was very keen and used to go out from Swordanes after dinner. It was about a half hour's journey and then she would fish late up to midnight. She was often successful with sea trout. Betty particularly enjoyed The Tail or The Vee – as it was sometimes called, before it ran into the rough water of Moggie Mull. She also was keen on the Burnmouth which was the extreme downstream part of the beat.

There were two tennis courts at Swordanes and a croquet lawn. For those who felt inclined, there was a good golf course, too, in Banff.

Mopsie had a caravan for journeys up to Banff on occasions. Pay, the chauffeur would drive, towing the caravan and taking five days, with Aunty Bee and a young John Dawes travelling up, also Betty sometimes. Pay would sleep in the car and the rest of them in the caravan. At the end of the Banff season the caravan was shipped out from Aberdeen to Tilbury and so returned to Kent.

If parties got too rough at Swordanes, Mopsie would simply sit upon the hapless culprit, until they were flattened! She weighed 18 stone.

There were some strange family traditions at Swordanes. Even as an old lady, Mopsie would still swim in the North Sea. The family was always staying in strength on 1st September, her birthday. Even after Mopsie's death, every member, young or old was forced into the water, always at 8.00 am, in celebration; even if the weather was freezing!

JOHN: *On Grannie's* [Mopsie's] *birthday, Reveille was 8 o'clock and you had to immerse yourself. You didn't need to stay in. You could then basically come out. You then breakfasted on good but thin porridge, followed by a full cooked breakfast.*

Betty on horseback, sidesaddle with the Blean Beagles

Chapter Twenty
Two dashing youths

Two young men whipped-in for the Blean Beagles in the 1930s. In the late 1990s, Peter Godwin and Stuart Boult cast their minds back to remember this period. Both also became lifelong friends of Betty's.

PETER GOODWIN: *You ask me for my memories of Betty. Easier said than done! The memory is there, but the exact detail and names concerned after more than sixty years is not quite so easy.*

In 1937 when I joined a new company in Canterbury, I discovered that I would have time to again go beagling [as I had done previously]. *So searching a copy of 'Horse and Hound', I found that 'The Blean' was the nearest pack and the next meet was at 'Mall House' in Faversham. Arriving at the meet, I found myself being greeted and invited into 'Mall House' by the owner's son who introduced himself as Maurice Wix. Very sadly Maurice was killed during the evacuation of France in 1940.*

In Mall House, I was introduced to Mrs McKeever and so met 'Betty' for the first time. At the end of the day she said the next meet would be at Cleve Hill. This was near Waterham, her home and 'Would I like to come there after hunting and stay for dinner?' Accepting with pleasure, I then met Jean and Willie. Willie had been given a large, secondhand electric train set, the electrics of which required sorting out. Having explained what I thought should be done, I then received a further kind invitation to return again ASAP, bringing my soldering iron – and have a go at it.

From that day on, Waterham became a second home and Betty and Jean two very important people in my life.

I well remember my first 'Blean Beagle Ball', held above the old Regal Cinema in Canterbury. Sitting at dinner in company with the surrounding Hunts and their Masters and at an age when such occasions were still new to me, Betty suddenly leaned across and said: **'Peter, will you please propose the toast to the visiting masters.'** *Not listening to my protest and giving me only a minute or two to try and gather my wits, she smiled and announced me.*

*I have no idea what I said, but it was a hunt ball, lots of cham-
pagne and everyone in the best spirits. These are the sort of things
Betty could do, maybe just for the fun or the devil of it, or maybe
because she knew it was a good way for the young to learn – by
being thrown in at the deep end!*

*Remembering this and other hunt balls reminds me of Betty's
evening gown. I think she only had one. She would say:* **'Why do
I need more? I can only wear one at a time.'** *It was a black
sequin frock and had been rather battered in many Paul Jones
which left the threads holding the sequins in a frail condition.
The result was that one would suddenly break and there would
be a shower of sequins in all directions! Betty would dance all the
evening and most of the night. We would go one until 4.00 am
in the morning.*

Looking back before the war...

*Tennis parties at 'The Mount'. Sandys was very keen on tennis and
there were three or four courts to play on. Weekend tennis parties
would be arranged and I was often kindly invited. Betty played a
very good placing game and her returns would have you running
around the court. She was excellent as a doubles partner.* [Others
remembered how nice it was to be able to serve – with the
butler standing ready with refreshment.]

*Sometimes after hunting, a small number of us would decide to
go up to London for supper at 'The Trocodero' restaurant. In those
days there was no hold-up with traffic and you could get into the
centre of London quite quickly and park your car without trouble
in Lower Regent Street.*

*Arriving at Waterham one might find the local policeman
there. He and Betty would be chatting and enjoying a well mixed
drink. I am sure he always managed to manoeuvre his bicycle back
to the station or home. Betty, quite reasonably, always liked to be
friends with the police, they could be very helpful, especially when
a hound got lost or went astray.*

*Betty had a wonderful way with animals, especially horses.
She could take on an awkward bad-tempered horse and soon have
it behaving quite differently.*

*She was good with her hands and liked to make things and
would sit in front of the fire in the evening, knitting long woollen*

stockings which she liked to wear. She had a wood-turning lathe in her bedroom, plus lots of tools and made several cabinets. Drawing and painting were no strangers to her.

Not only good at handicrafts but also enjoyed reading and would talk and discuss a subject with anyone. However, if she did not know the subject, would be very prepared to listen and question you on its detail. With her tongue in her cheek Betty liked to take an opposing view point, to wind you up!

Betty could tell stories from morn to night. Over the years you would often hear them more than once. Not always with exactly the same detail! I think that Jean could have easily told them for her. However, the way she told them always made them interesting and worth listening to. Although after a day's beagling and a lot of fresh air, it could sometimes be very easy to fall asleep while listening, however interesting they might be.

Betty did not find it difficult to stay awake in the evening. However, at the other end of the clock she was not the earliest of risers and there could be quite a chase in the morning when she was due at a Meet or some other arranged event, even if this was not very early.

When one thinks of Waterham, memories of many people can start to creep in.

Jean Fraser had joined Betty at Waterham only a short time before I first met her. She had answered an advertisement placed by Betty, requiring a girl to assist in looking after poultry. However, in answering this advertisement, she said nothing very much about her special qualifications or background. Then Betty slowly gleaned the background of Jean, family and education. Realizing her abilities, she invited her to move from her lodgings into Waterham itself. Where she stayed for the rest of her life.

Jean was soon not only assisting with the farm but also running the house and being a great help in looking after Betty's son William who was still very young. Jean always refused to dance at the parties, but was otherwise fun and lively. [She was like a sister to Peter Godwin.] Without Jean Fraser, I am sure Betty's daily life could have taken quite a different pattern.

Harry Butler was kennelman and professional whip to the beagles. Then, at a later date, Jim took over the same responsibilities from his father. Mrs Butler gave a lot of time to assist in the house and was a great help to Jean.

Then there was 'Paddy' the groom. I well remember him as he taught me how to jump. Having been born in Newmarket and my father being a retired trainer, I had had every opportunity to ride, but seldom took advantage of this. Betty very kindly gave me the chance to make up for lost time and to go out exercising with her. She also taught me some basic dressage and then turned me over to Paddy for jumping practice. As I remember, it was 'The Tapir' who had to suffer all my mishandling, but he was a very patient animal. (Some years later Betty put my son Simon into the saddle and gave him lessons.)

During the war both Betty and Jean would often write and keep me informed of local events [as Peter was abroad, fighting.]

Betty enjoyed all Field Sports: hunting, shooting and fishing and was an expert at all three. She was a good correspondent and after my wife Kit and I had moved to Heathfield, always kept us informed of events and encouraged us to visit.

Stuart Boult has his own memories of before the war:

BOULTY: *I did meet her husband. Not many times but I helped buy an overcoat for him, at Canterbury. That was his last Christmas present, I think. She 'lost' a husband – he went back to Ireland. I was out with the beagles twice a week. They had me dressed in green. Oh, yes. They used to call me 'White Boots', because I always used to wear white lacrosse running shoes, to me – nice things to run in.*

Stuart Boult came to stay at Waterham on one occasion. His luggage was standing in the hall. Mrs Harry Butler, who was working there at the time, hid the luggage – as she thought that there was an illicit affair going on!

BOULTY: *If we beagled on Saturdays, Betty used to insist on me staying the night. It was after about the second year, she moved me out of 'Little Hell' the bedroom that looks over the pigs. She moved me to a bigger room, next to her room, I think. The one in the middle. Then, of course, on Sunday mornings, it was a suit (for me). And Betty would appear and would be wearing a hat. She generally had a flower in her hat and a very smart coat and skirt or dress. A dress rather than suit – she wore a suit all the week. But on Sundays she'd go to church looking very smart then go and have lunch.*

One of the wonderful things as a young man, I always remember. Cream was something that was a little special – was always something that had to be bought separately. Of course, Betty having the cow, we had milk in the house, and, if anybody came in, if a young man came in to have breakfast, Betty would always serve them porridge then she'd say, **'I'll serve you to cream, because you young people never know – never take enough cream. It's good for you.'** Then she'd drop in half a pint of cream! She was sweet like that. She was always terribly kind to young people.

We'd finish beagling – have tea or something like that, then, **'Oh, I want to go and see – up to the Mount. Come on.'** So up to the Mount we'd go. We all used to sit there chattering, then they used to go to see something outside. Then it was just naturally supper. Edwards [the butler] would come in and say, 'How many for supper?' Joan would count – '15 of us, 10 of us.'

Mount Ephraim was still 'home' to Betty. She lived at Waterham, but all her childhood had been there. It wasn't only all evening, you know. We'd sit there, and I'd half to go off to sleep, and she and Sandys would rabbit on until perhaps 12.00 or 1 o'clock in the morning. And then we'd go back to Waterham, and sit down and have a last cup of coffee, or something like that, and Betty would say, **'Oh, I forgot to tell Sandys such and such, so and so'.** She'd go across, pick up the telephone. She'd go on, talking to Sandys, for another hour, two hours – off they'd go. So they'd never stop talking together, those two, about the family and the farm and everything and the business. Tremendous friends.

Betty, you know, would never go past the Mount. We always popped in. It was her home. Just because we were at the farm, that was where she farmed, it wasn't where her home was. Mount Ephraim was her 'mental' home. Always 'popped in'. Everything was always centred on the Mount.

'Sandys couldn't blow the horn and had a reed put in!' Betty used to tell that one! Sandys of course, always supported the story – [as he had a great sense of humour. Sandys, in fact, was an excellent horn-blower and certainly didn't use a reed, but he was able to stand this teasing by his sister!] – wouldn't admit to it.

Lovely tennis parties at the Mount. How many tennis courts have you got now? Mopsie played tennis too. In the summer they used to have tennis parties – before the war. I was always terribly *lucky, you see. I was always included in all the parties that Betty went to. Eight hunt-dances or balls I went to each year. Eight. I was invited – presumably as a complementary, because I was a hunt servant, an amateur. I became her partner and she could waltz! For years and years and years she wore a black sequin dress. At all the balls.*

If I rang Betty at Waterham before the War, for some reason, before the telephone had even rung the other end, Mrs Somebody from the Post Office, would be saying, 'I'm terribly sorry. Mrs McKeever has gone to so-and-so tonight, and she won't be back till late.'

The blinking girl at the Post Office – the telephone exchange, [Miss Eves] *used to give me a full report on what everybody in the Family was doing.*

We went to The Star, Maidstone for the Mid-Kent Stag Hunt Ball. We stopped at the gate and bought a bottle of Champagne and sat on the staircase of The Star, drinking this bottle of Champagne with Betty greeting everybody from the sitting position, as they were coming up the steps.

There was a hill at Belmont, and an enormous great field that out beagling she always used to draw. This lovely field was always down to corn and absolutely bare in the Autumn. As Boulty was walking round there, he said to himself, *'Good Lord, that looks like a cannon ball!'* He picked it up and showed it to Betty who had no hesitation at all. **'Oh, yes Boulty. You see, they used to have the Napoleonic prisoners. They were up here, and of course, one of the things they loved doing was playing Boule. This is one of the balls they used to make.'** It was extraordinary the things she knew, straight away.

BOULTY: *On another occasion she caught her stocking on the screw on the side of the horse-box.* **'Damn thing.'** *She kicked it with her toe to try and get it out of her stocking. Of course it wasn't in her stocking at all, it was actually in her leg. She pushed her leg all the way down until she could get the screw out. It was through her flesh – extraordinary!'*

Gypsies

BOULTY: *No door in Waterham was ever shut. That was another rule of hers. The house was always wide open for everybody.*

Somebody might walk past wanting shelter. Her house was always available. Betty hated anybody locking gates and she never locked a gate.

At the time of year when the Gypsies would be going down the Romney Marsh, they would just go into her land, and spend one night or two there. After the Gypsies had been going past and staying on her land for years, this all came home to her through a Gypsy boy who worked for her.

She said, **'I never bothered about them. I never objected to them going there. I couldn't find anything. One day I said to this boy, "Gypsies' coming past this week?"**

'Yes' he said.

'You talk about marking houses. Is Waterham marked?'

'Waterham marked Ma'am? It's been marked for years. We don't even bother, now.' Then the boy said, 'You know you're not Mrs McKeever, don't you? No, you're Mrs Kleever. If you want to talk to a Gypsy about yourself, you say "Do you know Mrs Kleever?" They'll say, "We don't know her personally, but her land is always open for us. We wouldn't touch anything on her land."'
He was a nice lad.

Bookies

BOULTY: *At Point-to-Points the owners always go in the ring, stand there and chat about this and that. They tell the rider what to do and encourage him. I was very fortunate that Betty didn't leave me standing near the cars or anything.* **'Come on, Boulty.'** *And so I always went with her into the ring.*

One day, Betty suddenly looked round the ring. and said, **'Boulty, Got five bob on you'.**
'Yes.'

'Go and put five bob on a horse.'

There were only about five Bookies there at the Point-to-Point. So I walked over to the first one and said, 'Oh, 5-1. Can I have five bob on it, please.'

He looked at me. 'Certainly.' And he wrote out the card. Then he took a piece of paper, slammed a white horse out, wrote it in underneath, 5-4-on, or something like that.

So I said 'That was quick. I've only given you five bob.'

He said 'Ah, yes. But you walked across from Betty McKeever. She told you to put the money on that horse. It will win. If Mrs McKeever says it will win, it will win.'

I thought, even the book-makers know me as Betty's man.

Stomacher

BOULTY: *We talked about the elegance of Mopsie's generation and her kindness. One day, we happened to say something about a tiara. I said, 'Well, what I was always fascinated with, is the stomacher. What was that?'*

And Mopsie said 'Well, you know, it was part of the tiara that you took off, the sort of lower bit, and you wore across [the chest] *you see.' Anyway, time goes on, and war starts. Betty rings me up and said,* **'You're off I hear'.**

I said 'Yes. Sad but never-the-less off I'm going somewhere and it's all very exciting.'

Well, Mopsie said you're to come and have dinner, properly, because war is not a funny thing and she hopes to see you when the war's all over, but you never know. At the top of the hill, at Berkeley. So come and have dinner, and put your dinner jacket on. Dress nicely. Betty was always one to give you your orders.

So I rolled up at Berkeley – properly dressed and Albert opens the door and looks at me. He says, 'Good Evening, Sir. Yes, you'll do.' Takes me into the Morning Room and gives me a drink.

Betty comes in and we have a chat about this, and suddenly the door opens, and in walks Mopsie, if you please, in black velvet, wearing the stomacher. I said, 'Mopsie, I never thought I'd live to see one being worn'.

She said, 'Well Boulty, dear, probably you and I will never meet again. We'll have a nice dinner – all properly done, and I would wear my stomacher for you.' I thought how kind and thoughtful. Mopsie was a lovely lady. She was a great woman for hunting.

Albert was remembered by Peter, too.

PETER: *I suppose he must have had another name but I can't remember ever hearing it Albert was very much a member of the Dawes household. He had been first employed as a general house and footman at The Mount, had moved with Mrs Dawes to Berkeley and then over the years worked up to be her butler. He would open the front door to you dressed in a dark green cutaway morning coat with silver buttons.*

Chapter Twenty-one
World War II

When war broke out Betty was staying in Banff, with her sister-in-law Joan and her nephew John. Joan Dawes rushed home but would not let the 15-year-old John come south for a week.

The 'phoney war' then lasted until Spring 1940.

Slotty and Ivy by this time had three children, George, Jean and the baby Charles. The Brunton family worked for them and their child was called Lancelot, after Slotty.

The younger generation, consisting of Slotty's three, the Brunton child and the 7 year old Willie McKeever were removed from Kent.

At the fall of Dunkirk, Slotty decided the family would move up to Shropshire. They wanted to be near the stepping-off point, because the American Daweses had offered to take all the grandchildren for the duration and Liverpool would be the port of embarkation. George's prep school (he was the eldest member of that generation) had moved up into Shropshire. So they all set forth.

WILLIE: *We had an old pick-up van. Mother, Jean Fraser, myself and Jim Butler. All the signposts had been taken down to confuse the enemy. There was no signposts. We got into what was allegedly Warwick and stopped and asked some old boy the way. 'Didn't you recognise it as you came over the river bridge?' He wouldn't tell us what [the town] was. We had to surmise that it was Warwick from this damned castle! We were driven to Shrewsbury in the truck and we all booked into the Red or Golden Lion Hotel, and we (self, Mother, Jean) stayed there about four days. Mother then said she'd had enough of this. and we got in a train in the blackout, and we went on various trains from Crewe, through to Aberdeen and then to Banff. And Mother persuaded Jean to look after me, from when the war was declared onwards, virtually. And that was how it was to be. We stayed in Banff, Jean and I; and Mother came back home to Waterham to the farm. Jim Butler drivng the pick-up truck back from Shrewsbury.*

Jean Fraser and I stayed up in Banff from roughly the fall of France [June 1940] until 10th March 1943. Mother closed down

*Waterham and just used it to picnic in, and moved up to Mount
Ephraim. Sandys was in London all through the week because he
was in the Ministry of Economic Warfare, and was a member of
the Home Guard. So there was just Joan living in Mount Ephraim,
and the house was split in half. The military were on one side
and the family were on the other.*

*Mother lived there with Joan, and Sandys came down for the
weekends.* [John was also there in the holidays until August,
1942.]

About a fortnight after us, Ivy, [young] *Jean and Charles
arrived with old Ma Brunton and they rented Links Cottage from
Aunt Mary Henderson, Mopsie's sister.*

*I suppose the Daweses stayed up there nearly a year. We all did
lessons. Lancey Brunton, myself and Jean* [Dawes]. *Charles was
much too young to do lessons, because Grandma* [Mopsie] *had a
fear that if we went to the Academy, we'd bring home disease, so
that was forbidden at that stage. It wasn't until later, after Slotty's
lot went back that I went to the Banff Academy for about a year.*

Jean (Rowntree) remembered leaving home. Her father Slotty
wanted them all north of London in 24 hours: *'We all piled into
a Hillman's Pork. The cook, her dog, her son, Ma, me, Charles in a
carrycot.'*

Jean Dawes thoroughly enjoyed staying with her Grannie Mopsie
at Swordanes.

JEAN [Rowntree]: *There was a Banff gang of about 60 children.
We found a dugout at the end of the lawn,* [constructed in the
first week of the War by Betty, John Dawes and the Keeper,
Fife] *on the cliffs, deep down to the road below, the shore road.
And these gangs would come and throw stones at us and we'd
throw stones at them. And the police came, because we also broke
these electric fittings on the telegraph poles and Grannie swore
we'd never get the* [telephone] *back.*

*But Jean Fraser said, 'Now look, I know they' re throwing
stones at you, but you must not throw stones back.' And we put
wire over the top of our dugout.*

Along the railway line [which Swordanes backed on to] *we
put lumps of clay on the wall* [at Jean Fraser's suggestion] *and
allowed the sun to bake them. This was slightly more socially
acceptable than stones, but the baked clay was very hard and gosh*

the battles were terrific! It was wonderful when [my brother]
George came up [for the holidays] *we had another pair of hands,
bigger and better than ours. They never beat us!*

*Then one day I was riding my pony, Polly, who was absolutely
marvellous, back from Whitehills, and I came across eight* [local]
boys, standing across the lane. And to go another way was miles
[further].

The young Jean Dawes couldn't think of a way across. But
she definitely wasn't going to go round. She was 9. Eventually,
she charged them at full speed on Polly, and, thank goodness,
they scattered, and she got through!

JEAN [Rowntree]: *Jean Fraser was not a teacher by trade, she was
a poultry woman. We used a post system, a lot of children in the
War were educated by it. All highly organized. It was very well
done. The PNEU system.*

*I was very fond of Jean. Never fell out or had a problem with
Jean Fraser. I think she was quite fond of me too. We got on very
well together. I don't recall her ever doing any sport with us. I think
we were just left to run wild when it came to physical exercise.*

Jean Fraser became almost a mother to Willie.

JEAN [Rowntree]: *That's why she became the Governess. Because
she was so appalled at Aunt Betty's lack of interest. It was terrible.
She couldn't believe what she saw. She came from Edinburgh to
look after the chickens and was appalled at the way Aunt Betty
cared, or didn't care for Willie. She asked, 'Can I stay and be the
governess?' And she started to educate Willie.*

Betty was certainly up in Banff for the Christmas of 1940. In
January 1941 she was driving Aunty Bee's car along the Cemetery
Road to Colleonard from Swordanes, and slithered into a ditch. The
Colleonard horse was commissioned to pull the car out backwards.

Sandys and Joan would go up to Banff for a fortnight's fishing.
They stayed at Swordanes or Sandys on his own would stay with his
Simpson godmother. *'He was very fond of Aunt Anne.'* Willie remembered. *'He used to tease her a lot – nobody else did. Sandys would blow
on her neck from behind. She was an old tiger and was deaf, but they
were great together.'*

Whilst Waterham was closed, Betty had her own permanent bedroom at Mount Ephraim and was very grateful to Sandys and Joan

for having her to stay. The south half of the Mount was being used by the military.

In 1940 Bill Dawes married Mary Finn (whose mother Madie Finn was Joint-Master of the Tickham with Sandys). Mary remembers going down to the basement air-raid shelter at Mount Ephraim in the middle of the night. There was Joan (Sandys wasn't there in those days), herself, Betty, Florence the cook and another maid. But Betty had quite a long way to come and hadn't got her warm clothes on, so she took a pair of combinations with her.

MARY: *It was dark, there was no light, and there was Betty, in the dark, struggling to get into her combinations – with the help of Florence. Suddenly there was sort of extraneous noises! Two of the soldiers, who were* [stationed in the north] *end of the house and, unknown to the family, were also in the basement, listening to Betty struggling into her woolly combinations!*

Betty was a member of the Kent War Agricultural Committee which helped encourage people to grow as much food as possible. She was farming, and got involved with some sort of defence work where they stored emergency rations on Monks Hill.

It was all very hush hush, but it was believed that if an invasion had happened there would have been a policy in Kent of 'scorched earth', so the Germans would find no provisions. Local farmers were recruited – people who knew their way across country, without having to use the roads. Betty was one of the farmers involved in this. If invasion had happened, she would have laid waste to the land. But she signed the Official Secrets Act and never gave anything away.

Betty was prepared to retreat into Blean Woods and 'shoot it out' with the Germans. To this end she was prepared, not only with her gun and ammunition, but with a bag of Scottish oatmeal and a bottle of whisky!

She had an unused box of shotgun cartridges labelled 'WD – Ball Cartridge – (for defence purposes only)'. These were issued apparently to all farmers living in coastal areas in anticipation of the then, almost certainty of invasion by the Germans. Betty's friends could imagine her confronting the Nazi panzers like Queen Boadicea, brandishing her trusty 16 bore at the enemy! She certainly didn't lack physical courage.

During the war, Betty carried a long pole in her car or tractor, fitted at one end with a grappling iron in order to extricate pilots or aircrew from crashed and burning aircraft by hooking them. She actually witnessed a Hurricane fighter make a crash landing on the marshes, however, the pilot managed to wriggle out before Betty could reach him with her long-handled grappling iron.

Willie: There was a landmine [a deep unexploded bomb of 2,000 lbs], *down in the fields* [about 150 yards from the Mount Ephraim lake]. *The bomb-disposal man came up, who beat upon the door, and Fred Edwards* [the butler] *answered it and the bomb-disposal man said, 'Can you get all the windows open in this house, you've got 20 minutes.'*

And Edwards turned around and said, 'What do you think this is, a bloody bungalow!' The idea was that the windows would blow [out when the bomb was exploded].

Now, one of the windows, in what is the pantry, got blown out during the war, and it had got a bit of glass still left in it, and a large bit of hardboard or plywood. The American cousins came down at weekends, and they got a 2.2 rifle, and a hole you could poke it through, and then lift a flap up. Because your grandfather [Sandys] *had chickens out near the fountain, and the rooks used to come down and pinch the eggs. And they used to sit there, the Americans, taking pot-shots at these rooks, through this hole in the pantry window.*

In a one-horse open sleigh

JOHN DAWES: *In January 1941, when it was very cold, Betty suggested that we drive over to Lorenden about four miles from Waterham – which was the Finns* [Mary's parents] *house – with The Tapir and the sleigh which had lived up in the barn roof behind the piggery, unused.*

In those days roads were not gritted, therefore were a lovely surface for horse and sleigh. It was designed for two sitting on the front seat, there was a place you could put luggage behind. I don't know if it is still at Waterham.

So it was a lovely day out. It didn't take all that long. Perhaps an hour and a quarter each way. We were well rugged up. It's the only occasion when I have been sleighing – in a one-horse open sleigh – I suppose you can say.

Slotty was first posted as a 38-year-old 2nd Lieutenant to the 89th Heavy Anti-Aircraft Regiment where Stuart Boult was Adjutant. Later he was an un-posted senior Lieutenant or Captain at Woolwich. He was called in and offered a Command. It was a mixed anti-aircraft battery – men and women, which was fairly unheard of until then. Slotty thought about it. It was made plain that he would have a dull time if he refused. So he accepted and served in Southampton, Dover, Derby and Manobier.

He found that when it came to doing the sums: for altitude, direction and range of enemy aeroplanes, the girl gunners were very quick at it. These sums were needed to give angle and elevation to the guns, and to set the time fuses on the shells.

When the V-1 'doodle-bugs' started coming over in June 1944, he had a lot to do with trying to shoot them down. Slotty always took Brunton, his groom as his batman. And if Brunton wasn't posted at the same time as he was, Slotty would take Brunton with him, march up to the Commanding Officer and say *'Hmm, and I have got my batman with me. Would you please sign the papers to move him officially.'*! He did that time after time. So Brunton served with Slotty until '44.

> JEAN ROWNTREE: *Sandys became Master of five packs of hounds and had a very gay lifestyle, so Pa asked permission to get out [of the army] because he was not needed by 1944. He got permission to come out and rescue his business, which was actually on the floor. Sandys had got the business down to 15 employees, I always understood, and Pa set about re-building it. Of course a lot of ships had been lost in the war. And Brunton went out to Italy as a driver.*

Sandys had been Chairman of Westrays and was attached to the Ministry of Economic Warfare and the Ministry of Transport. He was nobody's fool. Anyway London, during the war, was virtually closed as a port for Westrays, who were London Agents/loading brokers for the New Zealand Shipping Co. He was also involved in preserving the local hunts.

> WILLIE: *Mother visited Scotland about twice or three times a year. Because it was difficult to get up on the train. Trains were few and far between. Sleepers were reserved for military officers. It was an awful job to get a sleeper. There were very few civilian sleepers. But*

it was interesting. The Finns managed to come up to stay in Banff at 'The Fife Arms', fishing in '42.

Inverboyndie Distillery was at the bottom of Colleonard. But my Gran had a job to make money out of whisky, and Grandfather Willie Dawes was Chairman of the Distillery. He got them contracts to sell whisky in certain London pubs – but it never really got going. So they sold out to the Distillers' Company when it was formed in 1928 or 9. And the Simpsons retired to the farm and did not produce whisky, but they did have the foresight that when the 'pin' (the 4½ gallon barrel living just down the stair cupboard at Colleonard) was empty, it was loaded on to the horse and cart and went down over Josie Allan's Brae to the Distillery to be refilled. Whisky was very difficult to get during the war, and Sandys liked his whisky very much. So Uncle Tom provided the whisky, which was loaded into the bottles out of his barrel, and sent by post to Mount Ephraim – as and when required.

As a kid in Banff, we used to go over on a Saturday, 'cos it was Saturday mornings that the barrel was sent over the hill to be re-filled. I remember, I was fascinated to watch it being re-filled, at the Distillery.

Whisky Galore!

WILLIE: *The Distillery was bombed in the Spring of 1941, which was all written up in the Banffshire Press and Journal.*

Well, I was standing on the doorstep of Inverboyndie Cottage with David Green, Betty Green his mother, and Jean Fraser. And this plane had flown around, twice or 3 times it had circled around – a misty March day, March or February. School was out. It was about half past three, quarter to four in the afternoon, and the plane wasn't very high in the sky. I would think 200 to 300 feet and you saw two things come out of the plane, these were two bombs.

I can remember that we heard machine gun fire as the plane went round again. Wonderful story. We all retired under the dining-room table at Inverboyndie Cottage, being the safest place to go, having drawn the curtains to stop any glass blowing in. Because there hadn't been an alarm. There was no air-raid warn-

ing siren had gone off. Dear old Albert Butcher, Grandmother's
butler, was out in front of Swordanes by the clock.

And the baker's horse was there. Lemmens from Whitehills.
Scottish bakers in those days had these baker's carts with all selec-
tions of baps and cakes and breads – in great drawers that slid
out. The bakers horse was jumping up and down, because of the
[bombs], and had to be restrained.

And they were machine gunning, because there were Military
based at the Distillery. But they hit a bonded warehouse, and it
had got whisky in it that was a probably three seasons old – and
therefore not fit to drink.

There were awful tales. It was the Highland Light Infantry
which were based there, with the Ghurka Regiment. Lord
Rowallan, who later became Chief Scout was the Colonel. He was
a teetotaller, I understand, and he went and paraded everybody
and emptied water-bottles which had got filled up with this.

But some of the local fire-brigade, older men – because they
were all volunteers virtually in those days – they'd taken and drunk
some of this whisky, because it was all running everywhere. They
were taken very ill and, I gather, they had to go into the Chalmers
Hospital in Banff and be stomach pumped – or they'd have been
in a terrible state.

That was another tale – but the thing that was interesting
about it, was that it generated it's own heat with the wind.
Because it was a spirit it ignited, and the individual barrels
exploded. And so this fire raged for a considerable time, and bits of
it floated down the burn like a Christmas pudding alight. We went
to have a look, and below the warehouse was an old marshy bit of
ground – probably called the water-meadows if you were kind. The
farm on the hill above – all their ducks and geese used to go down
in there. Anything funnier that seeing a goose and a duck drunk on
the fumes of whisky – had to be seen to be believed!

The firemen were emptying maturing whisky into the
Inverboyndie Burn, to stop the fire spreading. Troops had had their
heads in the burn, or were using their tin hats to drink the green
whisky, and then had to be stomach-pumped. Cattle also drank
the burn waters and toppled over, poor dears. Their milk had to
be thrown away for several days after.

The Germans claimed that they had hit a major arms store in the
North-East!

Jean Fraser had a young suitor. At that time, there was a well-known shampoo advertisement out:

Friday Night's

'Amami' night.

(Ready for your date on Saturday.)

Betty, teasing Jean about her young man Marmaduke, would look soulfully out of the window and sigh, **'Every night is a Marmy night!'** Both she and Sandys could sometimes over-tease.

WILLIE: *Jean was engaged to an RAF chap from Lossiemouth in the War, and it was expected to proceed and be married after the War, and he was killed in a bombing raid over Germany in the winter of '42/'43. And that was the end of that.*

Waterham had been closed from after Dunkirk until Betty and Mopsie travelled south together on the night train on 10 March 1943. They stayed at Mount Ephraim for five weeks until Waterham was opened up. During Waterham's closed period, Betty just picnicked there sometimes, and Jim Butler firewatched.

WILLIE: *We came back down here in the Spring of '43 for a month. Berkeley was inhabited by the Military – the house half way up Boughton Hill. Grandmother came back to Kent for a month and we all stayed at Mount Ephraim. This house wasn't open. We then went back [north] for another month, then Jean & I came back down here [to Kent] in nice time to get accustomed to the doodle-bugs – flying bombs – when they started. And I was down here, and Jean then gave me lessons because I was not sent to Hernhill School. It wasn't until my Prep School moved back from Bruton in Somerset (the people who ran it were friendly to the family – called Whitfield), that I was sent to school in Autumn '45 when they came back.*

Willie had his 13th birthday the autumn after the war ended.

Chapter Twenty-two
Betty – middle stories

Dunkirk!

There was a small fishing boat, which came back into either
Peterhead or Fraserburgh. When the fishermen landed at the quay-
side, they discovered that everything was terribly quiet. All the
womenfolk then came forward and berated them and said, *'Get
waa away into Dunkirk'*.

The fishermen said, *'Vhat, Dunkirk?'*

And the women said, *'Aye, Mr Churchill said ye'r awaa doon in
Dunkirk, to pick up the so'jers and bring them hame.'*

So they re-fuelled as quickly as they could, and off they went.
*'We're going down to the Dunkirk place in wee boats to bring in the boys.
We're no' going to the fishing grounds.'* And finally, after a huge journey, they arrived off the beaches of Dunkirk – the day after the
evacuation was called off.

The skipper got the boat in as close as he could.

Now the crew consisted of a young loon (youth) who was a
muckle glaikit (big idiot). Now the skipper, nea' waa was he going
to get in the dingy and row in to the shore! as it was too dangerous.
So he directed the loon to do the job, and explained to him exactly
what was required. And *'Did ye understand all that?'* *'Ay, aye. Aye –
aye.'* And so the loon took the dingy, rowing as close as he could to
the shore. He jumped out and shouted, *'Anybody for Peterhead and
the Brugh?'* [Fraserburgh]

And by chance, there was indeed a Gordons' Battalion within
earshot. So they picked up six jocks, which was all that they could
fit in the fishing boat, and took 'em a' awaa hame, back to North
East Scotland. And it was months before the Army managed to
catch up with them!

This story was told to Andrew and Randall Nicol by Betty. Randall
had the story confirmed to him by an old skipper from Buckie or
Portsoy.

Ploughman

Liz Neame – A tale told by her brother-in-law.

A man was ploughing. Betty was out hunting and fell in a ditch almost under his plough. The ploughman unhitched his team and hauled her horse out of the ditch. Betty thanked him and rode on. 30 or 40 years later Betty met the ploughman's son. She tipped him. **'I didn't have any money on me at the time – but here, have a drink on me!'**

Launched

Betty was present at the launch of both *Ruahine*s, 40 years apart. These were passenger-going liners of the New Zealand Shipping Company. The first *Ruahine* would have been broken up before the second one was launched. Mopsie launched both ships. Betty was about 8 (or 10) or so for the first launch, so missed all the parties as she was too young. So Betty stayed in the nursery with a much younger girl.

HMS *Blean*

During World War II a new type of destroyer was introduced. It was a Type III Destroyer – Hunt Class. To be named after various hunts, mostly foxhounds, but two of the destroyers were named after beagle packs.

It pleased Betty immensely to have one called HMS *Blean*, so she presented them with a piece of silver. HMS Blean was commissioned in August 1942 and completed on the 23rd of the same month. She worked up at Scapa, in Orkney and then in the Mediterranean. HMS *Blean* escorted a convoy to Gibraltar 2 November 1942.

The whole of her active service was with the 58th Destroyer Division, based at Algiers, escorting 'Torch' convoys. (Operation 'Torch' was the code-name for the invasion of North Africa in late 1942.)

On 11 December, 1942 HMS *Blean* was hit by two torpedoes from the German U-boat U443. She sank in four minutes. Eight officers and 60 ratings were picked up, but 89 ratings were lost – they would have been in the bowels of the ship. HMS *Blean* had had the shortest career of any of the Hunt Class Destroyers. Barely commissioned before the Germans sunk her.

The crew of HMS *Blean* had been proud of the special piece of silver that Betty had presented, but it went down with the ship.

Meet of the Blean Beagles at Westwood Court, Faversham

Chapter Twenty-three
Blean-Beagles [3]

Hunting didn't really happen during the World War II but a nucleus of all the East Kent packs were saved.

The Blean Beagles hunted during the 1939/40 season from Waterham, then moved over to Mount Ephraim where the Mid-Kent Staghounds were kennelled behind the stables.

In the first months of the war the Tickham and some of the Ashford Valley Foxhounds were kept at the Tickham Kennels at Wrens Hill, with Frank Ruffles in charge.

Frank Ruffles then moved over from the Tickham. He lived in the Stable Cottage at Mount Ephraim, looking after the nucleus of the Mid-Kent Staghounds and the Blean Beagles.

All the packs were moved to Mount Ephraim when the big flap was on and thoughts were that they were going to be invaded after Dunkirk. It was easier to have everything there, because the kennelling was adequate. They all were amalgamated into the Tickham and a lot of hounds were put down because hunting stopped.

Sandys did a tremendous amount to preserve all the local packs during the war years. He was Master of the Mid-Kent Staghounds completing 22 seasons by 1949; was Master of the Tickham Foxhounds 1921–22 and Joint-Master with Maddie Finn from 1940 to 1945; Master of the Romney Marsh Harriers from 1934 to 1940; was amateur-huntsman to the Ashford Valley Foxhounds at various periods; and he gave a wartime home to the Blean Beagles. (Although he had been involved with Romney Marsh earlier, they didn't come over during the war, Clem Ramus had them.)

The reasons for having all the hounds in together were the problems in gathering flesh. The hounds survived on fallen stock and scraps. With petrol rationing there was a logistics problem in moving the carcasses. To all be in one place was far more convenient.

Then later on the kennels at Mount Ephraim needed work done on them, the kitchens, etc. – for two or three months.

So Jack Kirby returning from the war was taken on to start hunting the Tickham at Wrens Hill.

The beagles left Mount Ephraim after D-Day. Willie remembers Stella, a lemon and white beagle bitch, with her puppies, on the lawn at Waterham in the Summer of '44. The Blean returned home to Waterham about the time of the D-Day invasion. During the winter '44/spring '45 unofficial hunting started – as soon as they could get staff.

Faversham Riding Club had an event the beagles attended on the Mall Grounds in the town, July/August '45. With Mumford Cook and Harry Jackson – a prisoner of war running it. All the packs of hounds were back at their proper kennels by summer of '45 with more helpers available after demobbing during the spring of '46.

The Stag Hounds were kennelled at Mount Ephraim, pretty well up to the time they were disbanded. They stopped hunting in about 1961. Hubert Allfrey was the last Master.

Peter Goodwin whipped in for 1946–48 seasons. He remembers a Beagle Ball at Mount Ephraim just after the war.

Chapter Twenty-four
Floods!

Living near the huge Thames Estuary at its outlet into the North Sea can have its dangers. In 1953 the sea came in – over the sea-wall.

It had rained heavily with westerly gales until the Spring tides on 30 January. The wind then swung around to the East. It blew very strongly, causing the tide to back up. The flood water coming down the Thames was met by sea-water holding it in.

The water rose higher and higher. The sea-wall gave way and much of low-lying Kent was under water, including Betty's marshy bits.

Sandbags were being put up at Seasalter where some of Betty's sheep were. She hardly slept at all that night. Very early in the morning she was warned by the police or somebody to take the sheep off. She heard that the water was over the wall and that the marshes had been flooded. So she got her horse saddled up and was soon gone down to Seasalter with her hunting horn and woke everybody up – at 4 o'clock in the morning! She rode up and down, blowing her hunting horn, waking everybody up and alerting the villagers that the sea-wall had been breached.

At Mount Ephraim, Bill and Mary had got an early telephone call from Betty.

'Bring boats.'

'What?'

'Can you not see the sea's in.'

Bill and Mary rushed upstairs to the bedroom named the 'Director's Suite', as it was the only room in their end of Mount Ephraim which overlooked the marshes. The sea was in as far as the Coastal Road all the way to the 'Duke of Kent' pub.

They collected cousins George Dawes and Brian Selby, a GP14 sailing yacht and another boat. With these, they drove to the Coastal Road opposite Waterham. They could see some of the sheep on an island, which was Ladd's Hill.

A pulley system was devised. The boats were heaved to and fro with three or four sheep on each journey from this 'island'. Betty was directing operations.

Ivy Dawes, Slotty's wife, attached a rope around the horns of one cow and dragged her into the water with the Land-Rover, so as to encourage the herd to follow her. This worked, although it was thought that the cow being pulled would almost certainly drown, as her head went right under the water; but she shut the flange over her nose and so not only survived, but gave birth two days later! All the other cattle followed her and swam to safety.

Mary Dawes's father, Lewis Finn, had previously been Commissioner of the Sewers. Mary felt that if her father had still been in office, the flood system would have been properly worked, and the sea would have been contained. Joe Butler was working for Betty at Waterham.

JOE: *I know that particular night, January I think, there had been a warning. Peter Webb, he was the Foreman there then, and Jesse, they come and call me out, at Seasalter, I'll always remember it. We went in just under the bridge over there. Stopped the Land-Rover there and went in the field.*

There wasn't no water much on the grass then. The little inlets had sort of been filled up with water. We could see the sheep out there, so we decided to go out there and drive 'em on to the road which was higher. So we goes out there, and we'd only walked, you know, 50 yards or some'in' out there, and the water started to come up round our boots.

I remember Jess saying, 'Christ! That's coming up quick now.' But do you know what, we'd run back against the gate and by the time we'd got to the gate the water was coming in the top of our rubbers. It really put the wind up us. A huge force and it was coming in! We got up on the road and the sheep then had, sort of, drifted up on to the road, because obviously that was the way the water was going, and it took 'em up on the road there, and we drove these sheep along the edge.

Talk about as silly as a sheep! Some of the sheep walked along the edge, like, one or two slipped off into the water, and the other bloody things followed. didn't they. I didn't think they had any sense. The bloody things were going to their certain death. Although I must admit, they'd got to go a hell of a way from there to the Thanet Way, before they hit higher ground – and some of them survived and some of them didn't. We managed to drive the Land-Rover off the road then, and back on to higher ground. And we was all right, but it was very scary, that was, I must admit.

What did we lose? About 120 odd sheep, down over here and at Monk's Hill. The railway line from Faversham to Whitstable, well, the railway goes through, and each side there is a fence. Well, sheep was the other side. When the water come up, all these poor sheep was stranded on the fence. If, in actual fact, there had not been a fence there, they'd have just drifted up on to the railway line and walked away quite safe, but they was hung on the fence, see. In that place it was about 6 feet deep. The sheep wouldn't have a hope.

The flood had even, in some places, washed the ballast away from underneath the railway line. In actual fact the rails were just suspended in mid-air, you know. Most of the sheep were lost down here at Waterham and at Monk's Hill. 'Cos the flood's come up right over the other side of the line, and there were these little lumps of sheep, 'cos [to the north of the railway line], *the hillocks were 15 feet higher. So there's places where there's bullocks and sheep stuck on top of these mounds, stuck on top of the water and we had to rescue the sheep. We managed to get 'em off with a boat.*

Well down at Seasalter, Ladd's Hill we had this Sussex herd that was surrounded by water, so we had to get them off there. So Lancelot [Slotty], *he brought his boat down. So they rowed it across here, and rowed us fellows across there, and we made a pen. Got some gates and that, that was already on the hill and made a sort of corral, sort of thing, so we could drive these bullocks down and get them close to the water, and then, make a hell of a noise and that, and rush 'em into the water so they'd swim across; about 300 or 400 yards of water till it come to where the old dump used to be down Thanet Way.*

They would be out on this boat and they would try to drag the cow across to the other side, 'cos once one or two went, the others, they thought, would follow. Which was quite true, it did work. We got 'em across the other side.

[None of the cattle travelled in the boat.] *It was only a very large rowing boat. And there were two or three of them in there, rowing this boat, so as to direct the cows. It was OK with the bullocks.*

Then of course, we had to go along the railway line and collect all these dead sheep up. We laid them out, up in the orchard up the top there. Of course, you can imagine what a good job it was,

it bein' in wintery time then. Because most of them we bought
down and was fed to the beagles, which was one way of getting
rid of 'em. But obviously there was too many and they didn't burn
them. They put them in a lump up here and covered them over
with manure, so they rotted down and that, you know, but you'd
find all bits and pieces – the foxes had 'em.
  Oh terribly smelly. Anyway we cleared 'em up down there and
they eventually, you know, got it into the railway bank, filled in
the holes and so on.
  [Land cannot be grazed after the sea's been over – it gets
too saline.] *They put tons of this gypsum over there, it helps. It*
was usable after some time and they got compensated for so much
damage done.

Betty remembered being told about a 'rope of moles' swarming
along from the seaward side of the railway line, until they could
cross over by the sleeper level-crossing at Graveney. The moles were
so close together that they looked like a firehose. They crossed the
line inland just before the great flood invaded during the night.
  She looked back on that period nostalgically.

**I remember in the floods of '53, people I'd never heard of,
sent me loads of hay and straw. One man at Ringwell took
in my cattle, another man at Iden in Sussex took in my cattle
– all for nothing. My sheep were at Sir Thomas Neame's,
Mr Gaskin at Selling – all for nothing.**
  **When we rescued them, all sorts of people turned up.
They weren't all farmers or farm labourers by any means.
People passing on the roads, people down on the Sunday.
In the country there was a different feeling.**

After the floods, clay was put into shoring up and hightening
the sea-wall. Fifty foot was taken off the top of a local hill, Clay Hill.
So those who knew the landscape did a 'double take' when looking
at the much lower hill.

Chapter Twenty-five
The fifties

At the end of the war Betty was back in Waterham and life returned to a more normal existence.

Jean Fraser came back and stayed there and helped run the farm, after Willie went to school. But she also did Betty's paperwork – ran all the paperwork and generally coped with things.

WILLIE: *If the War hadn't come on, I would have thought she would have moved on to higher things within the poultry industry. She lived there until she died.*

JOE BUTLER: *Miss Fraser, I think she does marvellous to even stay here. I remember one time I really did feel sorry for Miss Fraser because, well, back to Mrs McKeever, she was a really hard person. And she said,* **'Jean, you can be sacked, the same as anybody else!'** *And honestly, Miss Fraser was in tears. It was really hard. Miss Fraser could be nasty too at times – and she was with me, but I managed to hold me own.*

Betty considered sending Willie to Stowe and in August 1946 she asked John Dawes to write to his old headmaster, but Willie was eventually sent to Loretto, where Sandys had been.

Slotty's daughter Jean did her first horse purchase from her Aunt Betty. *'It was about £900 but I think I paid about £1,000 because she said 900 and then said Guineas. Very sharp.'* (£945.) Of course, thoroughbred stock was always bought and sold in Guineas (£1.05) and probably still is. Jean cleared £2000 on the horse later.

JEAN: *Aunt Betty used to embarrass us as kids. She was quite cruel, because we were very susceptible at 16, 17. We would sit down to a big family dinner-party, and she would shriek with laughter and say,* **'How did Little Minx go?'** *Tim Rootes was my boyfriend at the time.'* [Minx was a make of car the Rootes company made.] *And you'd go scarlet with embarrassment. She always knew how to hurt us!*

Betty went over to Malmains a lot, as they were a close family. During dinner, she would sometimes tell scurrilous old family stories about the previous generations, to really embarrass her straight-laced brother. She would laugh her head off. Poor Slotty! Jean Rowntree didn't think he really enjoyed it much when his sister Betty came to dinner.

As an old lady, when Mopsie wanted to go to see somebody, she would get in the car. Her butler, Albert, would say goodbye to her, then dash and ring the police. *'Madam's out – watch out!'* All the local police were warned. Mopsie shouldn't really have driven at all.

But there were changes ahead as the board was clearing – all in a fairly short space of time.

JOHN: *Father was diagnosed as having cancer of the lungs which required an immediate major operation. He had one last day's hunting on Belinda and was operated on next day. Sadly it was unsuccessful.*

He had galloped off the hunting field at 2 or 3 o'clock and never rode or hunted again afterwards. Betty said that Sandys told her, 'It's a short life, but I've had a jolly good one.'

Sandys died aged 56, on 5 February 1949, just three weeks before his son John's wedding day to Jill, whose father Gordon Mitchell had also been a Master of the Mid-Kent.

Betty closed his long running-account in her Ledger book but continued renting land from the Mount Ephraim Estate. Whenever Betty told stories concerning her brothers, she would say **'My brother Slottie'**, but when talking of Sandys it was just **'My brother'**. She always adored him.

And then the whole generation of Simpsons passed away. Uncle Tom Simpson died in the late '40s, his sister Aunt Anne Simpson died '51/'52 and Budsie in '55.

All her life, Aunt Bee Simpson had lived in the same house as Mopsie. She was Betty's governess and had helped run the Mount Ephraim Estate.

WILLIE: *She was quite young. Died before Mopsie, suddenly, which was not expected. We went to Slotty and Ivy's Silver Wedding – '53. Bee wasn't well enough to go. She had gone to bed not feeling very well. Albert and whoever was cook at the time, found her at Berkeley. When we got home, we found that she was dead. That*

was the end of that, she died in May of the Coronation Year 1953.
She was buried in Banff.

Mopsie died in Berkeley on 22 November 1953, the same year as her sister. Mopsie was 84. Her funeral journey went round the Tower track road, her coffin riding in a pony and trap. Every yard travelled was on family land.

Betty told this story about her mother's funeral:

Mopsie had engaged a private secretary, in the period up to her death – somebody ex-naval. Then when she died in 1953 he organized the funeral.

The cortege set off from Berkeley to Hernhill. The naval chappie took up his position at the head of the cortège.

Slotty said to him, *'Look, Commander 'Bloggs', you should be doing so and so.'*

And the chap said, *'No. I should be here.'*

There was a hell of an up and downer – more or less at the coffin – about where this chap ought to be. It ended up with Slotty saying, *'Well, you damned fool! What do you know about organizing funerals?'*

And the fellow said, *'Well, I have organized one before, Sir.'*

Slotty jumped off this huge precipice without having checked. *'Well, whose was it?'*

And the naval chappie – as I think it was the job of the naval people – said, *'King George VI'*. Which was the collapse of Slotty. Apparently at that stage, Betty said to the carter, **'Drive on'**. Slotty was left speechless after having firmly been put in his place.

Being a Scot, Mopsie had not been brought up with the idea of Primogeniture. She had had a good dowry (on marriage) and so left all her money to Betty.

Betty also inherited Mopsie's and Aunty Bee's clothes. Lots of well-made tweed 'coat and skirts'. These clothes lasted Betty for her own lifetime.

Mopsie left her land around several descendants. Betty was left Bridge Wood and Dargate Common. Albert, Mopsie's butler, moved from Berkekey, after it was closed, to help Betty at Waterham. He lodged with Mrs Butler.

Mopsie left the house Swordanes jointly between Betty, Slotty, and their nephew Bill Dawes, Swordanes continued to run, sometimes being let to a family member over the next few years, but it was sold in the late 1950s.

Betty also inherited Linksfield Farm in Banff. This was sold, eventually, to the sitting tenant, as there was a hassle over death duties, owing to Scottish inheritance laws. From the row of cottages – fishing huts – in Banff, Betty kept one cottage for 10 years more. Old Stewart lived there.

WILLIE: *Father frequently asked Mother in the immediate post-war years, through Ivy Dawes's brother (who was Father's solicitor in London called Trevor McVeagh), for a divorce. And Mother refused and said she was not going to divorce him, and never did.*

So in consequence, Father went back and lived with a person I got on very well with, but she was a bit sour-faced. A well-known pre-war Irish woman tennis player, called Sydney Parr.

I didn't see anything of Father during the War. I didn't see him again until 1950, I suppose. I went across – I'd finished school – and I went across [to Ireland], last time I was going across to Haver. I was about 17 or 18. I was 18 in October 1950. And I went across there and I got my driving licence, it was great. And I decided to go across and see my Grandmother who did correspond and send me presents.

Father ran Parson's Town Farm during the War (for the Irish National Provincial Bank). They grew blackcurrants and things because Vitamin C was unobtainable in any other way.

And after that, he, Father, sold Parson's Town at the end of the War to Sadruddin Khan – one of the Aga Khan's sons, as a blood-stock farm. Not Ali Khan but Sadruddin Khan, the other brother. The house was let to a Major Naylon.

Father and my Grandmother amassed enough money by 1946/7 to hold the bank off [as they were still bankrupt]. *And the money from that he invested in a restaurant in South Leinster Street, or Nassum Street, along by the Trinity Hall in Dublin ~ from which he conducted an outside catering branch. Mainly because Sydney Parr, whom he was living with, was into that sort of thing. She was a good administrator, Sydney.*

Father (who was Protestant Irish) *ran the restaurant, and when he had chefs there – when I was first over after the War – it was an up-market restaurant that did good dinners. Latterly, it finished up just doing lunches. He did lunches for his Stock Exchange cronies, and people from out of Kildare Street Club, which was just round the corner. Then he also had the contract, up until his dying day, for the Kings Inns, where the barristers eat. Mainly because the lawyers of that time were all Protestant, and the Government was all Catholic, and even Trinity at that stage was Protestant. So he did two restaurants inside Trinity – supplying the staff, the food and the chefs. Doing catering then – to the catering at the Kings Inns. I've been with him with some of my kids – Margaret and Tom, listening to the speeches – in the background, whilst they were doing out the dinners for American Bar Associations, and people like that. They had a wonderful cellar at the Kings Inns.*

And that was his life latterly, and he also had one restaurant at the Royal Dublin Society, that he ran – at Balls Bridge Showground.

He lived just outside Balls Bridge in a flat, he and Sydney. I used to go up and get on reasonably well. We used to drink Pol Rogier Champagne and eat smoked salmon sandwiches, whenever we went over. That was his staple diet – if you were having a party. And I've always stuck to it. It's a very good recommendation, I assure you.

Rudolf had a restaurant called the Cherry Pie. He was very fond of his food. Betty herself wasn't so interested in fancy foods.

By the early '50s Bill and Mary Dawes were installed in Mount Ephraim with four children. (They had begun their family whilst living down the road in Mount Farm.) Mary's family had regularly beagled from the early days.

Betty continued visiting Mount Ephraim as a very close family member. The widowed Joan Dawes remaining in the Granny wing, the north end of the house that she had occupied during the war.

JOHN DAWES: *After the Second World War, Slotty was jealous of Father being Chairman. Slotty took over as Chairman of Westrays in 1948, just before Father died.*

Since the turn of the century, Inchcape had owned Gray Dawes, which still controlled Westrays with 51%. Bill Dawes joined Westrays and was invited to transfer to the New Zealand Shipping Co., eventually becoming chairman.

Westrays – the insurance branch of Gray Dawes Westray, employed John Dawes after he left the Army in 1955, and George Dawes also followed his father, Slotty, there for a few years.

JEAN ROWNTREE: *Pa re-built the business and travelled a lot to New Zealand. Malmains was constantly busy at weekends, entertaining business people from New Zealand.*

[Slotty did very well in business]
JEAN: *He wasn't a director of hundreds of companies, because he was too outspoken, and would 'create'. He was too straight but he was on Hays Wharf and on Union Lighterage. Dalgety's he was director of – but very few. But some very good ones.*

A Westrays man all his life, with New Zealand as a second string. He was never a director of the New Zealand Shipping Co.

Slotty always used to bring New Zealanders and Aussie business people to Mount Ephraim and Waterham. Betty was an interesting person for them to visit.

Willie's career took a different direction to the Dawes boys. He was three and a half years in the Army as a tank transporter driver.

As he was born before 1 January 1933, he didn't have to do National Service if he was in a reserved occupation. Willie was never called up and soon after he could decide what he wanted to do, he joined up. Before he was of age, Willie would have had to do what he was told. He joined the forces in the January/February 1952, following his twenty-first birthday in October. Having always been interested in transport, he knew exactly what he wanted to do. Willie joined the Service Corps, signing on for a 22-year engagement with a 3-year option. And did an extra 6 months for Suez as everybody got held back then, which he found very interesting. He served almost entirely with the 2nd Unit.

In 1957 Willie McKeever married Anne Mount, who was from a successful local farming family – the other side of Canterbury. Locally, it was said that 'Canterbury was a City entirely surrounded by Mounts'!

JOE BUTLER: *They had an almighty row, Willie and Mrs McKeever. That's why Willie went off into the army. I think he went down with Lancelot when he left here after the row. I don't know the ins and outs of it, but about farming here. He went off in the army and that was it, like.*

He come back and then went off farming away. He got married and that was it. I think Mrs McKeever was a bit put a'back by that. At the time she had bought Monks Hill (I think it had belonged to Dawes in some way) when it finished with Bones.

After the war when Willie was away in the army, Mrs McKeever had always wanted Monks Hill Farm, thinking he was going to come back and run the whole shooting match, but I'm afraid it didn't work out.

WILLIE: *I got married and we moved to Monks Hill and tried to farm with mother for about 6 to 8 months. It wasn't to be, unfortunately. We couldn't see eye to eye.*

So I got a job as a working foreman on 1200 acres of Bedfordshire, and I moved up there. I was up there for 5 years, and was also involved with the haulage business.

It wasn't market gardening. We didn't involve ourselves with vegetables. We were milking cows. We dealt in livestock – sheep, cattle, cereals, all tenant farmed. Part of it from the Bedford Settled Estates and part of it in cahoots with the shooting tenant on the 2300 acres of the estate.

After my brother-in-law decided to become a medico, (having worked on farms and taken a degree in Agriculture at Cambridge and [then] decided that farming wasn't for him), I was invited by my father-in-law [Jim Mount] to come back and do the job he should have been doing, at Little Barton and Renville, Canterbury. That is virtually what I made my career at. I was there 36 years.

Betty told the Women's Institute:

Just after the war there was a period here [in Hernhill], when people didn't know each other, much worse than it is today. I can remember when Brian Bones came back. He came in [to the bank] with the cheque and asked, 'Who lives in the council houses opposite the school? I know two people.'

'I don't know.' This happened when he went into the bank on a Friday. He really didn't know and he said, 'When my father was alive he'd have known everybody.' Which is true.

'With the changing population, he wouldn't,' said the bank lady. She said 'Go down to Mrs McKeever. I bet a quid she knows who lives in all these houses.'

Brian lorst a quid. He came down and bought a pig off me. After the Village Hall was built, this side of the village got to know each other. That and the W.I. It's always pretty good.

Betty had always banked and shopped in Faversham. However, a year or so after the war the Council installed parking restrictions in many of the streets. This meant that Betty could no longer stop and park outside her bank or certain shops. Her car had to be parked, possibly some distance away. She was furious and complained, but to no avail. So she transferred her bank account to Whitstable and from then on did all her shopping in that town, where there were no parking restriction.

Betty would always count her money in the bank – in the corner. Although she had watched them count or weigh packets of money, she insisted on counting her money before she left the bank.

In 1958 Bill and Mary made a protracted trip of about 5 months to New Zealand and Australia and left their three eldest children in the care of Betty and Jean. They were early teenagers called Mary Ann, Wonky (her brother couldn't say Veronica), and Sandys (Edwyn Sandys Dawes again!).

Shooting was still a major sport for Betty. She taught a young neighbour, Jeremy Jacquet, to shoot.

On a trip up to Banff, Betty and Jean played golf at Duff House against Willie and Anne. They took alternate shots and no quarter was given. The young couple were winning as Anne has a good eye for a ball. Betty didn't expect this and got angrier and angrier, as it was always important for her to win and do the thing properly, but she and Jean lost the match.

In March 1958 Betty made a final trip up to Swordanes, stopping 4 times for petrol on the way up for:

4 gallons petrol Macknade	£0	18	10
7 gallons petrol Long Bovington	1	12	10
7 gallons petrol Ecclefechen	1	12	11
1 pint oil		1	11
petrol Forfar	1	8	6

And 5 times on the return:

3 gallons petrol, etc. Banff	2	9	5
7 gallons petrol	1	14	7
and 1 pint oil Falkirk	–	–	–
8 gallons petrol Durham	1	19	3
8 gallons petrol	2	1	3
and 1 quart oil Biggleswade	–	–	–
4 gallons petrol Chatham		18	8
Totalling	£14	18	2

They spent two nights on route each way, at the Bell Hotel,
Long Bovington and the Brechin Hotel on the northern journey;
then the Braid Hills Hotel and the George Hotel, Grantham coming
south. They had the laundry done and bought fish. Basically Betty
was clearing up Swordanes prior to selling it. She charged the
Swordanes estate (of herself, Slotty and Bill) £64 10s. 7d. for the
journey. Swordances was duly sold after that.

In 1960 Slotty Dawes competed in the Olympic Games sailing in a
Flying Dutchman yacht. He created the Flying Dutchman Class and
brought the design back from Holland. His first boat was made at
Whitstable. Over the years Slotty created it into an International
Class and everyone fell in love with the 'Dutchman'. Luckily, a new
dinghy class was needed for the 1960s Rome Olympics.

The Flying Dutchman was chosen against the '505s' which fell
over in strong winds whilst competing and the Dutchman did not.
The Sailing Olympics were held in Naples.

Because, unlike other competitors, his kit didn't break, the
Committee invited Slotty to sail – a Grandpa of 56 years of age.
Slotty had enabled 49 nations to compete in this class and it was
the biggest collection of Dutchmen ever.

Slotty came 1st in the second heat. His overall Olympic position
was 9th. His spinnaker let him down so he made his own after that.

He was always a great do-er – with his hands. On one occasion
Slotty shot off half his thumb. This happened when he had tried to
fire a pistol which was strapped to a gate by remote control. It mis-
fired and he blew off his thumb. A decade or so later he sawed off

the top of his forefinger, with a circular saw. But he still made things.

John Dawes and the whole of his family emigrated to New Zealand for four years. At the last moment a goodbye family picnic was held on the field, New Zealand. A halcyon day, with Betty in great form. We went up there, I remember, with fifteen people and two dogs in one car!

Betty kept in touch with John, writing the news in her own style – enjoying the company of her nephews – and the sport:

15 Dec 1959

I had a nice day's shooting with George on his new estate at Ham Street. We got 9 pheasants, 1 woodcock, 2 hares and a rabbit.

Bill had a day which he was on holiday and we went out, but the fog so thick the birds never got up and when they did we could not see them.

From what I hear the Mid-Kent seem on their last legs but I hope they will recover. It seems that quite a lot who still hunt with them, say the position of letting out a deer on highly farmed land & then chasing it is indefensible. Perhaps it is but I have enjoyed lots of good times with them.

24 Feb 1960

I got to Banff in June for a couple of weeks with Lillian [Simpson – her cousin] but the river was too low and I only got a couple of sea trout for my 14 days.

It was rather fun fishing the other side of the river from Scatterty on the Hotel beat.

We are all very busy trying to shoot wood pigeon at the weekends. There are clouds of them but they are still hard to get.

Chapter Twenty-six
Farming [2]

At various stages during the war and afterwards, Betty had acquired more bits of land as they became available. Hers was a fragmented farm.

Pudding Lane had been farmed by Knowles. Betty took it over in conjunction with Mopsie after he died. Also Dargate Common and the bits around Bridge Wood which she inherited from Mopsie in the '50s. She farmed more land around the pylons.

Monk's Hill had 175 acres. Betty had bought it in 1942 from Sandys, but as Willie had not stayed very long to try and farm, it was sold in the '60s (for £13,000).

Her nephew George had inherited Holly Hill, which Betty farmed for him until 1961. She grazed Sherwood Park, Hubbles Bank, Pottery Bank, and took on Crockham. She kept sheep from Sonstoll, Upper Sonstoll, and Tunstall, right through to the New Zealand banks, which she rented. Betty kept and preferred her Kent (later called Romney) sheep, which suited the district. They were good mothers and had excellent wool, even if they didn't produce as many lambs per head as other breeds.

Sometimes the sheep would have a Border Leicester Cross ram put on them.

Extracts from two letters written to John Dawes, whilst he was living in New Zealand:

15 Dec 1959

With the very long summer with no rain until November it has meant a very long and protracted year. Fruit has been a very bad market, so there was far too much of it about. Pigs have also slumped but we are looking up again now.

I have taken the rest of the Sherwood Parks off Bill & hope I clean them up.

24 Feb 1960

It has been a very hard year on the farm. The weather was wonderful but fruit was a glut, and had to stand up to European fruit, where the men work longer hours for less

cash. Pigs have also been down and sheep were unsaleable owing to the drought and lack of grass.

Colin West came to work at Waterham in 1959 or '60, as a young man. There were twelve people working on the farm then, who included a shepherd and fruit people coming in on a seasonal basis.

Colin remembered that both double cottages were occupied by farmworkers. Douglas was one real character who worked at Waterham, Manigers another.

Betty could frighten people if necessary. She would shout up and down the orchards, and could make grown men quake!

Colin said, *'She was a fair old girl. She was straight. Played down the middle.'* Colin stayed at Waterham until Betty's death and is there now.

At one stage in the '50s, Betty had a gentleman farmhand. Granville Wheler from Otterden was at Waterham for a while. He was sporting mad and had lots of money. Whilst working for Betty, she encouraged him to go to university at Oxford.

Granville Wheler was excitable. They were all out shooting one day and a rabbit went scurrying past. He swung his big gun round and went with both barrels. Jean and Betty both got their bums peppered! Everyone screamed with laughter!

PETER GOODWIN: *There was 'Bob the Gypsy' who might one morning – just not be there. Then a day or two later would turn up. Betty would give him a good dressing down but would still keep him on as he was a very good worker, especially with livestock.*

There was 'The Russian'. Am not sure that he was really Russian. Jean always thought he was rather a slacker and I remember her suggesting to Betty that he should go. To which Betty replied: **'Oh! I like to see him around. He's easy on the eye!'**

Many people who worked for Betty were characters in their own right.

Betty was a typical farmer and a real hard bargainer, whether she was selling a pig or buying a horse. This acts as a reminder of one quite friendly conversation she had at Faversham Market. Talking with the market owner, she said, **My morning is just the same as all you men. I have an early breakfast, load up my pigs, drive them down here and then have to see they are penned and recorded. This means that a lot of time has passed since I left home. It would be very useful if I could find** a toilet. **You have one marked 'Gentlemen' but you don't think of the ladies. I have to seek cover in my empty pig trailer and make use of the straw.** *I understand this produced some confusion on the part of the market owner. Soon afterwards there was a 'Ladies Toilet' in the market.*

Mike Reed, who nowadays has a prize herd of Sussex cattle, started his herd off after the war when he bought a splendid cow from Betty, E-41 – with a crumpled horn. After the cow had died, her horn was put on Mike's walking stick and used by him for some years. Eventually he claimed that he gave the stick to the chief cattleman of Mexico.

When John Dawes returned from New Zealand, he bought the 50-acre Holly Hill Farm from his cousin George, took over the 6-acre Thread Farm (left him by Mopsie), acquired Sonstoll Field from his brother Bill, and he and Jill had their own house, Sonstoll, built. They took over the steep and shaggy grazing on Middle and Lower Sherwood Park, Hubbles, and Pottery Banks.

Betty would not sell John the loo at the back of Thread Cottage (found to be on her land – just!) unless he sold her the equivalent few feet elsewhere in the Blean. **'Thread Cottage,'** she said, **'was the house in my farm.'**

Mr Barton of Little Waterham did farming business with Betty. She charged him for grazing and other services:

	£	s	d	
157 Ewes Barton @ 1.0/– per score =	12	17	6	in April
Wash with Lead Spursil	16	10	0	in April
2nd Spray with Nicotine	21	0	0	in May
Cutting Hay J C Butler 16½ hours	10	6	3	on 29 July
25 Gallons Lime Sulphur @ 107/6	2	17	2	in April/May
18¾ hours Washing 48 gallons Dispersable Sulphur				
6 gall Nicotine 3¾ Agrol in May				
4 Washing @ 26/-	6	0	0	
42 Wetable Sulphur	1	9	0	20 May

In 1949:

	£	s	d
Fruit washing @ £1 6 0 – 34 hours	44	4	0
Mangold 1 ton 18 cwt @	3	15	0

Washing Account 1954:
DNC 6% 54 Gallons DNOC
March 19/20 – 7 hours Spraying 3 tanks 900 Gallons

April 5 – Lime Sulphur @ 3% 27 Gallons Lime Sulphur/900 gallons water.
April 16 – Lime Sulphur @ 2% 18 Gallons/900 gallons water.
Washing (spraying) for Little Waterham. Using DNOC and DDT, Nicotine and Lime Sulphur.

All these fearsome mixtures would be used for spraying the fruit or the fields and dipping sheep. She also charged him for:

Fencing 1961:

	£		
131 5ft 6 inch stakes @ 7/-	£9	4	0
4 Rolls Ryelock 3/11/8 a roll	14	6	8
25 yard	1	12	3
3 Rolls Barbed wire 431- 250 yards	6	9	0
75 yds barbed wire		12	9
Staples @ 1/7/6 a 1000. 650 staples		18	0
2 Workmen – 5 days	17	0	0
Divided by 2	50	2	8
(They probably shared the boundary)	25	1	4

She would hire out services such as hay bailing and carting. Also combining and rotavating. She sold turkeys, cockerels, capons, potatoes, and cartridges. In 1961 Betty sold:

	£		
2 large white Gilts (pigs)	£52	10	10
1 Pedigree Kent Ram	£8	8	0

She would hire out her Service Boar for £1 1s. 0d. a time, for two night's service, a guinea.

Slotty always purchased a Christmas turkey for the Whitstable Yacht Club Draw from Waterham.

Joe Butler

Joe Butler always worked for Betty. She claimed to have delivered him at his birth. *'M'father died in 1938, so I just started on the farm.'*

The Butler family had lived in the bottom lodge at Mount Ephraim, then moved to a Waterham Cottage in 1931, when Betty started farming. As the tied cottage belonged to her, the Butlers had to work for her or lose their home.

JOE: *Before the war, there was a servant's side, my mum used to work over there, like everybody had to in them days. This was a tied cottage and you had to. Jim my eldest brother was working down the road at Saddletons – where the greenhouses are now. So obviously, when m'father died, Jim had to come back and work on the farm to retain the cottage.*

And me m'self, I didn't want to work on the farm, but I didn't have an option. It was part of the times. I wanted to go to Faversham into engineering. There was a job there, the Schoolmaster up there had got me an interview – and that's all, you know...

*When I said to Mum about it, she said, 'Oh – all right.' And I suppose she must have said to Mrs McKeever about it. And then – orders come. '***You're over on the farm.'*** You had no say in it. It doesn't matter whether you 'liked' it or not. If the job was there – you had to do it.*

I come on the farm in 1942. During the war everything was ploughed up for corn. Down here we had Monks Hill and ploughed up the marshes. Quite a lot of corn and that growing and we still had about 200 or 300 sheep.

Miss Fraser was here some of the time or in Scotland. In actual fact, when she first came here, she lived next door with Mr Cassels. She come to look after the chickens. And then it sort of progressed from there. Miss Fraser went up to the farm and lived over there after a while. Then Miss Fraser took Willie over like, sort of thing.

The chickens fizzled out and then we went into pigs and there always has been a few sheep like, and that's gradually progressed on, sort of thing. Mrs McKeever done well with the large white pigs. She took them off to the shows like. I used to take 'em off – after the war.

Joe found Mrs McKeever was a bit reluctant when it came to making improvements on the farm. When Monk's Hill had been acquired the land had all been arable and was wanted for sheep grazing, so they did a lot of fencing up there.

JOE: *We made a road from Monk's Hill, right the way down over to the marshes. We got a lot of them big flints, put in the road. I remember I used to go up to the papermill at Sittingbourne and get ashes out of there, to put on top, like. So, made quite a decent road, really. Never spent much on the farm here at Waterham. It was a*

shame really. I mean to say, the beagles was was her big love –
and she loved the horses, like.

I always remember Mrs McKeever driving on the road and that,
with the sheep. I don't know why she always used to do it when
there used to be a holiday or something, and a lot of traffic. **'We'll
move the sheep today.'** Where would we go? There she was with
a walking stick. She used to own them red handkerchieves, tie it on
the top, and there she is walking down the Thanet Way and us
driving these sheep. And all the cars, you can imagine, there,
honking their horns. **'I don't care about them,'** she used to say,
'the sheep and that, they were here before the motor car.'
Sometimes she asked the police to come along on these occasions to
see about the traffic, but ususally the local copper kept well out of
the way.

We had a Sussex herd of cows and that and used to show
them. The herd was up at Monk's Hill because Jesse Richardson
lived over there. He used to look after them. We used to bring on
young bulls like, and lead them about and get 'em ready to go to
the shows and everything. And old Jess was, you know, a bit of a
Foreman then. I must I felt sorry for him, for she did used to give
him a right stick, sort of thing. The one thing I disliked about her,
was the fact she would love to give the foremen here a dressing
down. Make 'em look small, in front of the work people. I think
that's very bad. Undermines your authority, don't it. I don't think
that should be.

She used to with me sometimes. I used to have rows with
her very often and the one good thing about it, that if you had a
row with her today, tomorrow it was all forgotten, we was back
to normal like. Any local disputes, I'm sure she used to enjoy, she
seemed to get a kick out of it, making you feel small, like, 'Cos
she always used to say to me, **'You're only half the person your
father ever was. You'll never be anything like your father
was.'** Really that hurt.

Now Mrs McKeever was never one to worry about going in the
house in dirty boots. We'd come in through the front door and I 'd
been out with Mrs McKeever and she walked straight through into
the office. Miss Fraser was up in the kitchen, see, looking down the
hallway. And there's me stomping. **'Come in'** Mrs McKeever says.
She went across there.

Miss Fraser looked at me and said, 'I hope you don't go into your own home like that?'

I says, 'Well no. Not exactly.'

Mrs McKeever was just hearing of this, and so she waited for a while for me to get a right rollicking off Miss Fraser. And she was laughing, you see, and then she all of a sudden piped up and said **'All right Jean, I told him to come in like that.'** *But she waited!*

WILLIE: *There were pigs here until the pit for Monk's Hill was sold up in the mid '60s. She used to sell a lot of pedigree stuff locally. Sell so many boars a year – pedigree large whites – the great Yorkshire pig.*

We certainly 'showed' in a lot of the national shows, post War. This started off with the Royal at Lincoln, in about 1947. They showed at Windsor, at Shrewsbury and we used to regularly attend the Royal County Show (as it was then). It is now the South of England Show at Ardingly. In those days it travelled and it was a very nice show.

ARTHUR FINN: *You know she always went to all the shows with Jean in her horsebox with the pigs. They went to Peterborough and always turned the pigs out and Jean and Betty slept in the horse-box. '50s and '60s. It was only latterly that she discovered B & Bs. Because she used to show her pigs quite a lot. She always went to a Shell garage and asked the people where to stay.*

She went to Reading Market. Reading was one of her places, with her large whites. There was an important sale at Reading every year.

JEAN ROWNTREE: *At the farm's height, Betty showed her pigs at Peterborough. Possibly also at Edinburgh.*

I think the fun thing was when she had pigs outside the bath-room window. She had her bath at 8.00 (or 10.00) in the morning, and she would shriek through the window, stark naked, apparently, at the blokes. So the story used to go.

Betty never went to Europe, but would do business with anybody. She sold pigs to the Italians. They couldn't speak a work of English – so they used sign language. She sold ponies to a Russian, also. They had no common language, so it was all in mime. The

Russian took off his shoes and waded across an imaginary river to illustrate where he lived.

Welsh Mountain ponies

Betty kept a herd of Welsh ponies. They really took over from the Sussex cattle.

ARTHUR: *You know about her going down to select Roland, the stallion at Col. Watkins-Williams-Wynn's in Wales. Betty went to get her stallion. They all came down the mountain and she chose her bunch of horses, boxed up. John Beach was with her and maybe somebody else as well. They brought him [the stallion] back and she broke down in London, with that wretched horse-box and the Zephyr. The policemen got all the accoutrements to Blackheath Police Station. The Land-Rover, horse-box, Roland in the back. He was really an unbroken stallion off the Welsh mountains. They're very, very handleable, incredible things, so its not quite such a wild animal as you think, but basically – wild. Roland was taken out of his box and walked up and down and John Beach was sent off to get a replacement vehicle. And Betty went off somewhere else. The last we saw of the stallion was – the policeman walking him up and down in the yard of Blackheath Police Station!'*

JOE: *They were very wild when we first had them ponies. It started off quite small, there was only a dozen or so, with a stallion. Terrible things with the land – they pick and choose. When its wet, they destroy the turf. We used to take 'em to Ashford. When we first took the first lot there, they was literally unbroken, and there was hell to play. It was chaos, and the auctioneer said, 'Well that's the last time you're going to bring them down like that, you got to have them handleable.' So from then on we used to have to get 6, 7, or 8, and have these, week or two, leading them around. Get 'em so you could lift their feet up and get an 'alter on 'em and lead 'em. My God! Why me and Colin and whoever else was here never got hurt, I don't know! We used to get them in the middle of the stables down there. And honestly, they'd go up the wall! We had to jump around in there and get a rope on 'em, and Ooo, it was hell to pay. But anyway, touch wood – we survived. We had one or two kicks and bangs, bruises and that.*

Moving the herd

In about 1965 several of the family were summoned to help move the whole herd of Welsh Mountain ponies from Waterham into the Blean. This involved crossing the Coastal Road which stretche from London towards Whitstable and Ramsgate with fast-running traffic. Jill Dawes and her family, Jane,t myself, and James (who was 10 or 11) were there, also Wonky, Bill's teenage daughter, on her thoroughbred mare, Golden Pheasant, Gil (reputedly a half-gypsy, with not many teeth), and Joe Butler. Betty herself came in her Land-Rover.

Two of the ponies were leadable, so Janet and I led Roland, the stallion and Rosemary, a mare. Roland took a fancy to Golden Pheasant and tried to mount her. **'You need a step-ladder!'** said Betty. Wonky then had to keep her horse behind the herd of about 20 ponies. Roland and Rosemary pulled us girls in pursuit. Eventually we could not hang on to them any longer and they broke away. The ponies ran in a confused fashion towards the speeding highway.

The police held up the traffic on the Coastal Road, so that we could drive the whole herd across. The horses dashed across, all save one pony which fell into a ditch nearby. Betty (never one to miss an opportunity) shouted **'Wait, wait. I need to ear-clip her'**, and insisted that the ear-tag equipment was fetched. Betty thought this mare the least likely to be captured again because she was so wild. So the mare was ear-tagged whilst trapped, keeping waiting all the traffic on the Thanet Way.

The mare was then hauled out of the ditch. **'If I sent for the RSPCA, they would probably break its neck,'** said Betty, who knew how to carry out this manoeuvre and the mare was duly extricated.

We then all crossed the road and drove the animals a mile and a half further up into the Blean. There was a corral in the field, Tunstall. All the ponies needed to be caught for ear-tagging. The men and Wonky caught the ponies by grabbing them around the neck and hanging on – all three together until Betty, waving the ear-puncher succeeded in putting the tag in. Wonky was pushed along the fence where there was some barbed wire. It ripped a long tear across her bottom. Thereafter, nobody had any success catching ponies until after she was sent home!

The herd was safely deposited in the Blean for many years. Everyone was tired that night after a most exciting day.

Ashford Market

JOE: *Ooo, it amused me that she used to get down there when they was auctioning them off. Noone else would do it, but where the auctioneer stood, yelling out for bids like, she would be standing up there behind him, giving him what this one's done and that, and I don't know whether he liked it or not. Noone else would have been allowed up there.*

COLIN WEST: *She would get away with murder parking – especially at Ashford Market.*

She would park her Land-Rover and horsebox across the yards, but would obligingly leave the keys in so any of the market men could move it.

Betty let fly at the authorities when they tried to put a road through New Zealand. She said **'You'll never do it, because the land won't let you.'** They had about four shots at it – but the clay always slipped down the hill.

The farmyard at Waterham was always a fair old mess. My grandfather Gordon Mitchell visited Betty one day, and exclaimed, *'£40,000 worth of rotting machinery!'*

In the 1960s – through lack of attention and lack of standards, Betty's sheep were struck off from the Kent Flock Book. Her attention probably wandered to other things, possibly the village hall.

Betty and Jean had a few ducks. One drake rejoiced in the name of 'Sweaty Armpits', owing to his habit of flapping his wings and pecking under them. He frequently did this on the roof of Waterham. Some of his wives laid their eggs up there on the roof. Occasionally, weeks later, these eggs would roll off the roof and burst. The stench was unbelievable!

Chapter Twenty-seven
Blean Beagles [4]

Immediately after the war a decision had to be made by a committee as to whether to continue to run the Blean Beagles. At the time there were only six hounds left. These had been kept at the Tickham Kennels and Mount Ephraim during the war years. Hunting had not been possible, particularly as the land had been mined quite heavily around Kent.

The decision to disband the beagles was very near. There was one significant factor which helped re-start the pack. It was a donation of £40, stuffed into a paper-bag that smelt to high heaven, which was specifically for starting up the Blean Beagles again.

The donation was from Boswell. Between the wars this man had lived in West Street, a poorer area of Faversham, then he had lost his job and been 'down and out'. He was going nearly mad with frustration, and would come out beagling, as it kept him sane. It made a great difference to his life. He then 'struck it lucky', made good, and moved away.

In those days Bill and Mary Dawes would go out fairly frequently with just 2½ couple of beagles. Bill as the huntsman would carry the horn, with Mary whipping-in. They were often the only field.

On one hunt, the hare got driven into a flock of sheep and was lost there. The whipper-in drove all the sheep along the ditch, one by one past Betty, but with no luck. There were very few people out that day, but as the beaglers were all leaving, Betty turned back towards the flock.

I saw the hare walk out of the sheep: she'd been there all the time, how we didn't see her I don't know because a real shepherding job had been done.

Mike Hicks heard this story from Betty in 1984, and to show the span of time involved in beagling, he described a time when a hare got into a flock of sheep four centuries earlier, when hunted by Jacques Du Fouiloux in France in 1573.

There were unemployed people who would come out beagling. Fox-hunting could be costly. Beagling was an inexpensive sport, needing only a pair of boots. If someone could not afford the modest subscription, Betty would make sure they would 'do' something to help – like whipping-in. It gave people occupation, fun, exercise and self-respect. Often followed by a delicious tea as well.

Pupils from a 'home for difficult girls' would come beagling, with Betty keeping an eye, to make sure they behaved. She never had any trouble, and the other followers were none the wiser.

Boys came beagling from St Lawrence Junior School, Ramsgate.

On 12 May 1956 a Presentation Scroll was given to Joan Sayer to mark her 25 years assisting. This is a wonderful document showing Joan as a sportswoman. She hunted (with the Tickham and Ashford Valley); beagled (Blean Beagles); and she raced in Point-to-Points. Also Joan became a shepherd during the war years, she hunted with stag-hounds (Mid-Kent) and she ran races, never being beaten. Betty painted six miniature scenes depicting these events on the scroll. They are superb.

The Blean Beagles had started off in the '20s and '30s in the 'Beagle & Harrier Association' Stud Book with pedigree hounds being tatooed on their ears, but Betty once used a good, but un-registered, working beagle. There was a supplementary index she could have used after the war, but she did not bother to register again, because of the new rules.

Having a marvellous knack of communication with all animals, she brought the best out of her hounds by a few gentle sounds of encouragement and without ever raising her voice.

Sometime in the late '50s Betty gave up the horn and riding so she stopped being the huntsman. She had always been lacking the athletic build needed for a foot huntsman. Betty found it inappropriate to ride to beagles any longer. A lot of youngsters came out as followers, and from horseback she **'couldn't control the children'**. Also she was nearly 60 years of age. The countryside was changing. As Betty herself was no runner and never had been, reluctantly, she had to hand over her horn to Colonel Verbi and Arthur Finn. Since when, the hunt has always been run with amateur huntsmen and whippers-in.

'She took to her feet, relying on her vast knowledge – and short cuts by car – to see plenty of the hunting. Now, she could take as much interest in the people who followed the hounds themselves.' Gregory Blaxland wrote in the *Kentish Gazette*, 7 February 1969.

Noel Watson, Betty, Mike Bax, Mike Taylor, John Beach, Anita Edwards,
Joan Sayer & Helen Bouch

Betty 'enjoys nothing more than to see people of all ages and from
all backgrounds thrill to the cry of her beagles'.

JOHN BEACH [whip]: *She didn't care who you were. The important
thing is good fellowship. Betty developed good feet/car (or Land-
Rover) knowledge of hunting. She always knew her way across
country far better than round by the roads.*

The Dawes, Finn, Neame, and Amos families had now been
supporters of the Blean Beagles for four generations.

Arthur Finn was huntsman in the late '50s. Most of this time
Paul Marsh and Andrew Parry whipped-in.

Colonel Verbi hunted the hounds during the early '60s.

Mike Hicks (who lived in Canterbury then), occasionally hunted
during that period. In 1956 he was the ninth person that season to
carry the horn.

ARTHUR FINN: *When I hunted the hounds on Saturdays and
holidays, Col Verbi and Noel Watson hunted on Thursdays. In
the early years I never paid a Sub. Betty never asked for one. I had
no money and there were several others in the same boat. If any
gymkhanas or other beagle events were to be held, that could be*

difficult depending on how many boys there were around as there was National Service as well. 1950s – to about '60.

We started hunting towards the end of August. The problem was Betty disappeared (for the shooting and fishing) for all of August to Swordanes (and possibly longer), for quite a long time. And old havoc used to occur in her absence. With dilatory hunt servants – whoever they were at the time – and the boys trying to catch up. What we were trying to do, was find out how many bitches had got served during the week.

Betty would come back and they'd write the studbook up, and they knew exactly what sire for each hound was, they knew – or a very good guess, so that was quite a full objective.

Noel Watson was the main huntsman – late '60s, early '70s. He really enjoyed the sport, getting very excited at the time of the kill. Others involved were Reg Gore in the 1950s, Mike Adams and David Neame in the late 1950s.

These keen huntsmen were all taught to make the special beagle 'pudding'. It was no longer made of pinhead oatmeal as it had been in the early days. By this time, the pudding was made of Maize flakes, called 'Kositors' rice.

Electrified rail

There was much building development and the railways were electrified. The lines were now dangerous for beagles and on occasions, a few of the hounds had been killed on the electric line.

On 15 December 1959, Betty wrote to John and Jill Dawes, away in New Zealand:

We are hunting on Wednesday down in Thanet as with both railways into Faversham electrified it wipes out a lot of country. The live rail is very high and it is only fenced by the usual wire fence net mesh. I have been out on my cob quite a lot, as at the moment we have a girl groom. She is no rider but feeds calves, Beagles and the horses and is capable of riding anything I want now.

And on 24 February 1960: **'Arthur Finn has been hunting the Beagles and shown good sport.'**

One day in 1961 Arthur hunted the Blean Beagles as Betty was attending a wedding. The hunt went down to Ladd's Hill marshes down on Seasalter, with David Neame and probably Paul Marsh and Andrew Parry as the whips.

One hare was well hunted for a time then another hare was put up, followed by a third. The beagles followed the three fresh hares as they crossed over the electrified railway, three at once and followed by most of the pack. The hounds were running faster than the young men could. Few of the beagles were injured on their way across but as they returned, they checked and put their noses down to sniff. As a result 4½ couple (that's 9 beagles) were lost.

It was a disaster. She arranged to meet the 'Guesser' man from the Railway Board next morning to show, him what had happened and say, **'You must fence the line,'** or whatever. He turned up in city suit and highly polished black brogues. Then he was taken to tramp across marshes to the site of the disaster. Unfortunately, they came to a barbed-wire fence and the man was disconcerted as to how to get over. So Betty took off her wonderful hairy tweed skirt and laid it across the top of the barbed wire to climb over! She said **'Don't worry, I'm perfectly decent!'** With elastic bands and elastic things here and there. Perfectly decent and that terrific double quality silk pants she wore.

Other beagle packs rallied around, the West Surrey (or West Sussex?) giving her 3 couple and the Wye College – a couple. Betty bred from some of these beagles; one of the few times she used outside blood. Breeding from the Wye hound, Wizard, helped retain the full, deep, throaty cry – which Betty liked.

Arthur said that his mother had done quite a bit of illicit courting of his father, Tom Finn with the beagles and the Tickham. Tom had been Chairman of the beagles and had followed them, but like Betty, he didn't run. Bill Finn, Arthur's brother had been Chairman but he didn't ever run or ride.

The beagling country was the same as the Tickham hunted plus a bit more. All of Thanet and Sandwich. Betty had started to move out of just the small area she had hunted pre-war, because she had lost so much of her beagling land to roads and railways.

The Blean Beagles had a varied area to hunt. From Dover there was cultivated arable land on chalk – and small woodlands halfway up. Then the beautiful marshes of Sarre – full of different birds. More arable land then fruit trees. Then again more arable and fruit towards Sittingbourne. So there was a certain amount of both marsh and arable. Sarre also had Irish hares (descendant of those imported for coursing) which ran very strong and straight, and were difficult to catch.

The A20 was a division line.

ARTHUR FINN: *It should be our country, but the Wye go there, because the Wye would get invited. So there was no point in falling out about it – they are there. Its not actually on the map as their's, but they get invited by the farmers. Its no good saying: 'Oh you can't go there, its our country.' Pointless.*

Other whips and potential huntsmen were Ray Cutchee, Laurie Kay, and Mike Bax.

Betty's interest in, and rapport with, young people all her life had kept the age-group of the beagle followers young. Pupils from King's School, Canterbury, have followed the Blean Beagles for several decades, including David Gower, the England test cricket captain, when he was a fair-headed youngster.

Betty's public relations'skills continued apace. The town of Whitstable – very unusually – became supporters. For many years the Beagle Gymkhana was held in the town grounds; the hounds were paraded at the Whitstable Show and the Beagle Ball was held at Tankerton (just beyond Whitstable).

During a hunt, the beagles would travel about 15 miles and followers would get well exercised. Betty always knew which way they would travel and would walk that way. She walked about 5 miles, but was always in at the kill.

The beaglers could enjoy the countryside. A day out in other people's fields – coming across all the trees, flowers, and birds in their habitat. Then often a delicious tea at the end, kindly made by local supporters – in the area beagled.

There was one occasion when the usual delectable spread was set out at the home of General Sir Philip (who won the VC) and Lady Neame. Unfortunately a door had been left open. The upshot was, that the pack rushed in and the beagles ate the tea! Well, it was a beagle tea! They got there first on that day. Suprisingly, not a plate was broken.

There are plenty of beagling stories.

Anita Edwards, a beagling whip for many years, fell and broke her arm. Betty set the arm with the aid of two spanners. The hospital wouldn't touch it as it was set properly. Mrs Edwards used to collect the 'cap' at beagling Meets, which followers paid if they were not annual subscribers.

SANDY ROGERS: *We were out beagling and I was absolutely dying for a pee. We were in this huge field and you know how Betty just stands there. I said 'If you'll excuse me Betty, I'll just over there...'* *She looked me up and down and said,* **'Look! What you understand is – a woman might see you peeing but a lady never would!'** *So I didn't really have much choice. I had to relieve myself there and then, while talking to her in the middle of the field!*

John Hills – (who jointly with Mona Finn was Master of the Tickham) remembered a Betty story.

JOHN: *Years ago – we fell out with Lord Harris. The Masters of the Tickham went to Betty, to see what to do about it. I persuaded her to write him a letter, which she did. The Masters copied it out and she signed it and sent it to Lord Harris. Lady Harris then met Betty in Faversham one day and. said: 'Lovely letter – but you've learnt to spell!'*

She could tell that the letter didn't just come from Betty, but was really from the Tickham Masters!
Mike Bax, one of the beagle Huntsmen, married Jan Aston.

JAN: *When I was 6 months pregnant, with my son William, having to sit in the trailer to stop the beagles from fighting. Betty gave me a deckchair (normally I wouldn't be allowed a deckchair). At the last minute, she suddenly decided to come and sit with me, so another deck chair was got. We both sat in the back of this trailer, going miles, full of stinking old beagles, for about an hour. We were going to some Meet, sitting side by side, me heavily pregnant! It was hysterical.*

Betty did not like the thought of the pregnant Jan being in there alone. On another occasion Jan was in the beagle trailer when they were involved in a slight accident and she had to keep mousy quiet as she shouldn't have been there.

GEOFFREY NEAME: *I went to King's, Canterbury. I bumped into Guy Hindley my first day. We both decided to go beagling as our sport – every Thursday afternoon.*

We were all taken in a mini-bus from school by a master. I was there 1974–79. We wore scruffy gear, jeans tucked into socks. We always called her 'Master'. Never anything else but Master. Nobody called her Betty. It was great. Used to smoke fags behind the haystacks. There were loads of hares.

A lot of the King's, Canterbury Old Boys, who were former beaglers, still turn up at the Beagle Ball.

On Boxing Day, 1962 the Meet was at Perry Court, the home of Hugh and Norma Curling. It was the year of the big freeze. The beaglers returned early as it was freezing up because the beagles' pads were sore and they wouldn't run. They didn't hunt for three months as the thaw didn't come until 7 March. In the end they just used to take the beagles out for exercise. There were one or two Meets at the end of the Season and it was always tea round the diningroom table at Waterham, because Jean was there to cope. They had Battenburg. Norma's son Simon would say *'I'll have a piece of window cake, please.'* Jean would cut round cakes into squares.

If there were flies on the tea table and you tried to wave them away. Betty would say: **'Don't do that we like our flies.'**

One Boxing Day, on the Cleveland marshes, Betty's favourite beagle, Willow got herself torn. She was laid upon the kitchen table.
'Where's the needle?'

Jean Fraser suggested various places to look.

'We have to use a darning needle.' Betty sewed Willow up and applied some spray from the vet. The usual young men were present – Simon and Mike, Guy and Geoffrey. They then all had tea at Perry Court with the Curlings. Willow was healed and back hunting a month later.

On another occasion Willow was lost in the woods at Throwley. Betty tried several times to entice Willow out, but the beagle had possibly been picked up by gypsies, so that was that.

The last Meet of the season was often held on Grand National Day at Heel Farm, the home of Jack Hills and his children Marjorie and John. They would always be sure to finish hunting and box hounds early, so that all could crowd into the sitting-room where Marjorie would supply an excellent tea and watch the race on television. It was always enlivened by their own sweepstake and John on the telephone placing any last minute bets which members might ask him to make.

ARTHUR FINN: *There was a vogue for – everybody started getting donkeys. At many shows you got all these tartie fel-artie donkeys – amazing colours. So we had to have a class at the beagle show – for donkeys. And we got down to the committee which we held in the Whitstable Yacht Club. Who's going to judge the donkeys?*

Betty said **'Oh, Robin Hooper will do it, 'cos he was our Ambassador** [in Greece] **and he should know about donkeys.'** *So Robin, being a good sport, did. He even put up stickers for the Blean Beagle Horse and Dog Show in Athens.* [Arthur told of his time serving on the Beagle Committee.] *We used to go down to the Yacht Club. When I was first on the Committee I was working for G W Finn and Sons as an Articled Clark getting paid £3 a week. This went mainly on bus fares, and I'd always pay my round. So, when it came to paying for my round, it was a complete wipe for me for weeks.*

The Whitstable Yacht Club [meeting] *was a particularly difficult one. You'd got everybody down there. Joan Sayer, Jean Fraser, Betty, Mrs Edwards – eight or twelve of us. In those days the old ladies – Joan Dawes would go as well – she wasn't a great drinker. Joan Sayer and Betty and Jean, they'd all have a large gin and French. So each round they'd have a large gin and French, which is two gins and the French has got alcohol in it as well. So after the end of the evening, they'd probably had ten large gin and Frenches. And then they all went home, including Joan Sayer in her little A30. We were ritually worried about her getting back to Egerton.*

NOEL WATSON: *As the decades passed, Betty became more and more popular in the hunting scene and ended as doyen of the beagling world.*

Arthur Finn with Betty

Chapter Twenty-eight
The sixties

In the 1960s Betty had a beagle called Debbie. She was the most enthusiastic, best at picking up the scent, always in the heart of the pack, the fastest. In fact, she wasn't a beagle at all, Debbie was a poodle. It was comic to watch her find the scent when the beagles had lost it. Go 'Yap! Yap!', the beagles would then overtake her, and when they lost it, she would find the scent again. She got tremendously muddy, and was the properest dog you ever did see.

I was around during this period. In the early '60s John and Jill Dawes, my parents, plus Janet, myself and James had returned from a 4-year sojourn in New Zealand and built our house, Sonstoll in the Blean. We were half a mile from Mount Ephraim. Betty farmed all around us, so would pop in for tea or a drink on a very regular basis. She and Jean often came to supper or lunch. We went frequently to Waterham too, and always got a warm welcome. Mrs Richardson was the cook. David Sorrell remembered her cooking: *'She had those beautiful cheese straws. Mrs Richardson used to make the cheese straws – worth going to dinner for.'*

They kept canaries in the sitting-room bay window. The collie in the kennel was 'Dog', with one white side to his face. He always let you in – you didn't know he was there when you went in. And whoever visited the place, he definitely killed them when they came out!

Betty would swim in the pond behind the house, until the advent of a dead cow one year. Noone swam thereafter! Some time later, her granddaughter Lilian fell into the pond and nearly screamed the place down after being stung by the nettles as well. Granny Betty thought she was making a great fuss, as there was nothing wrong with her! She put the reluctant child in her own shirt.

Handbells

Betty and her sister-in-law, Joan Dawes, bought a set of fifteen handbells. Beaglers were not necessarily frightfully musical, so Betty numbered the bells, and caused various of them to ring out carols in pubs and private houses. Once she asked Janet, Anne and James Dawes, John and Sue Johnston, and her shepherd David, to come and play to a few old dears. All were taller than average. Janet remembers arriving at a hall to find that there were 120 'old dears' . Up the aisle they walked, accompanied by comments such as: *'Cor! What did your Mother feed you on?'* Janet recalled, *'We managed to play in time! Most of us were in early to mid-teens.'*

They used to play the bells for a Carol Service at Whitstable Church, two carols or something. They all got the giggles.

'We were pretty bad, I remember', Mike Bax said. Then Betty used to cart them round in the car, visiting friends.

MIKE: *Firstly, she'd do the Pluckley area, basically visiting Slotty. Then descend on one or two others. Then she used to do the Eastling area, and we'd call at four or five houses, have lots to drink, and collect money for Cancer Research. Completely unexpected or uninvited or anything. We would just turn up and play bells.*

Certainly I, myself (who was considered musical) would have quite a lot to do with the bell-ringing at Christmas time, going out six times in 1966. We went to Seasalter Church, Whitstable Church, the Roman Galley pub, an old folk's party at the League of Friendship, Swalecliffe. Private households such as the Crooks, Daweses, Berrys, Samuelsons, and Sayers. Also at Waterham for Willie's young family. Lots of fun, plenty of drinks and an occasionally recognizable carol! Betty did not play, it was for the young. Andrew Parry and Gay, Paul Marsh, Jane, John Beech, Felicity, Mike Bax, Patrick Neasham, Sue Sorrell. Penny Bryant, Hilary Ruddock-West, John Johnson, Laughlan Shakleton-Fergus (Australian), Janet, myself, and James Dawes, and any passing young people.

We went out bellringing many other years, too.

Betty had a collection of different 'Mayday' shepherds at Christmas time, who would ring handbells also. They always accompanied Betty and Jean to dinner at our home, Sonstoll, on Christmas Day. In 1966 there was Paddy (who's teeth I socked out when he fell headfirst on to the ball, during a hockey match after the feast!); '67 –

Jim Adams, '68 – Edward Watson, '69 – Alan Evans and one called Fred – over the Easter period.

Driving

Betty was not always a brilliant driver. Coming to visit at Sonstoll she always sent the edging stones to the drive flying.

In 1966 Janet and I remember being taken to the Eridge Hunt Footraces by Betty. She thought it would be a good idea to tell us youngsters some facts about driving – as we were about to start learning how. Betty held forth on the subject of drivers who looked in their mirrors too frequently. She thought it was unnecessary, that one should be able to drive without looking in the car-mirror. This message would have had a greater chance with us girls if our necks had not been getting colder and colder ~ and then stiff. The reason for this was that the day before, Betty had failed to notice an object whilst backing her car out, and as a result – she had no back windscreen!

We ran in the Eridge footraces. The shepherd, Jim, won a race and Janet finished second in another and won a coffee table. I (as usual) finished last.

Betty held an annual Christmas Draw for the beagles. In earlier times it was held at the Three Horse Shoes, in Staplestreet. In later years it was held at The Dove in Dargate. Another well-attended social event.

The Beagle Gymkhana was held at the Westmeads Showground at Whitstable, yearly on about the third Wednesday in August. 'Dog' would be released to guard the ground during the preparations for the event. He came back once with a piece of somebody's trousers in his teeth!

Slotty would tip young Simon Curling ten shillings at the show. My brother James and I would attend the Gymkhana on our ponies, taking part in the egg-and-spoon, musical-sack, and trotting races, and also a showjumping course. There were classes for dogs too. It was a well-attended and rural event sponsored by Whitstable Town. The Blean Beagles were the only hunt to receive a subscription from an urban council.

Betty was always an awesome figure to the groups of lads milling around the town. Years later as an adult one of these lads, Martin Almond, still remembered her as a forceful character.

Whitstable Carnival

JANET: *At the Whitstable Carnival, Betty decided to have the beagles accompanied by a beauty queen and handmaidens, to emulate the beauties from Margate and Ramsgate. Instead of being raised up on three lofty thrones, she squeezed four of the beagling girls through a hole in the netting of a beagle trailer. They had to crawl through straw and sit on apple-boxes in their, by then, rather tatty long dresses. Half the trailer was wired off for the Blean Beagles Bitches – the inevitable comments arose! Sue Sorrell, who is very pretty, instantly became Beauty Queen, whilst Janet and Anne Dawes – who had fewer pretensions to beauty, and a French girl – who was going through the ugly-duckling stage, were the handmaidens. They were very popular and pennies and ha'pennies were showered upon them. The beagles were sick on their shoes.*

Whitstable Carnival: Anne Dawes (author), Susan Sorrell, Janet Dawes, Simon Curling & Hedwige

This was on Wednesday 14 August 1968 with Simon Curling accompanying, dressed up as a page. Quite a lot of money got collected. It was dark coming back from the carnival. There were no lights on the trailer of course. Betty just tied a torch on the back, covered with a workman's red handkerchief which she always used, and trundled down the Thanet Way. Norma and Simon had also attended Betty at the Herne Bay Carnival in August 1966.

Carpentry

'She was a key figure in the building of Hernhill Village Hall, carrying out a large part of the carpentry herself,' wrote the *Faversham Times* in 1990.

The village hall was very much a do-it-yourself job in the late '50s. There was a good theatrical group in Hernhill – that did a play every year which Norma went to with Betty and Jean. Betty enjoyed doing woodwork and did a lot for the village hall making the flooring and the staging up there, and, when any repairs or woodwork were needed to be done – she always knew how it should be done. It had been Betty's idea to have the enormous tables – which were heavy to move about – but they could be pushed together to make a substantial stage.

> JOE: *'Cos the stagin' was made up of half a dozen or so, it may have been Eight large tables. This wide, this high. I know she was makin' them down here in a shed she used to have for carpentry, next to the garage, where they used to have the little chicks, years ago. That was all right for a start, then the floor began to go. Well you can imagine, sticking a foot through there. After that, everything was sort of moved up into the bedroom.*
>
> *One of these electric circular saws was there. Up one end, there was a large table that was always littered with tools of every description, bits and pieces of wood and whatever, up there. Oh yes, it was littered this table. I don't know why in her bedroom, I'm sure. But – not the sort of thing you'd associate with in the bedroom.*

The walls were lined with racks of chisels and other woodworking tools.

Betty made the coffee table at Mount Ephraim with the Dawes coat-of-arms on it. She made two beautifully fitted-out drinks trolleys, one went to her great-niece Mary Ann as a wedding present; the other a special one, for Bill and Mary.

At 'the Mount', it always took a long time to have a drink. If Betty was having whisky, the bottle would be collected from one room, the glass from the pantry, the soda from another wing, and the ice from the kitchen. With more than one person, Bill (who was very sociable) would have to look in other places, too. So Betty made his drinks trolley with fitted places for large bottles, small bottles, drawers for different~sized glasses and an ice box. Also a lid which could open to become a bar. There were large wheels one end and a pushing handle the other. It looked good and was very well used all Bill's life and saved him miles of walking.

She used to make the old Scottish types of cradles – for her groom, Anne Clinch, and also one for Susan Sorrell. She made a set of jumps for the horseshow – and Norma painted them on one occasion. Betty had a chap staying there one summer – a farm student. It was a very, very wet year in the early '60s. His father was a builder and he knew about carpentry. He and Betty between them made a set of jumps that are still used. Really thorough and good quality workmanship.

Betty was also very good at painting and drawing – flowers and hunting scenes. And knitting. The wonderful stockings beautifully knitted, and she'd turn the heel while talking all the time. She always had a piece of knitting going. She'd come back from beagling and the boys would all be sitting around after tea. And Betty would be talking, talking, talking the whole time, and they'd be absorbing it and she'd be knitting the whole time. Betty copied her special pattern for ribbed stockings into the back of her account book.

Anne Clinch

Betty always laughed and said Anne was her god-daughter, because she had to be confirmed just before she was married to George. Anne was Betty's groom from 1961 until 1963.

ANNE: *A friend of mine told me about it. Told me Mrs McKeever wanted someone. I was working for someone else but I didn't like the job. My friend gave me her 'phone number, so I went down for an interview and that was it.*

When I went to work for her, I bumped into the person who had worked for her just before me. He said that she was horrendous to work for, that she never stopped going around the stables and finding fault! When I went there, she never ever came near the stables. I used to have to come and get her, to come and look at her horses. [Anne knew her business.] *We just got on very, very well.*

Mrs McKeever bred quite a few good thoroughbred horses over the years. Point-to-Pointers – Balkan Windfall and Balkan Seabreeze were two of them. They were nice horses, before she took up breeding the Welsh ponies.

Weren't allowed to mention her husband. If you mentioned him, it was instant dismissal. There was one time when Willie wasn't allowed to be mentioned!

[After my marriage] *she made a lovely crib for me, a rocking crib – sideways, from a stand. It's still in the loft – in case I get any grandchildren.*

Orchids she grew. Wore one at the Ball every year.

This is how I saw Mrs McKeever: She always made everybody feel the most important person in the world. I think that's the main thing I always thought about Mrs McKeever. It didn't matter who you were. Whether you had a lot of money or just had nothing. She just made you feel so much better than you were. And she also had a great sense of humour, which I always saw the funny side of. Not everybody did.

We was going to a Point-to-Point once, when I was riding for her. I think she thought I was getting a bit worked up. There were these signs saying SOFT VERGES. **'There you are. Soft Virgins!'** *Made me laugh!*

I was married from Mrs McKeever's place in 1963. Firstly, I couldn't get married because I hadn't been christened or confirmed. So we all had to go off to the church to be christened, Hernhill Church. There was only Mrs McKeever, Miss Fraser, my godfather, and George and I. Because I wouldn't let anybody else come. I felt a right prat! We were all squashed into the same pew, and the Vicar said would we like to move out a bit and be more comfortable.

'No,' *says Mrs McKeever,* **'We're keeping each other warm.'** *Then we had to go straight on from the christening to the confirmation and that was at Faversham.*

*I think there was a pub in-between places, because my god-
father seemed to get lost on the way to the confirmation. Mrs
McKeever and Miss Fraser stayed the course. Then we all went
back to her place at Waterham for dinner.*

*She gave me an engagement party, then I got married from
there. She always said it was the best wedding she'd ever been to.
We just did it ourselves – nothing flash. She helped to organize.
I got married at Hernhill.*

MARY DAWES: *At Chelsea Flower Show* [one year – with Betty]
and my mother-inlaw [Joan], *we sat down somewhere on some
chairs to have lunch. Something out of a paperbag. As soon as
the paperbag was empty, Betty with a very casual air, blew it up!
Popped it with the most enormous noise! Of course my mother-inlaw was mortified. I will never forget that.*

One day Betty needed a new lavatory seat, and was spotted
sitting and trying them out for comfort, in the shop window of a
hardware store window in Faversham!

Willie's growing family continued at Renville – just the opposite
side of Canterbury. In the '60s, Willie used to fly over to Ireland for
the day and buy cattle, probably sixty to eighty head at a time.
Willie would see his father, then after sorting all the cattle out they
would come in by boat to Holyhead and then down to Canterbury
by rail.

In the course of time, he and Anne had had four children.
Tom, Margaret, Sheila, and Lilian. Betty was delighted to be a grandmother. She would play Happy Families and other card games, but
would give no quarter to the young ones, if her memory was better
than theirs. She always played to win, so it often ended in tears.
However, she had a great affection for her grandchildren.

Betty always had great faith in the vet rather than the doctor.
She was badly bitten by a pig or cut her leg at a Point-to-Point,
and her leg wouldn't heal. So she went to a doctor and it went
on for months and months. Eventually, on a visit from the vet to
Waterham, he went up to her bedroom and said, *'Oh, what's wrong
with you.'*

**'I don't know what's gone wrong, but it's Purgatory now. It's
very bad.'**

The vet replied, *'Oh, I know what's happened. You've been stitched up with cat-gut, and you're allergic to it.'*

'Right, quick! Get at it! Open it up and change it.' She was fine after that, and the vet stitched her up.

MY DIARY: *Saturday, 27th April 1968. At 12.30 went to Waterham (as we were going to Wye College Gymkhana). But foal fell in ditch so fetched Aunty Betty and had lunch whilst she caught its mother, then spent ages trying to make the foal suck. It turned out Aunty Betty had cut her foot badly. Janet and I drove her to Faversham Cottage Hospital – 12 stitches. Home soon after.*

In '67 Betty had a coffee-saucer sized lump on her neck, but it cleared up.

There was always a tremendous social life associated with the beagling existence. There was the annual Beagle Ball, held until 1967 in Faversham soon after New Year. This was often considerable fun, with a great mixing of generations. Then from 1968 onwards until the late '80s, her Ball was held at the Marine Hotel just beyond Whitstable at Tankerton; often on the second or third Friday in March. A mixture of old and modern, always with an 'Eightsome' and 'The Gay Gordons' danced. We would always take a party along. Another ball Betty much enjoyed attending, with other family members. was Princess Olga Romanoff's 'coming out' Regency Masked Ball at the Dorchester. The 18-year-old was a local Faversham girl, with illustrious Russian ancestry.

From this time on, Betty would shave her own whiskers – if necessary! She liked eating fish and roast beef. She was not so fond of roast mutton or pork.

Chapter Twenty-nine
Jean Fraser

Jean was a tall upright Scotswoman of about 5 foot 8 or 9. She held herself well, wore horn-rimmed spectacles and had blue eyes. Her hair was short, dark, and wavy.

Jean was very well educated, and had her Diploma in Poultry. She was Betty's companion and was an important figure in the running of all aspects of Betty's life.

She acted as secretary for the Blean Beagles. Quite a lot of paperwork was run by Jean. Gymkhanas, balls, Blean Beagle Draws, the schedule of all the winter Meets, circulated to all beagle supporters took a lot of organisation. Jean kept the paperwork going for both the farm and the beagles, and generally coped with things.

She never drove a car, owing to bad eyesight. Also, Jean didn't want to learn to drive. *'I'd just be the chauffeur,'* she would say.

The 'beagle teas' – such a feature of the pack, were given by many different hostesses. Well inevitably lots of these teas happened at Waterham, they were delicious and were made by Jean.

If Betty was invited anywhere, Jean always came too. She was not a rich woman but she was generous and gave lovely presents, as a 'thank you' for being entertained so much by Betty's family. She had inherited and clung on to many bits and pieces from Mopsie. Bit by bit she would give these special pieces out to younger generations of Daweses and McKeevers, on marriage and at Christmas.

For instance she gave us a handsome antique wooden clock as a wedding present and a silver tea-caddy with lions heads. She gave Janet, Mopsie's silver-white brocade wedding dress and train (with Betty's permission), which Janet later remade to use in a large panel, at her own marriage.

Jean was very kind. She had lots of time for the young, and had strong views on bringing up children.

Betty and Jean always sat in armchairs either side of the fireplace. They had droves of visitors; family, beaglers, friends, and Jean was the housekeeper, the organizer of any indoor servants, dailies who were employed. She got the supplies in, and generally kept the show on the road for all Betty's tastes and activities. She became 'family'. *'Oh Betty!'* was a frequent utterance of hers.

> MARY DAWES: *One of Betty's little petty economies was not to turn the heating on. Eventually, Jean would say, 'The orchids aren't looking too good.' And after an inspection, the heating would go on – for the orchids!*

She and Betty were a good team, keeping the whole Waterham enterprise on the road.

I remember Jean giving me lessons in taking off a turkey's leg after plucking: Jean cut lightly around the leg-joint, then shut the leg in the kitchen door and pulled really hard, thus removing the tendons and making the leg much more edible. Waterham kitchen door showed signs of much use in this way. Jean helped run the farm and her participation in it went a long way to producing the excellence of standards, and keeping it going.

Then there were Jean's dependants, her mother and aunt. Mrs and Miss Fraser had (like Jean) originally come from Inverness, but had later moved, living together, first at Edinburgh (Jean's uncle had been Chief Constable) then at Joppa, a suberb of Edinburgh near Portabello. Later they moved to Lievenhall. But they were getting older, and had lost their money.

In the 1960s, Betty very kindly provided Mother and Auntie Fraser with a cottage to live in, near Waterham. Betty took them everywhere around, as they neither of them drove. So she kept all three Frasers together as a clan.

Mrs and Miss Fraser stayed in Kent for about ten years, as Betty's dependants. First, they lived in one of Betty's Monk's Hill cottages, which she provided for them, situated at the top, up towards the railway line.

Later, after they could no longer manage on their own, Betty invited them to stay at Waterham. Auntie Fraser remained in good health until she was 88, then died on the loo. Mrs Fraser was hard of hearing and had some sight trouble. She had a stroke, aged 92 and was resuscitated in hospital afterwards, somewhat unnecessarily. Thereafter, when visited she *'just wanted to die,'* but did actually survive for another eighteen months/two years. Mrs Fraser eventually died in June 1968. Betty housed and fed each of these ladies for all that time.

Jean kept the ashes of Mother and Auntie Fraser in the powder room off her bedroom for years. Eventually the ashes were taken to Scotland in the late '70s and laid to rest at Tom-na-Cross Kirkyard, which is just outside Beauly, near Inverness.

Noel Watson (front) as huntsman of the Blean Beagles

Chapter Thirty
Noel Watson – huntsman

Noel Watson, huntsman from 1967 to 1970 described Betty as *'One of the greatest characters I have ever known, a real relic of a bygone age and class.'*

Noel first met her in 1966, when the huntsman, Ray Cutchee, invited him to whip-in to the beagles. After feeding the hounds at the end of a day's hunting, she always insisted that he stay for tea, a meal that usually dragged on till supper, and ended with whisky and sodas, late at night in front of the fire.

Betty would talk about anything, from family and local matters, long-forgotten boundary disputes and never-ending hunt politics.

NOEL: *I was privileged to carry the horn for the Blean Beagles from about 1967–70 during which time I learnt more about actual hunting than I have from a lifetime's hunting with other packs. For a start, Betty, who was a beautiful horn blower, taught me all the twelve correct calls on an English hunting horn. She also taught me how to feed and care for beagles. She had a 'hands-on' approach to all kennel problems, and many is the squirming beagle I've held down on her kitchen table, whilst she cheerfully stitched a gaping wound caused by barbed wire, after a day's hunting.*

Every Sunday during the off-season the Watson family would exercise the hounds.

NOEL: *Apart from that I don't think the beagles were ever let out, unless it was to be paraded at local shows. Betty was a firm believer in the adage, that the only way to get horses and hounds hunting fit, was to take them hunting.*

Betty told Noel the story of a farmer who fitted false teeth into his store cattle in order to falsify their age and collect the subsidy. The farmer's crime came to light when one of his bullock's teeth fell out on being knocked on the head in a slaughterhouse!

NOEL: *Betty was a true member of her age and class – quite an autocrat. She had been brought up in an era where most, if not all*

*the land she hunted over belonged to her family or friends. She
didn't have to ask permission as the farmers were her father's tenants and she naturally enjoyed all the sporting rights. With this
in mind, she never asked anyone's permission to hunt or even bothered to let them know when she was likely to beagle across their
land, even though times had changed, and by the 1960s most yeo-
man farmers were now freeholders of their land. This often resulted
in land owners asking what we were doing on their land. Betty
always met such queries by saying,* **'Ah, I knew your father well,
and he and I were great friends. He won the championship
for Sussex Cattle in 1923, didn't he?'** *(Or* **'He was the best
shot'** *or* **'the best horseman'** *etc...) and always won them over
with her undeniable charm. One day when hunting the beagles, I
was accosted by a farmer who was incandescent with rage at the
sight of us hunting over his land. Betty came bustling up and was
promptly sworn at in foul and abusive language. At the end of the
farmer's tirade, she politely and calmly asked his name which, we
shall say, was Mr Fulford. She replied* **'Ah, Fulford, Fulford. Oh
yes, I remember your father well and I didn't like him either!'**

Perhaps Betty was not strictly adhering to her correct upbringing
of writing to and seeking permission from the farmer every time she
hunted, but by this stage, she was in her sixties and was very sure of
her status within her the community.

NOEL: *Another time a thick fog came down whilst hunting. A real
pea-souper which literally cut visibility to arms-length, making
hunting impossible. I decided to call it a day, and groped my way
back to where I thought the meet was. However, I was completely
disorientated and went in the opposite direction! I climbed over a
hedge, still calling for the beagles, when a window opened out of
the murky smog and a woman's voice said that she 'Hadn't got
anything for you today – thank you.' I then realized that I had
blundered into her back garden, and she had thought that I was
the local rag and bone merchant calling for custom! I humbly
explained my presence, and she kindly took pity on me and all
my 'cold little dogs' and insisted that I brought them all (about
15 or 16 couples!) into the house to get warmed up. The beagles
were isolated in the front hall of her cottage whilst (after phoning
Betty, where she was having tea at the pub where we had met)
I was regaled with tea in the kitchen.*

When Betty called to collect us all, she was invited in as well
and being a great one for tea, promptly plonked herself down for
a chat and a second tea. It was then that our hostess's husband
returned from work and had hysterics when he opened the front
door and 30 odd wet, muddy beagles poured out of his cottage
barking wildly at him!

On another occasion, after a long hunt, the tired hare led the
pursuing beagles into a thick covert, where a lot of men and boys
with long sticks appeared and joined in the chase. To my horror
I realized that they were beaters and the Blean Beagles had gate-
crashed into the middle of a formal pheasant shoot. However, the
beagles were close on the heels of their quarry and there was no
stopping them. They rattled round and round the covert with great
cry, until suddenly there was an abrupt silence broken only by
the muffled growling sound from the hounds that denotes a kill.
I pushed my way out of the covert into the adjoining field where
the scrimmaging pack were worrying their prey, only to find that it
wasn't the hare they had caught but a cock pheasant! At this point
I was surrounded by irate gentlemen with shotguns and the shoot
captain who asked me what the bloody hell I was doing ruining
their sport! I replied that I was frightfully sorry and shamefacedly
handed him the pheasant. Suddenly, seemingly out of nowhere,
Betty bore down on the assembly, seized the cock pheasant from
the shoot captain's hands, and shoved the somewhat mangled
bird into one of the copious pockets of her aged trench coat with
the explanation of, **'Master's percs, don't y'know!'**

By now Betty was not a very good walker and certainly could not
run. During the course of a day's beagling she just leant on a gate or
stood on top of a hill, but it was the right gate or the right hilltop.

Betty did an immense amount of work with local children pro-
moting hunting and other rural pursuits, encouraging them to come
beagling and dressing the more eager ones in green coats.

Noel Watson had to retire from hunting as he had contracted TB
in both kidneys. Betty volunteered to give him one of her kidneys
for a transplant, but the surgeon refused her offer.

Betty & Jean Fraser at weddings

Chapter Thirty-one
Weddings

Here are some stories, sayings, and one-liners that Betty used to utter – during weddings.

Walking into church a friend remarked on what a nice scent someone was wearing, Betty replied, **'My favourite scent is the nice smell of fresh horse manure!'**

The bride's mother was walking up the aisle in a hat adorned with pheasant feathers. In a loud aside to the bride's father Betty called out, **'Ranald – Been shooting lately?'**

At my wedding in 1972, my brand new husband, Colin commented, *'That's a nice hat, Aunty Betty.'* She was wearing her 1920s Ascot hat, which was black straw, crumpled now, but history says it used to have roses around it. **'Been to a good many weddings,'** she barked. **'A good many funerals too.'**

Willie and Anne McKeever's wedding – 1957: Slotty wouldn't attend the rehearsal. He was sailing. Would he make it in time for the actual service? He was in a race. This put people's backs up.

PETER GOODWIN: *I cannot date this event. It was probably in the 1960's. A. young lady from near Faversham was to be married. Betty was an invited guest to the wedding. The ceremony was in London, at St Margaret's, Westminster. Wearing her best point-to-point tweed costume, she drove to London in her Landrover which was rather bespattered with Waterham mud. The police, who were directing the chauffeur-driven Daimlers and Rolls's, tried to turn her away. It was not until she showed her wedding invitation card that they believed she really was a guest! She was delighted and lon her return had great joy in reciting the event.*

James Dawes and Annie Broughton's wedding – 4 October 1980.

ANNIE: *As a wedding present, Betty pulled out a rolling pin from her kitchen drawer – unused.* **'I don't suppose you'll ever make pastry, but it will be bloody useful to beat James with!'**

When she was invited to our wedding, Betty quite firmly told my father that she didn't drink champagne, she only drank whisky. And my father laid on whisky, especially for Betty, which she drank very happily.

Arthur and Annie Finn's wedding.

RANDALL NICOL: *Betty, Sandys and myself were present. Mary Dawes said 'We're going off. Would you like a lift, or stay with the young? Betty said* **'I'll stay with the young.'**

Andrew Mineyko and Janet Dawes's wedding – 5 November, 1983.

On the night before Janet's wedding, Betty had a friend of Andrew's to stay. She gave the girl directions to her bedroom that evening. But a little later she said, **'Oh dear! You'd better not go in there, as my godson, a blacksmith sometimes comes, and always uses that room.'**

Alan Warner was also staying. He was faced with a dead sheep on the kitchen table at breakfast time which was being chopped up for the beagles. The stench was too much for him so he was shepherded out.

Hon Bernard Lever and Annie Ballingall's wedding – 6 July 1985

BERNARD: *On my wedding day I set up camp in a rural hotel about seven miles from the church. By chance, John, Jill and Betty stopped there for lunch.*

Just before I was about to set off for the church, I went to the Gentlemen's loo downstairs, to meet Betty, with her white stick, being as blind as a bat in it.

I said 'Hello'.

'Aren't you the grum?' *she asked. 'Yes,' I replied.*

'Well, you're a very good-looking young man.' *She said – waving her white stick!'*

Chapter Thirty-two
Michael Bax – Betty's hero

Michael Bax first met Betty when he was about 10 at a firework party at Sonstoll. She lectured him on the night sky, which he found fascinating. She invited him to go out with the beagles, but he did not do so for another couple of years, when he went to a Meet at the Plough at Lewson Street with a friend.

The following year he went to the Boxing Day Meet in the Market Square at Faversham. Betty made an enclosure for the hounds out of baler twine, but two hounds managed to get out.

Michael caught one immediately and brought it back, and Betty recognized him as the boy she had met two years before. As Michael's family was driving to Westwood, up the Whitstable Road, Michael saw the other hound running across the Recreation Ground, so he caught it and delivered it to the Meet. Betty said, '**By God, you're a Devil with the hounds. You must carry a whip from now onwards**'. Which Michael described as a dream come true, and from then on he was a whipper-in.

His first duty as a whip was to walk from his home, Gushmere Court to Luton House in Selling, where Betty was a guest at the wedding of Katherine Morrison. He arrived at exactly 12.45, and asked for her. Betty thought it would be the ideal excuse to have some small boy turn up at the wedding reception and ask for her, and then she'd say, '**I've got to go. I've got to get this boy to the Beagle Meet,**' and get there herself in good time to start an enjoyable day's beagling at 1.30.

Towards the end of the next summer, Noel Watson became ill, there was no one to hunt the hounds at the mid-week meets. Twice in January 1969 Betty asked Michael, then aged 14, to hunt the hounds. She brushed aside questions of whether he could manage the job with: '**Perfectly all right, perfectly all right. Don't be so silly.**'

MIKE: *It was a classic example to us all, when you give a young person a job to do. She completely ignored me, said* '**Ready, off you go Mike, it's half past one.**' *Then she kept out of the way the whole time, and I didn't see her till the end of the day, and* *it all went well. It was amazing. Start of something rather special for me. Betty insisted that I have a beagling coat, and my mother made me one out of some very light-weight cotton material.*

Shortly after that, when Michael was hunting the hounds, one of them was electrocuted on the railway line at Selling. There were no recriminations from Betty.

Michael was very impressed with Betty's fitness. She was then in her late sixties and would join him on long walks exercising the hounds, and could lift the tailgate of the horsebox in which hounds were transported much more easily than he could.

When they were together she would talk to him as one adult to another on any suject, including giving him a demonstration of water-dowsing with coathangers.

Michael Bax was at King's School, Canterbury, and in the early '70s beagling was made a non-corps activity on corps day, which was Thursday. Betty moved the Mid-week meet to Thursdays so that

Guy Hindley, Betty & Mike Bax

the boys and masters could attend. *'Guy Hindley who's now a Master. People like Geoffrey Neame, who's a master now, were coming out as 12/13 year olds.'*

By the time Michael got his driving licence in 1974, Betty's sight was beginning to go, and she was happy to leave all the driving to him.

Beagling for a day

MIKE: *As huntsman, I would have to pitch out. We would usually meet at 1.00 to 1.30, except during the King's School period, on a Saturday. Most of the Meets would be three quarters of an hour, to an hour away. Except for the local Faversham Meets.*

We'd have to leave Waterham at 12:15 for a one o'clock Meet. I would get there at about 11:15 and would go into Waterham. Betty was totally clued up in that period of what was going on in the kennels and would know exactly what was lame. She'd know all the hot bitches and tell me. Bitches on heat and lame hounds got left behind and otherwise, sick hounds. She'd give me a pencil and piece of paper. And I would go over to the kennels, usually on my own, and take all the hounds out.

We used not to have a hound list. When I first started doing it, you'd take out 14 couple or something, and she'd know exactly what was there. Later on, I think we'd probably left a few out, on occasions. She began insisting on Hound Lists so that she knew exactly what had gone out, and who was missing at the end.

I would very often give them a walk up the lane just to settle them down before they were loaded. I would come over with the horsebox and we'd load them, and drive to the Meet.

1 o'clock, you'd arrive at the Meet, and the field were there. You might have a drink somewhere. If it was a Lawn Meet, then Betty would make a real fuss of the host, and entertain everybody for quarter of an hour or so. So we'd always get off rather late, which irritated a young, eager huntsman!

Off we'd go hunting and, as the day starts, your host farmer would tell you where to go and draw and look for a hare. He'll tell you the three or four most likely places, and you'd draw those in order. I'd take about half an hour to draw the hounds.

And if all goes well, the hounds find a hare and run it in view for 100, 200 yards till it goes behind a hedge or over a fold in the ground, then they'd go down on to their noses, and start hunting by scent.

As huntsman, you've got to try to stay in touch with them, so that you're watching and anticipating which way they're going to run, so that when they check, you've got a good idea of where to cast them, to hit off the line again.

If all goes well, after an hour or an hour and a half, you've got a tired hare in front of you. Which, because their scent begins to go when they get tired, you probably lose, or sometimes catch.

We never used to catch an awful lot of hares though. The best season I ever had was about 12 brace. Betty in her heyday, hunting the hounds from her cob, she killed 17–18 brace, several times. But they were always small beagles, and it's not an easy country with roads and railway lines and fences and so on.

The afternoon would carry on in that vein. You'd probably hunt 2 or 3 hares in an afternoon. You'd go on until half an hour before dark, and then collect all the hounds up, load them up, check them off against the list.

Very often you'd have a beagle tea in somebody's house. Betty would sit down and hold court for half an hour, three quarters of an hour. Half past five, six o'clock, she'd say **'Right, time to go.'**

Off we'd go and drive the hounds back to the kennels. Take them in, feed them. She would always come out and supervise the feeding of the hounds. We'd either feed them pudding, or raw flesh, or bibles. Bibles was one of her favourite foods – sheep's stomachs. Betty used to go to the Charing Abattoir and collect horsebox loads of sheep's stomachs, which the hounds would devour. One or two per feed. They liked it too. They were horrible things to handle.

Then half past six, quarter to seven we'd probably got through all that, and she'd say, **'Right, come on in,'** – and have a cup of tea. Or as I got older, one would sit in the sitting-room, and have a glass of whisky. I would be exhausted, glaze over and Betty would tell stories endlessly. Then one would struggle to get away about 8 o'clock.

That was the pattern, but it was a wonderful experience. Fantastic.

Houndsman

MIKE: *Then I began regular visits to Waterham from that moment, as a sort of huntsman. I used to go over 2, 3 days a week in the holidays, exercising the hounds. Feeding the hounds, skinning, learning how to make puddings. Nailing up the weather-boarding on the kennels, repairing the concrete, repairing the wire to runs, exercising the hounds.*

The big long walk took us round over the Thanet Way, along Plum Pudding Lane side, then right the way round by Hernhill, and back over the Thanet Way at the Hernhill end. Betty would come on those walks, so there was another example of how fit she was. She would be on those hound exercises on her feet and some-times Jesse Richardson would be on those walks as sort of kennel-man, as a retired farmworker in those days.

The hunting territory of the Blean Beagles

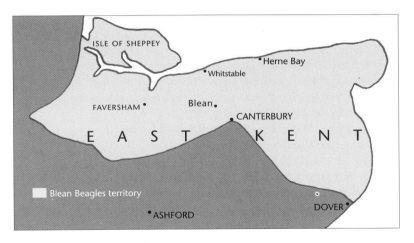

The original Blean country was Sittingbourne to Canterbury, that is to say, mostly north of the A2 and the A28.

The Boxing Day Meet was always a big terrific affair based at Faversham. From 1972 to 1989 it was at the former Fremlins, now Whitbread Brewery, Court Street, which is on the opposite side of Abbey Street to Shepherd Neame. In 1990 we crossed the road to

Shepherd Neame. Nowadays it is at the Shepherd Neame Brewery, in Abbey Street, Faversham.

The Meet would be 11.30 in the morning. You'd get 200 or 300 people coming from Faversham to the Meet and the Fremlins brewery would dispense beer and cherry brandy to the hunt followers.

Then the hounds were put in the horsebox and taken up to Westwood Court, up by the A2, at Faversham. The Westwood Court country gradually became more and more difficult and Betty became more and more worried about the M2 motorway, so it was stopped.

Graveney Marshes, a Meet since 1909, is the oldest main meet of the beagles with many terrific Meets there. Mike Bax is in no doubt it is still one of their best bits of country.

In Hernhill, all that orchard country used to hold hares. The Hernhill Meets were at Mount Ephraim, Sonstoll, the Red Lion opposite the church, and The Three Horseshoes at Staplestreet. Now, unfortunately there aren't any hares there. So the beagles haven't met there since 1990. They always used to hunt that country quite a lot and find hares down at Crockham, just below Sonstoll, which used to run straight up the Blean and into the Tower. The hunt would lose them in those big woods, then would have to come out and find another hare. These were regular Meets.

Further away, Sheldwich Corner, Selling Church, The Plough at Shottenden, Chislet Marshes, Blue Bridge, Preston – Wingham and with the Doubledays at Rodmersham – were all regular Meets.

Also Roman Galley, Thanet Way, but no way could they go anywhere near there now, because of traffic.

The Beagles did not go there until 1970 or just after, when Betty opened up the Sheppey country with two or three Meets in Sheppey. One was at South Leas, Minster, another on the Sheerness Golf Course and at New House Farm, Leysdown. Nowadays, Sheppey is one of the most important parts of the Blean country, with six separate Meets on Sheppey.

The Dover Country is the country between Canterbury and Dover. It is another bit of country which, at the turn of the Millennium, is very important to the Beagles, places such as Sutton and Studdal, and Waldeshare. This gave Betty new bits to beagle which she would not really have got to at all before about 1970.

The original Blean country didn't extend beyond Canterbury. The line went into Canterbury and then up the Amery Hill Road towards Herne Bay.

When the West Street Harriers ceased, Betty started hunting that country. In the early 1970s, she did apply, at last, to the Master of Harrier and Beagles Association to register it. Mike Bax thought they were a bit iffy about it because The Wye College Beagles wanted it as well. But she said, **'No, I've been hunting there anyway for a number of years'.** The Master of Harriers and Beagles did register it to her. So the hunting country actually doubled in size.

Previously, there would have been plenty of room in that original Blean country, which was Sittingbourne to Canterbury, mostly north of the A2 and the A28. Then the railway was electrified and the M2 constructed.

John Hills and his family at Heel Farm, Throwley, were great fans of hers. So it became another of the main Meets – another piece of country Betty opened up and the Blean Beagles have been able to extend. They always had a Grand National Meet at the end of every season. The Meet would be early, 10.30 or 11.00 in the morning. After the hunt, the Hills's would have everyone into their kitchen to watch the Grand National. That became the traditional finishing day of the season.

Betty would have hunted with Lord Sondes in the old days and was a great pal of his – the last but one Lord Sondes. Betty could go where she liked on the Lees Court Estate. Then Henry Sondes came along – became the next earl after George, in about 1972. He was mad keen on shooting. He had a keeper called Fountain – still alive (his son is still keeper on the Sondes estate). Betty didn't get on with Henry Sondes.

Fountain wound Henry Sondes up about the beagles. *'Sir, you can't possibly have the beagles, they're going to disturb the pheasants.'* and so on. And there were one or two incidents. The beagles did not get in on shooting days, but they did get into the Lees Court area among the pheasants. There was one blazing row on the telephone, between Betty and Henry Sondes. When Betty tore him off a frightful strip, and said how disappointed his father would be in him, etc, etc. But that was the end of going anywhere near Sondes, particularly in the shooting season. They still have that problem, although Henry died in 1998. You never know, the Blean might get back there.

If the hounds killed somebody's chickens, Michael, as huntsman would get a frightful ticking off from the irate owner.

MIKE: *Betty would walk up to them, and just check out who they were, and whose son they were, and whose grandson he was, and tell these people all about their ancestry – you know – how she used to drink in Faversham Market with Grandfather, or Grandmother or whatever. And within 10 minutes, these people were as sweet as pie.*

As she got older, she wasn't great about 'clearing' the country – things that began to slip that showed her age. We definitely turned up at places where we weren't expected, no doubt about that. We always got away with it. We were never sent home from anywhere, but I became aware of turning up at places, and people looking rather amazed.

The hound breeding slipped, and we began to get mistakes. The pack of the late '70s was only half the pack it was in the early '70s. In 10 years the breeding went to pot – and that was age, I'm quite sure. She just couldn't attend to the detail, and the planning of it, and there'd be a mistake. As she got older, she got softer, and a litter was kept that shouldn't have been kept. It doesn't take long for a highly bred pack of hounds to go downhill in those circumstances. And the same happened on the farm, I am sure. Which is all perfectly understandable.

Paul Stern, the blacksmith at Wittersham was a huntsman of the beagles for two or three years in the late '70s, with people like Chris Hill.

I stopped hunting in 1980, once we'd had children. So I hunted them for eleven years. Then I eventually became a trustee. In one of the last meetings she said: **'Right, I may not be around an awful lot longer. The Beagles must be kept going. If you don't keep the beagles going, I shall come back and haunt you.'** *And she would!*

Chapter Thirty-three
The seventies

SHEILA JUDGE: *I suppose I knew about her as a child. She was the same age as my mother. She apparently knew a lot of people my father did. Well, we started going to shows, to Blean Horse Show when my daughter was riding.*

The first time I saw Betty, I took a short cut through a ring and got bawled off. I thought, 'Oh God'. It was a long time ago. I thought I'd put my foot in it, I'll keep out of it. But I realized afterwards – she never remembered it. I was going round there buying horses, and going to shows and I got friendly with her. She was awfully good to us because we had a riding school at the time.

We used to take Riding Club children out to see the ponies. Mad about the ponies and things and she'd always give them tea and make a fuss of them. She was really good. Anything for children. She used to have children down from London to show them the farm. **'You' got to teach the young, or you'll lose your hunting,'** *and all this. All for it.*

Bill Dawes had had a successful City career. He had become a well-known personality in British Shipping. Bill had been Chairman of the New Zealand Shipping Co. since 1966 and became Deputy-Chairman of P & O between 1971 and '72. He was a director of nineteen companies at one stage. After this phenomenal career, he did manage to retire.

Both he and Slotty had always brought many New Zealanders and Australians home for the weekend. Taking them over to Waterham or having Betty over, was still often included in the entertainment.

Betty wrote to John Dawes on 15 January 1975: **'Sandys would have been 81 today. How I wish he was with us still.'**

The Hernhill Craft Centre

The Queen's Silver Jubilee was a time to launch new activities. A meeting was held in the village and suggestions were made for future projects, such as to whether to make a seat for the old folk, or to plant a tree.

Betty suggested a Procession of Hunting through the ages. This was partly so that Janet Dawes, who was ill, could take part, whilst riding side-saddle on a led horse. **'When I was young everyone had a family member with a wing down. Take her about with you.'**

John Dawes had the big idea of starting a Craft Centre in Hernhill. Somewhere where people would actually use their hands and make things out of wood or iron, incorporating the skills of the past which were fast becoming forgotten.

> JOHN: *The Craft Centre should be a place to practise and learn the use of hand tools, and hopefully acquire the joys and skills of Do-It-Yourself. In particular – carpentry, rustic crafts and the use of wood, grown locally… Other crafts such as blacksmith, metal work, and basket work should be included. The idea was to use hand or treadle tools but to have no power tools or electricity.*

If a responsible adult was present, children could also use the Centre. Retired people could use it and make something. Indeed, any who wished to impart their skills to the young were encouraged to do so. Those who were unemployed might find it a help in removing their frustrations.

John suggested they could both make the seat and plant the tree. Bill Dawes provided premises at Mount Ephraim's stable block for a peppercorn rent. £1,000 was found to set up anvils, different types of saws, many other tools, looms. Betty was very enthusiastic. This scheme was very much in her spirit of enterprise. Something the young people could actually do. She promoted and supported the project.

On 8 October 1977 at 3 pm Betty opened the Hernhill Craft Centre. She spoke of all the different trades in her youth, the potters, blacksmiths, woodworkers and spoke so well, that her speech was remembered years later.

The centre became a permanent and on-going enterprise. Betty loved her village. She would attend and help at the Hernhill Horticultural Show.

The subject came up one day about successful gambling. Betty said: **'I'd rather lose my money in Hernhill, getting people to work.'**

Betty wore trousers once. She had to climb a gate at Holly Hill. Her nephew Sandys had to almost take the trousers off before she could negotiate the gate.

Her home was functional and comfortable, rather than stylish, and she painted the sitting-room at Waterham a bright beagle green.

PETER GOODWIN: *Betty had a wonderful knack of getting you involved in whatever she was doing at the time. You were, perhaps, just returning a book on a Sunday afternoon. You would find Betty in the garden, weeding. She would involve you in conversation which slowed your immediate departure and Betty would then say* **'Just get me the wheelbarrow from the barn, please'.** *When you returned with the barrow, you would find yourself holding it while it was being loaded, and next you would be pushing it away to the compost heap to empty before returning for another load. You would soon find you had been there for an hour or more. Then Jean would come out and suggest you both came in for tea.*

The East Sussex Point-to-Point which was run at Heathfield, gave my wife Kit and I a chance to return hospitality. Betty, Jean, the Hills and other friends and family would descend on us at 'Glendale' for tea/supper, before returning home at any hour. Betty always keeping the conversation alive!

Other local hunt Point-to-Points that Betty always attended were the Tickham and the Ashford Valley; also the Romney Marsh Footraces, the Erridge Footraces, and the Wye Gymkhana.

Jean herself had troubles. From being the efficient heart of the Waterham establishment, something was going wrong.

People would ask, *'Jean, have you been to the doctor?'* This she needed to do, but first, it was against her nature (a dour Scot) to go. In the past Betty had had to call the doctor out if Jean needed him. And secondly, it meant having to persuade Betty to actually take her there – as Jean was entirely dependent on her for transport.

Jean had been rubbing her eyes and saying they were dreadful.

Then one Sunday afternoon two days later, Jean went walking in the orchard. Dog was with her but came home on his own. Betty was worried. After two hours she went out to search as Jean hadn't returned. Poor Jean had gone blind.

PETER GOODWIN: *Jean had an eye problem and one day, on her own, apart from one of the dogs, she was walking in the home orchard when a curtain fell and she became totally blind. It was*

only the concern and dedication of the old dog that made Betty,
on her return, follow him and so find Jean, wandering and lost.

Diabetes was the verdict. This was a difficult period for them both to adjust to. Jean had no pupils in her eyes, and couldn't tell whether it was day or night. She ate all the wrong types of food for diabetes.

There had always been lots of clutter at Waterham – footstools and little tables. The clutter had to go, so that it was possible for Jean to get about without falling.

Jean went to blind school. After that she could hang out washing. Seven steps in one direction, six in another. Jean managed – although she could be a bit of a no-hope Scot sometimes. But if she was interested in something, she really blossomed.

SUE BOULT: *Jean got clever. She did everything. Pouring boiling water into a teapot! I used to watch her cooking in the kitchen. She was absolutely amazing. I suppose because it was gradual.*

But Jean did not sit down under this affliction. She continued to tackle every job which she thought she could do, especially household duties, including preparing and cooking meals in the kitchen. Perhaps things did not always work out right and she could easily burn her fingers on the cooker, but she would just grin, bare the pain, and carry on, often refusing assistance . Betty would say, **'Go and do that'** or **'Get that'**. Jean could manage everything except fried eggs.

SUE SORRELL: *I reckon that Jean got blind in '78. 1978 was when they went to Scotland. They probably took Mother and Aunty Fraser's ashes up to Tom-na-Cross on this trip.*

In 1980, Sue holidayed in Scotland with Betty and they went to stay with her friend near Aberdeen.

SUE: *We then went to see Swordanes, the house on the beach, then Colleonard and into Banff. Then on to Aultmore which Betty used to take as a grousemoor in the summer to shoot, south of Cullen. We drove across to Tomintoul along a road that can be shut off with snowdrifts – right out on the moorland.*

Betty's eyesight was very poor, due to a shooting accident described later. My sister, Janet Dawes would visit and read out titles of book-tapes to Betty and Jean. In the late '70s these were few and far between and done by 'Calibre Talking Books'. They both went for biographies and things they could listen to together.

If they went to dinner at Sonstoll, Jill Dawes would tell Jean, *'Your plate is a clock'.* Then she would describe all the food on it relative to a clock's face.

Bill's daughter, Wonky (who had married and moved away) was staying back at Mount Ephraim. She went down to Waterham to cook a meal for Jean and Betty. Opening the fridge, Wonky was very surprised to discover garden tools in it!

SANDY ROGERS: *Betty and Jean had all these Magyars who came down to the farm at Christmas time, as agricultural students. Betty had to tell me this one. She had come out of the bedroom. She said* **'I never bother to dress in the morning, just – you know – go to the bathroom.'** *And this poor lad came out, and there was Betty – starkers! She said,* **'Gave him quite a shock, probably put him off women for life.'**

Catherine Miller was in a party of children ringing the handbells. On returning home, she got bawled out by her family for being delivered late after bell-ringing with Betty. She said it was well worth it, she'd had such a good time.

SUE SORRELL: *There were long great queues at the Ladies loo, at the Swan in Charing. So we stood there I should think, for 10 minutes. And Betty said,* **'Oh, I'm going to the Gents. It's ridiculous – all these women. It's the mirror in there. They stop and powder their noses. You don't have all this in the Gents.'** *And off she strode, into the Gents. All those surprised-looking men coming out. I didn't follow her in, needless to say. I waited and queued.*

A story was told once, when the lads from the council estate were trespassing on her land and probably scrumping apples, or ferreting, or doing something they shouldn't do. She apparently used to go out and shoot them with salt pellets. She would load her gun with salt and blast off at them! If the salt goes in under the skin it itches and it's pretty stingy, but it doesn't do lasting damage.

Betty was always out and about with her band of young men. Simon Curling was around primarily in the '70s as a beagler. He is son to Hugh and Norma and was mostly away in London and Gloucestershire thereafter. (Since Betty's death he has become local and prominent with the Blean Beagles.)

SIMON: *About 20 years ago, I'd bought a little Austin Seven special car. Bought it on a trailer but I didn't have a tow-bar. So I ended up ringing up Betty and saying 'Can I borrow the Land-Rover?' to go and get this thing. She was always ready for an outing and said,* **'Oh, I'll come with you'.** *So she came out on a day trip down to Brighton somewhere; carting her round there.*

I used to drive her round on occasions. Another occasion was Guy Hindley's 21st birthday. Geoffrey Neame had volunteered to drive Betty and Jean Fraser. And they both flatly refused and said 'No' – they wouldn't have Geoffrey drive them. They wanted Simon to drive them.

So I got deputed to take these two old ladies to Guy Hindley's 21st drinks party at lunchtime. Which was just as well, as Neame, in true Neame style had allowed Anthony Talbot to borrow his car keys to move Neame's car. Anthony then went home with them in his pocket! So if Geoffrey had taken Betty and Jean, I think they'd have still been there at midnight.

When Jean was being driven by Betty she knew when Betty was swerving. She could feel it!

Betty took Simon out as a beater at a fairly informal day's shooting at Provender. Arthur Finn had put some birds down, and just rung up a few people to say, *'Oh, let's go shooting'.*

It was before Simon had passed his driving test in 1978, Betty arrived at Perry Court – in the days of the blue Land-Rover.

SIMON: *We went over there and trundled around, Provender is a rough shoot. The highlight of the day was that a fox appeared which Arthur shot. No one would have known, other than the fact that he carted it out. One of the other people out shooting was Mrs Joey Elworthy. At the time she was Master of the Tickham Foxhounds.*

Arthur, in spite of being host, got a thorough dressing down from Joey, for having shot this fox. Betty thought he should have done, but that he shouldn't have been so damned silly as to tell anybody! Should just have left it where it was.

The other highlight was on the way home. Jean Fraser had a Braille watch. Betty had taken to wearing it because it was much easier to tell the time than a real watch. That, of course, was at the stage that she was still driving! – which was a bit disconcerting.

Betty caught pneumonia one time. She was allergic to penicillin. She had an operation once and wished she had been reminded to breathe correctly – as she had practised – immediately she became conscious afterwards, instead of when she remembered to. It would have helped much more.

'I am a Christian'. Betty would say, and not let anyone narrow her religion down to any specific denomination.

In 1979 there was another big celebration as Betty reached her 70 Years' Mastership of the Blean Beagles. The event is described later at the end of this book. She was a good quarter century ahead of anyone else in the running – and it was quite an achievement. Steps started being taken to have this record officially recognized. So by 1980 we were all very proud of the fact that Betty was mentioned in the *Guinness Book of Records*.

Betty loved her garden. She came from a gardening family. Her mother and Auntie Bee had both been great gardeners, especially with the Rock Gardens at Mount Ephraim. Joan Dawes had once taken the American Dawes's around the garden, saying proudly to them, *'I planted this'*.

'Oh,' said the Americans, straight from Dallas. *'At home, the gardeners would do that!'*

The garden at Waterham had wonderful roses. It became an unusually scented garden – particularly for Jean.

The year 1982 was a sad year. Betty's nephew Bill Dawes had had cancer for a couple of years and finally died on 12 January. He was only 61 years old.

The stairs at Waterham are old and winding and very, very steep, with a rope handrail. Jean had been getting more morose and depressed as the diabetes progressed. Life was not much fun. One day whilst descending the stairs Jean had a diabetic seizure. She crashed down from the third or fourth step and hit her head. The fall was fatal.

This happened on 14 March. There was an inquest in Canterbury. Willie gave evidence. Jean Fraser's funeral was at Charing Crematorium on the 23 March.

PETER: *It was a very sad day when Jean died. It brought to an end a very long partnership, for although not always agreeing with each other, Betty and Jean were really extremely good and close friends.*

Betty was tough and managed well as always. She found she could empathize well with Mary Dawes, Bill's widow, as they were in much the same situation, and so she stayed at Mount Ephraim for a while.

Jean's ashes were later taken to Scotland to Tom-na-Cross, Beauly, and put with her own kin. She was 67 years old when she died and had been with Betty for 45 years.

Chapter Thirty-four
The 'anti's

There have always been people who disagreed with hunting. Possibly thought it a cruel sport. From the early '70s, the anti-hunting brigade started getting more organized. 'Protesting' became a way of life for certain people. The chasing of a small furry animal was a good cause to protest against.

LACS – The League Against Cruel Sports – was one organization which sprang up. In some of these 'anti' groups, people would collect money to send a group of protesters out on a day's anti-hunting, often providing them with a packed lunch (presumably veggie), an allowance and a very enjoyable day out in the English countryside with plenty of exercise, which didn't often come their way.

These hunt saboteurs would use substances to confuse the scent, have people calling out false information, using a false horn and generally do a 'spoiling job'. Like any other form of hunting, it was tremendously enjoyable for them. There were, of course, plenty of arguments between them and the hunt followers. A certain quality about the anti-brigade, led them to be called the 'unlovable unwashed'.

The Blean Beagles possibly suffered less than the larger Fox Hunts, but they did suffer. Betty, as always, would talk to anyone, and always argued about their points reasonably, according to her own integrity. A measure of her special character was revealed in her treatment of the saboteurs.

The beagle huntsmen would often have a very testing time, trying to keep their tempers. The hounds would get sprayed with 'anti-mate', to spoil the scent.

Betty had suspicions of one young man who had asked her for a Fixture Card and answered him thus:

Blean Foot Beagles March 27th 1973.

To the Occupants, the Residents Flat, Guy's Hospital.

When you attended our Meet at Great Paddocks, Challock, Kent on Feb: 10th – I promised to send you our Fixture Card.

I did not do so as I heard that you were an Anti Mate Society and that you spray the Followers and Hounds, with a chemical called Anti Mate. I understand that this only affects the males. I could not allow this or welcome you out with us, as though mating is only of accademic interest to me now – owing to my age – I remember it as Pleasurable.

In its best connection a Man and his Mate means Man and Wife – A workman refers to a friend and fellow worker as a Workmate and I use the word Matey to mean friendly.

You looked to me like young men who would belong to the so called Permissive Society and I am horrified to think that you would not permit Mating, particularly as your visit was only five days before St. Valantine's Day, the herald of Spring.

For centuries young men on this day have sent the lady of their choice Valantines. All the birds are reputed to mate on this day – though I am not sure if this is ornithologically correct. Certainly down the ages Poets and Song Writers have assured us that 'In the Spring a young man's fancy lightly turns to thoughts of love.'

Perhaps you are Doctors and allarmed at the Population Explosion. MY television tells me that the World Population will double by the turn of the Centuary. I agree that this must be stopped.

I have spent all my life trying to breed good live-stock, therefore I think you should spray the sub-standard and the very best males kept to carry on the Race. Naturally laws would have to be passed before this was done. I, therefore think it would be a tragedy if our young male Followers were sprayed. They are fit, intelligent and hard-working, and just what our Nation requires now to produce the future generation. If they were sprayed it would cause them great distress and if the young huntsman was sprayed the maidens of the Hunt would be heart broken. It may be that this spray has only a temperary affect and it might well have a limited use at what I believe are called 'Lovings' in the USA or at Pop Festivals in this country. Again my personal view is that no great loss would occure Nationally if you used a Perminant spray at these functions. Indeed if a temperary spray had been invented in my youth, it could well have been useful in the hands of the Vicar or schoolmaster when we danced on the Green Swad on Flower Show night. It could have saved months of anxiety, for I well remember weddings when the Proccessional Hymn could well have been 'Get me to the Church on time'. If I have been misinformed about your society I will send you our fixture card next season and we will welcome you out with us.

Our cap for coming hunting is 30p per follower. Naturally we will expect you to abide by the Laws of the Land as any other action is of course Anarchy.

Yours Truly

J B McKeever

Betty sent copies of this letter to various people:

Coupled with that really Permissive Society – the Landlords, Tennants, their workmen and the Shooting Proprietors and their Game Keeps. Also all the Ladies who welcome us to their homes during the season.

BOULTY: *When you're mentioning the meanest Master of Hounds chasing these poor little hares. Remember now, she's never enjoyed the kill, but it had to be done. All these anti-hunters came down and she used to have the police at the hunt to chase them off private property.*

But, on one occasion, there was a young man from the Daily Mirror, *who these anti-hunters had brought with them, and he followed them all round. As they were leaving, Betty went over to him and said,* 'I believe you're from the Daily Mirror?' *He said, 'That's right.'*

'Well, I hope you enjoyed your day.'

He said 'It's been most interesting. I've got quite a lot of copy.'

'Right well, will you come and have lunch with me, down at the house?'

'I beg your pardon?'

'Yes, they've all had their turn. It's my turn now. You come and have lunch with me, Sunday.'

Well, he was completely knocked sideways, this poor young anti-hunting press reporter. He duly went and after lunch, Betty took him round, to show what hares really look like. She explained to him when they went out, that wherever the puppies found – they shocked all the young leverets that couldn't run properly or were deformed and so they got killed and put out of their misery. In midwinter you had poor old hares, who hadn't anywhere to sleep except on the snow. She said life was miserable for them because of rheumatism and things. He really was humbled by her. That's typical of Betty, you see.

Of course it's cruel, but the cruellest of the lot is fishing. It can take an hour of pulling a fish around by a hook in its mouth before you land it. With hunting it's very quick.

The Horse and Hound Ball was picketed by hunt-saboteurs. With affection they would say as Betty entered, *'Ah, Mrs McKeever. How are you? Going to give up?'* She had been attacked one day out beagling and was arrested by the police. **'They thought I was in danger of being roughed up by the antis; so they took me in, and I followed the hounds in the police car for the rest of the day.'** One day a group of protesters sprayed the hounds and some of the spray went into her face. She was driven straight up to Harley Street to see an eye specialist.

Betty always said, **'Do be polite to them'**. She always used to get her supporters to divert them and tell them the hunt was somewhere else.

No-one has a right to break the law. You cannot break the law and have a country that is law abiding. And that is what is wrong with the country today. I'd put everyone in prison who broke the law. When the law says I can't hunt, I shan't hunt.

If that time came, Betty would up and leave Kent and go and live in Ireland.

Chapter Thirty-five
Nearly shot my head off!

All her life Betty preached 'safety' and its importance when going shooting. She taught many youngsters to shoot, emphasizing safety and the importance of good footwork – her son, all her nephews. Jeremy Jacquet was one boy she taught, James Dawes another.

MIKE BAX: *She taught me to shoot. I've never had a shooting lesson, ever in my life, except from her. I remember the first day she took Ric Neasham and me out shooting, walking up the ditches of the Seasalter Marshes, and we put up two mallard. And you know, young boys who had never shot anything flying before, I remember taking an absolute age to get the shot off. She was shouting,* **'Shoot! Shoot! Shoot!'** *And by the time we shot they were 60 yards away. Of course, nothing happened. We got a frightful wigging about* **'being so slow. How vital it was, you don't aim at a moving target. Just put your gun into your shoulder and pull the trigger, and your instinct and everything else points the gun.'** *We then had to go out the following Thursday. We put a duck up out of a bomb hole, in the middle of a marsh. Both our guns hit our shoulders, and this poor old duck had probably got about a foot off the water, and was slaughtered! And she was absolutely delighted with that. She said,* **'Yeah, that's what it's all about. Speed and instinct.'** *But this poor duck! Received about four shots from Ric and I, before it had hardly moved. But that was absolutely right and that's how you should shoot.*

But I remember her prowess. She used to take Ric and I beating. Whenever she was invited shooting, she usually had to take beaters and we would go as beaters. I remember her shooting and I don't think I ever saw a man shoot better than she did. She would mow 'em down while the men were missing – all over the place. We'd have been 16, 17, 18 then, so that would have been 1971, '72. She was 70 years old plus, then and still shooting better than anyone. It was fantastic. All the lessons on safety were before we were ever taken out anywhere.

But one day in 1978 she got caught out. She was probably careless because she was alone. Betty was horrified with herself as she had committed a cardinal error. She was practising for the Christmas Shoot in early winter with her Canterbury-made silver-barrelled 16-bore shotgun. In 1979 Betty described the incident with a laugh!

A good year to talk to me. I nearly shot my head off last year! If I'd been shooting with anybody else I wouldn't have done it. I stood the gun against a very broad gatepost on my own land.

The men didn't tell me that, eh, the ride on this 14 foot triangular thing was broken, and when I couldn't get it open, I stuck the gun in 'this way' [gesturing the gun vertically before her] **and took both sides and pulled it. And it walloped down (you can see the scars on my hands). It walloped down on top of my hands. And all would have been well if the trigger guard had held, but the trigger guard broke – and, of course, it fired the right barrel right straight up into my face. An awful lot of blood. I walked home to the car and drove myself home. Got one of the men to drive me into hospital. That was all.**

In fact, Betty had 28 pellets in her, fired as they were from point blank range. She had heard someone on the road before getting into the car, and called – but they had fled in horror at the bloody sight of her!

Having driven home without being able to see, she carefully didn't tell Jean Fraser (who was blind), what state she was in.

She had, in fact, pellets in her breast, chin, lower and upper mouth, cheeks (most of which she learned to live with), and, strangest of all, six pellet holes through the crown of her rainproof hat – which she would later often show to an amazed audience!

It never impaired her talking at all. How she survived, I can't think. **'I always thought I had no brain. Proves it! It just goes to show, the fore-brain serves no purpose whatsoever.'**

James Dawes, Betty's great-nephew, visited her soon after the accident.

JAMES: *She was out of hospital very, very quickly, much to everybody's astonishment, I think it was about a week later after the incident that we went to visit her. She wore her hat, which was a green waterproofed Irish looking – sort of gabardine. A trilby-*

shaped thing, not a deer-stalker. You could see where the pellets
had gone through the brim of it. And looking at her face and skull,
you could see that a couple had gone in, right at the top of the eyes,
one at the top of the bridge of the nose, and had gone between the
plate at the front of the skull, no doubt ricocheting all the way up,
and come out of the top of the head but they hadn't. If you place
your fingers at the top of your head, you can find a gap there, and
that's where there were two 'out' holes. They hadn't gone right
the way through the thing, they'd gone in there, ricocheted between
the two plates, come out at the top and there were two holes. There
were two holes at the top of her head! I confirm their presence.
I checked – with some amazement. I saw the entry and exit
wound from there.

As far as I can see, it was one hand the gate walloped on to,
and it broke through the trigger-guard, 'cos she had the mark of the
bruise and the blood on her hand for the rest of her life.

JOE BUTLER: *She really looked in a state when she came back. She*
drove back. And yet, she didn't actually blame me for the accident,
but she blamed me because: What happened was, this gun of hers,
she put the gun, it was a concrete post, like that sticking up. She
put the gun up there like that.

Well, this gate was a triangle affair. The bottom hinge at that
end had been broken for donkey's years – ages. Well, she took that
off there like that, and of course it went straight down the barrel,
busted the trigger guard, bang. The gate, yeah, 'cos it slipped out
of her hands, see, she took the weight of it.

She said she went down the road and there was all this blood
pouring down round her face. She tried to stop someone. They sort
of swerved across on to the other side of the road and dodged.
Whoever it was (possibly a child) was frightened. Anyway she
drove back and she come in the farm and she says, **'I've had a bit**
of an accident', *and there was all this blood. But she was OK like*
– sort of thing.

I said, 'You want to go to hospital, see.' And **'Yes all right'**,
she answered. So we goes round to see Miss Fraser and that [who
was blind]. *Anyway Miss Fraser said, 'Betty, get to hospital, don't*
worry about anything.' Anyway, I think it must have been on a
Thursday or something. We was going to get paid on the Friday,
see.

'I must get things organized for the men to get paid on Friday.' *All she was worried about was getting us paid, writing a cheque or doing something. And it must have been – oh I don't know, twenty minutes or so before she would condescend – and I drove her into Canterbury hospital.*

And there, she's sitting up on the bed like this! [With clothing open.] *And there's me standing at the bottom of the bed and the nurses round her – sort of looking at one another. 'What's going on?' She'd no* [modesty] *to say the least. But she was still giving me orders, like.* **'Don't forget to do this and do this. Do something else'**, *and this sort of thing. And these nurses you know, were sort of laughing. You know – smirks coming across from one to the other. Of course she wasn't taking a bit of notice of what they were sayin'. Well you know what she was like about anything like that, she was not embarrassed about anything.*

And when I said to her about this accident, I said, 'Well it was your own fault' I said. 'Not that I've had anything to do with guns, but I always thought when you go through fences, over gates, through gates, you un-load.'

'I've had guns all m'life,' *she said.* **'I've always treated them as loaded and armed. I treated them with respect.'** *I said, 'You didn't that time'.*

'Well, that was your fault,' *she says. '* **If you'd a told me about that gate.'**

I said, 'I've told you dozens of times about the gate.' [She'd been through it hundreds of times.] *It's still like it now. It wasn't up afterwards, I know when you look at it like, you could put it down as being a pure accident, but its difficult to define an accident. She was very lucky. Really. Could a' blow' her head off, like, sort o' thing. She certainly did survive.*

Chapter Thirty-six
Late Betty stories

It became an annual pilgrimage to go up to the Horse and Hound Ball. As Betty got older, and yet older, she became something of a wonder. All those years of Mastership and her phenomenal hunting knowledge. I believe she used to dance a circle of honour, to applause. Some of these yarns embroider in different directions:

JEAN ROWNTREE: *Betty and Jean Fraser were travelling up, as usual, to the Horse and Hound Ball, at the Grosvenor House. All Masters of Hound have to be there early, to have drinks with master – the Duke of Beaufort.*

To keep her warm they had the bales of hay in the back of the truck for the homeward's journey. Of course, when they got on the pavement in Park Lane, the door wouldn't open. So in front of the entire – all these frightfully grand people who were arriving, Aunt Betty ended up emerging through the window of the truck! In her 1920 black dress and her amber beads.

Jean Fraser told me that one. In the '70s.

BOULTY: *Betty was the senior Master of Hounds. She used to be invited to the United Hunts Ball with the Duke of Beaufort.*

One year, she was put into a rather small car. I think it was a Volkswagen, but I wasn't there – just heard the story. Apparently when they got to Grosvenor House, they opened the door and Betty, being the size she was, having sat there for and hour and a half, couldn't get out! So they had to open the sliding roof and haul her out of the roof.

ANNIE DAWES: *Before we were married* [Annie married James Dawes] *she invited us to go with her to a party, at the Horse and Hound Ball. We duly arrived and it was dark. As we got out on to the pavement near Grosvenor House there were a lot of 'antis' yabooing and shouting at all the fur be-clad people in their long dresses or white ties, going in. All the antis seemed to know Aunty Betty and they weren't being terribly abusive to her. But they were shouting nasty things as they generally do. One young man was blowing a hunting horn and he blew it rather well, so Betty walked up to him and said,* **'Young man, you blow that horn extremely well. Would you like to represent my table in the horn-blowing competition?'** – *At which they all cheered her and she walked in.*

It was the first time I had ever seen her out of her tweed suit. When she took her stole off which was a rather tatty piece of fur – and had seen better days, to my horror, I found that Aunty Betty was in her long dress which was on inside out! So I had to take her, along with somebody else (I can't remember who) into the ladies powder room at Grosvenor House, and try and get her out of this dress – which was very difficult, turn it the right way around and then stuff her back into it! She was not amused!

Sue Sorrell had to deal with an 'inside-out' Betty at the Beagle Ball on another occasion.

Norma: *'Betty always wore her beagle green brocade.'* Norma and Hugh once drove Betty up to the ball at Grosvenor House. They got to Cobham, driving along the A2. At half past six they got a flat tyre. Norma wore a sheepskin coat and walking shoes on top of evening dress, having had the foresight to put them in the car! They changed the wheel – but the car was falling off the jack. **'Wasn't it in gear?'** asked Betty, sitting serenely in the passenger seat with Norma's miniature dachshund on her lap, quite unperturbed. But they were not late. The reception was held by Michael Clayton, Editor of *Horse and Hound*.

Frank Soames

JANET: *Frank Soames was dropped on his head as a baby. He was a little simple but enjoyed and was a regular beagler – because he liked the beaglers. Betty always said that the beaglers were well-mannered. Frank Soames came from a reasonable family but was virtually a tramp.*

On one occasion he was laid up in hospital. This dirty and smelly old man was visited by Sue Sorrell, the blonde Blean Beagling beauty.

Also Sir Robin and Lady Hooper – beaglers (he was former Ambassador to Greece. Lady Hooper always greeted guests out there in Greece, with: 'Bath first or dinner?') Various other beaglers visited him, and Betty telephoned his cousin Christopher Soames, the Tory Minister who also came down to see him. The ward staff were most impressed.

What sex?

JILL DAWES II: *When Betty's nephew George Dawes's children were young, Betty came over to visit them. Jill was walking out of the drawing room with her children Christopher, Alan and Jane. In a very loud voice Alan asked, 'Mum, is Aunt Betty a lady or a man?'*

Winnie the Pooh

Betty, going down one day to visit her great-nephew James in the Ashdown Forest – home of Christopher Robin, Pooh, Piglet, Owll, Tigger – and Kanga. **'Oh yes, I remember coming here and shooting kanga!'** Years before, some wallabies had been kept near by. They had escaped into the forest and so had to be culled.

Beagle green

JANET: *One of the beaglers (Harry Beasley, I think) went to collect drinks from the bar in a hotel. Two or three of Betty's other friends joined them. Harry went to collect more drinks. Onlookers were most impressed as he was clad in beagling green. You can imagine the whispers as time passed. 'Look, they still have liveried servants!'*

Sheppey

NORMA: *Betty didn't believe in going abroad but she had been to America, to the Everglades, but America was 'a colony' and therefore OK! And she'd hunted in Ireland. If people were going abroad in her later years, Betty would say:* **'I don't need to go abroad. I'm going to Sheppey. That's across the water.'**

Barren?

Sheila Judge recalled a slightly vulgar story:

SHEILA: *Someone came to the door, she'd upset some old fellow. He said 'You're nothing but a great fat white barren sow.'*

'Look here,' she said. **'Fat white sow I may be. Barren I am not! I've got a son to prove it!'**

Choking

JILL DAWES: *One day Aunty Betty had come to lunch with us. We were having 'poussin' – and quite suddenly she started choking – in the middle of her endless stories, and eating and drinking. She choked and she choked and she choked! John got up and thumped her on the back. I think [son] James was there. He got up and thumped her somewhere else. She then went out to the downstairs lavatory. I remember turning to Stuart Jardine and Roger Lean Verco – who were there, and saying, 'If she doesn't bring it up, you two will have to hold she upside down by the heels – at the top of the stairs, whilst James thumps.' However, mercifully, the small piece of poussin that was causing her distress, emerged in the bathroom. But she didn't stop talking. Neither did she stop talking when she came back and sat down and continued to eat, drink – and tell stories.*

Chapter Thirty-seven
Farming [3]

Betty was still very much a working farmer. Latterly she had just two permanent farm staff, Joe Butler and Colin West.

She farmed 350 acres of land. The farm sold sheep wool, ponies, fruit, pears, and straw. There were 400 sheep. She fed her ponies freshly crushed Scottish oats.

Betty had planted a beautiful pear orchard, a good going concern. **'Don't forget, you plant pears for your heirs.'**

Jean had been the one who produced the excellence. Betty was asked to leave 'The Kent Society' as her sheep were no longer eligible. Her flock was in the Kent Breeders Society until after Jean lost her sight. But by that stage Betty herself was well into her 70s.

The Welsh mountain ponies had really taken over on the farm from the Sussex cattle in the '60s.

Joe said she had done extremely well really. Although towards the end, she wasn't too bothered about things. She'd let Colin and Joe get on with things, but the farm wasn't being managed. Betty always said to Joe **'As long as I break even, I'm not too worried about it.'**

JOE: *'Well, this can't pay. Them ponies, well, can't pay.' I says. They'd have these ponies in and be leading them round for weeks. Then go down to the market and what was she making on them? Only about £50. When you think what she'd paid out on the hay and all the time that it took for the* [taming]. *Well, she must have enough money to do the job, otherwise, let's say she wouldn't do it… If you can't afford it, don't do it.*

Betty obviously just liked having the ponies around, and latterly they were mostly a hobby.

Tom McKeever worked on the farm for 18 months from the summer of '82 until winter, '83. He thought she had too many ponies, as they are very choosy feeders on the land.

Tom reckoned his grandmother (even with impaired vision) was good at her livestock. At market she could pick out, straight away, a sheep which should, perhaps, be in a different pen – as it didn't match the ones it was with.

She knew her animals, sheep, horses and after Tom had left, Betty expanded her sheep by buying a whole flock of pure Romneys (as Kent sheep were now called).

SHEILA JUDGE: *Her farming: she liked the Kent sheep. They were smaller that the others and they didn't have so many lambs, but they were hardier and easier. We go mad and have three or four lambs or breed big ones, but you lose out in other ways. She used to enjoy the fruit picking. When computers first came in to pay the men she said,* **'What' s wrong. To pay the men, I sit here at the kitchen table at night and work out everything for my fruit-pickers.'**

In the early '80s the farm was mostly sheep. By 1982: **'Pigs gorne completely out. An unprofitable gentleman. Used to keep about 24 sows here.'**

Willie to take over?

JOE: *I remember she saying once about Willie and Anne to come over, and said they'd want to run the place or do something. And I remember her telling me.* **'Humph. Bloody coming over here and telling me how to run... they can't run their own place over there.'** [Betty obviously had no real intention of loosening her hold on her farm.] *Their son, Tom, he come over for a little while, and he lasted a little while, because he wanted to change things.*

Tom had said to her: 'Really,' he said, 'you want to get rid of them ponies.' She put it to me, whether it's fact or fiction, he said. 'Here, the ponies go, or I go.'

'Well, you'd better go,' she said. **'I'm not having people coming over here telling me how to run the place.'**

Well it was her place and I know. [Joe reckoned he knew how to handle her tactfully] *I mean to say – go like that like a bull at the gate, well with her – you'll never get anywhere.*

Joe reckoned that the only way was not to make it your idea, but try and twist it round so it was her idea.

JOE: *We had to get certain things done, sort of make her think along them lines. Work it round so that you know, 90% of it was her idea, 10% was yours. Don't say, 'you should do this'. You'd got to be very tactful, like. At Monk's Hill, she spent a bit of money up there, doing the buildings and all that. Done that big Dutch barn, but all the time she was at Waterham, never spent any on the buildings. None of the buildings was ever done up. A few odd slates up on here and there. I mean to say, weren't until Willie's come on the scene that he's put some money into the place and righted the fences up round.*

Mrs McKeever, when it came to spending money, it always seemed a dirty word.

Doing up Joe's house

Some maintenance work badly needed to be done on Joe's tied cottage. Betty agreed to it so Joe got an estimate. '*Then she said* **"Um, Willie tells me its not a good idea for you to put money into the house. So I think I'll do it."** '

JOE: *Well, it never materialized, she kept putting it off and putting it off and I said 'Well, something's got to be done', 'cos you couldn't open the window. If you'd opened the window it would a' fell to bits. She wouldn't do anything and she passed away and that was it. It was never done. And after she'd gone, I said to Willie about it, and he said 'Yeh, I'll get it done'. And he did.*

She wouldn't spend no money, like on the farm. I mean to say that poor old oast round there fell down – the one in front of the house, well that got blew down. Nothing was done about it and I understood she got insurance for it, but she hung on to the money. Nothing was ever done round there.

I asked Willie if he had taken over Waterham at all before Betty died?

WILLIE: *No. We discussed it. Cost me an absolute fortune! Her accountant suggested to her (she was saying that it was getting on top of her), that it would be much better if I took over part of the farm. So we went into deep discussions with her accountant and my accountant on the feasibility of doing this. This was about four or five years before she died. We went in to her accountants to do*

the final thing and draw up the papers, they'd done all the paper-
work and worked it out, where Joe Butler would work for me and
I would run the sheep.

She would have Colin and do the kennels and that sort of
thing. Deal with the beagles and look after the fruit.

I would be responsible for all the sheep, the running of, the
financing of, and pay the bits into her bank account, having used
fertiliser and that sort of thing – to intensivize the sheep. When we
got there, well, we talked a lot about it with her accountant, and
*after about forty-five minutes, she said, '**No, it'll never work.**'*

Her accountant leaned over his partner's desk and said, 'What
do you mean, Mrs McKeever, it will never work?'

*And she said, '**My old boy giving orders to my staff. It**
won't work and so I'm not doing it.' And that was that! And*
she refused to pay her half of the bill. [Willie laughed]. *The*
accountant came to me.

*She said, '**Well, it was his bloody idea in the first place. I'm**
not paying a penny.' So I ended up paying her half! I still see him*
at the Farmers Club now – and we all laugh about it!

Willie did, however, farm some of Betty's Dargate Common bits
for her, latterly.

Betty could be impossible and a bad farmer. The rented land
was in a disgraceful state. She was a late and irregular payer of rent.
Willie used to have to deal with Betty at Rent Review time. She
rented all the old banks off Bill, then his son Sandys. He used to
have to put the rent up. She was not easy to deal with on financial
matters and it used to take Willie all morning and several glasses of
whisky before he could actually do any business.

The Daweses were pretty good to her and they realized they
weren't going to get anywhere, so better leave things as they were.
She got away with murder and played to it.

Ashford Market

I love Ashford Market. I love going down to Ashford Market.
If I haven't anything else to do, I like to go down there. It's
the sort of thing that if you're retired, you want to go even
more to keep you in with people you knew.

Betty became a character of the market from 1932 to 1989. She especially liked going there for the morning market, then having a pork pie in the pub afterwards. She had a very strong sense of humour and was very earthy. All the drovers – the people there knew her would all come up and talk to her, so she had a wonderful time.

Sandy Rogers was asked by Betty to be her Farm Manager once – when he had no job.

SANDY: *And I used to take her to Ashford Market. As soon as we got to Ashford Market, Betty would sort of disappear. What used to amuse me was that she'd wear things she wouldn't worry about at all, things that were getting on a bit, and yet she would still have extremely good, tasteful pearls around her neck.*

ARTHUR FINN: *We used to get her away from Ashford with all her shopping.*

Sue Sorrell remembers trying to back Betty's trailer with sheep in the back, into a parking space at Ashford Market, with about twenty sheep-lorries queuing up behind them. Betty kept saying **'No, think of it as a wheelbarrow,'** and getting quite cross which did not help the harassed Sue, who said, *'In the end, I think, I got out, and one of the lorry drivers actually backed it back. But that was a classic. I will never forget that as my most embarrassing moment.'*

There were two herds of Welsh ponies, with her favourite stallion Roland. Betty had bought several blood lines and weeded other blood lines out. She bred the ponies to 'do' on very little hay. She was inclined to fiddle the VAT on them.

SHIELA JUDGE: *Always had the Welsh ponies, I had all the pedigrees of the Welsh ponies and she used to go up to Wales. Betty had a lot of trouble with the man and you always do with the Welsh. She got the carried (cot) ponies. She found she'd bought a pony and they'd give her the wrong one – this sort of thing. Having got the ponies and got them established, she was exporting them all around the world, she really did well with them.*

Of course, in the finish she got in a muddle, I'll be quite honest – trying to sort out those pedigrees. She couldn't see very well, and everything was on the table in the dining-room. It went on too long.

'I was always 'done', every time I went to Wales.' *Blean Hills 'Jude' was another pony of Betty's breeding.*

SARAH BAX [Mike's daughter]: *I was at the Blean show on my pony, Bella, whom she bred. Betty remembered Bella so well, who had a wall eye – one blue eye, and then a black eye. Betty told me she would never go blind in the wall eye.*

Unlike other horse dealers who rush through it, Betty did the pony breeding carefully and knew what she was doing. She took pride in them. I had another pony of hers, a lovely chestnut mare, Blean Hills Pomander, who I did a lot of showing on – beautiful. Betty bred beautiful looking ponies.

She has 'a Welsh mountain pony stud which provides gymkhana mounts for dozens of local school-children,' wrote Peter Cook of *Farmer's Weekly*. 'Her fields are full of browsing mares, bulging with unborn foals or delicately nuzzling a new arrival, are a rare and satisfying sight among the regimented orchard-lands of east Kent.'

Sue Sorrell used to help Betty with the registration of the ponies for the Welsh Pony Society. Every year, when the foals were born, they had to be registered. So Sue had to go out and draw them, which was quite difficult. Joe, Betty, and Sue would go out into the field with a handful of charts and track all these youngsters down and drew on socks, colour, stars, and whether they were colts or fillies. Then all these registrations had to go off to the Welsh Pony Society.

The system worked quite well – with about a hundred ponies. A good stockman, Betty had about three stallions at one time. Roland, the founding stallion, Graig Fach Roving Star – a lovely boy and lived at Pudding Lane – Dargate. He was bigger than Roland and was always out with his mares there. Quality wise, he was Section B and Roland was Section A.

An offspring of Roland, Beau Bells became Betty's chestnut stallion with the flaxen mane and tail – Blean Hills Beau Bells.

She went to Midhurst with a hunting friend (who always came every year to stay with her and judge the horseshow) and bought there her last stallion 'Impersonater'. It wasn't her 'type' of stallion, but Betty couldn't see very well at that point.

There were two or three horses knocking about at Waterham. Betty always kept one line of thoroughbreds, until the end. They were related to the Balkan Green strain – steeplechasers. She had a mare and she bred a thoroughbred foal every year. Sheila Judge's daughter had one of the last ones, 1978/9. *'I don't know what happened to the horses in the finish. May have died or something.'*

Betty had a big bay horse and called him Fulmar – because he had a mark like a seagull. She just had this one strain of thoroughbreds.

SUE SORRELL: *We were in this field opposite Waterham and she was taking the colt round and round. Walking behind it on the long rein. Then we would go out on the road to get used to it, always on the long rein. This would be Seabreeze's offspring, one of the Balkan ones. Sunshine Girl was the last of the line. She was about 19, 20. When Betty got very ill, right at the end a woman took her in.*

SIMON CURLING: *When we started to get environmental – about fifteen years ago, the question came up as to whether the marshes at Seasalter should be ploughed?*

A man from the Ministry came down and said that it was 'undisturbed vintage marshland'.

'It was pretty funny. I'd ploughed it up for the war effort. Put it back down to pasture in 1963.' *Betty went off environmental people after that with their, 'ancient unploughed marsh for thousands of years'!*

By 1989 Betty farmed sheep, bred ponies and there were 24 couple of beagles. She had two men to help her – Joe and Colin. The ponies were more her hobby than a paying concern towards the end. She told Colin West **'When are you going to realize, I do not want to make money on this place.'**

Chapter Thirty-Eight
The Blean Beagles supporters club

The beagles had always had a social function. Betty was gregarious and so in the '60s she started organizing a coach-trip to go to the Derby. She filled up the bus and it became a very successful annual event. The coach was far easier to park at Epsom than a car, and you went with a group of like-minded people.

By the '70s the 'Blean Beagle Bus' trips started branching out to other occasions. One of Betty's favourite excursions, and in the middle of London, was the Chelsea Flower Show. It all took a lot of organization, with writing to people, to let them know the date, persuade them to come, and do so in time to hopefully induce them to bring a party of their own friends. Betty and Jean were good at this.

If people sent a subscription, Betty would always write a personal thank you letter.

Other bus trips were arranged, to the Grand National for instance, or the Horse of the Year Show. There were also Draws, the Ball, the Gymkhana and the Sponsored Ride.

Draw

There were two or three draws a year. One at the Gymkhana and one at Christmas, and possibly one also for the Grand National.

In earlier days, the tickets were printed but it grew more expensive. A Roneo 750 electric duplicator was acquired. The tickets were typed, then stencils were cut. These were put through the Roneo on paper to print them, then the tickets were guillotined. The next step stapled them together in tens. Holes were sewn through the tickets with a sewing machine. Then a numbering machine was used to stamp the ticket and the counterfoil.

SUE SORRELL: *I used to help her with the Draw Tickets. Betty used to like to have an 'evening'. Certainly, in the earlier days, a very lively evening where everybody was doing things for the draw. We used to be roped in as sewers of perforating holes on the sewing machine. I spent hours on this treadle machine. Norma did all the*

hard work. Then, of course, you had to do the big 'selling' of it.
That was always the thing. 'Oh, gosh, it's the Draw night, have we
sold all the tickets?'

But people who had never hunted, really got involved in all
this. A friend of mine Frank Cassels, those who were not really
hunting people, would turn up – for Betty.

Muriel Shaw and Brian Peek would help. It was all slave labour
for Betty's friends and non-stop chatter, followed by tea. Jean would
count the books after 6 pm.

The Draw tended to be held a week or so before Christmas, sometimes at The Dove in Dargate and the Four Horse Shoes at Graveney.
In earlier times it was held at the Three Horse Shoes, Staplestreet.

The Beagle Ball or Dinner Dance

SUE SORRELL: *When I first knew Betty, the Ball was at Delbridge*
House, Faversham. Then it was held at Tankerton. She liked the
Marine and kept the Balls on there until she died. [The move of
venue to Tankerton – just beyond Whitstable was in the late
'60s – before 1970.]

In the '60s, those were the really rosy days, the best Beagle
Balls. With Arthur and Mikey. Fantastic hunting days, and the
Beagle Ball.

When the venue was changed from Faversham to Tankerton the
ball was held at:

1970 Tankerton Hotel – 3 times.
1973 Punch Tavern – Sturry.
1974 Marine Hotel – Tankerton.

I remember the Ball being held at Tankerton annually in about
the second week in April, but it wasn't so invariably. For Betty's last
two years the venue went back to Faversham:

1989 Alexander Centre – twice.

SUE SORRELL: *We went from the Mellow Tones to Dave (David*
Jones) Band. That was a big change, but Betty did come round
to Dave in the end. The Mellow Tones were not terribly mellow!

The younger crowd thought we needed to have a better band.
Betty used to say, **'Well, you know all about these things. You**
find the band.' *David Jones did a wonderful job, basically played*

fairly modern music. Then met Betty, and she said, **'But you've got to be able to do an Eightsome Reel.'** *Poor David Jones – the first time he played, he was terrified. 'I've got to be able to do this Eightsome. It's too loud or they don't like it.' So he listened to instructions and finally, after he'd done it two or three times, he got the right balance. He mixed it in extremely well. They all learned to do an Eightsome and everybody enjoyed it.*

Betty still did the drawings for the Blean Beagle Dinner programme. In spite of failing eyesight.

Dress – usually, before the Beagle Ball, I would go over to Waterham, to help zip her in and put her fineries on, and make sure she'd got everything on the right way round.

For these Balls latterly, dressing was difficult. Betty had her own way of managing this. David and Sue Sorrell were an estranged married couple at this stage. Betty was friends with both of them equally. So Sue would zip Betty into her dress at the start of the evening, then David would take her home after the dance and un-zip her at the end! Betty, of course, enjoyed the irony of this situation.

Betty would wear an orchid at the Hunt Ball each year, from her own greenhouse.

Boulty would call out *'Right, who's wearing my coat?'* They always used to demand that he would put on his old beagle coat as a young person would be wearing it. *'I would try it on at every dance. I don't know where it is now.'*

Outings

In spite of her white stick and legs getting old, Betty would still get up to Chelsea Flower Show or the Derby.

SUE: *After she was fairly blind, she would use it to her advantage, whenever it was necessary.* **'Just flash the white stick in front of you, Susan.'** *Certainly at Chelsea in the wheelchair, people would get a certain sort of thwack. It was like parting the waters.*

MURIEL WILSON: *She always went to Chelsea and she always ordered new roses every year. The same year that she died she ordered new roses for the garden. Betty would hire a wheelchair to go to Chelsea Flower Show. She could get much closer to the blooms.*

The Chelsea trip would be in private cars, not a coach trip. Norma remembers going with Sue Sorrell and Betty. They parked at Battersea.

MURIEL WILSON: *At the Derby, she used to go in the wheelchair. The Derby bus was one of the best supported events. The Gypsies would come aboard and tell people's fortunes.*

In 1977 Betty organized a coach to Cowdray Park for the polo. The picnickers there were inclined to be upset by the advent of a coach. 'What's going on?' and were reassured when they knew it was Mrs McKeever.

Betty really just enjoyed day's out and had time on her hands. Other events she organized – not necessarily with a coach, but just someone who had a car and was willing to drive her were: Showjumping at Hickstead; winery; riverboat to Kew; Drusilla's Zoo Park, Alfreston; tea with Hindleys – and many more.

The Blean Beagle Horse and Dog Show

Betty had earlier, after the World War II, shared a show with the Tickham, but took on an annual show for the beagles from the early '60s onwards.

The Beagle Show became an annual event at the Westmeads Showground at Whitstable, on about the 2nd or 3rd Wednesday in August.

By 1972 it moved it's venue from Whitstable to Plough Lane, Waterham, in the field opposite the farm. The show was still held on about the second or third week in August, but by now was on a Saturday, not a Wednesday. Held from 9.30 until 5.00 – or 7.00 pm. The dog classes started at 1.30. More events were possible at Waterham. There was in-hand judging of horseflesh as well as all the gymkhana pony events and the dog events.

Pony events	Dog events
Best childs' pony	Sporting dog
Junior walk trot gallop	Best child handler
Open trotting	Dog with most waggy tail
Musical sacks	Prettiest dog
Fancy dress	Bun race
Tickham Foxhounds parade	Dog most like its owner
Blean Beagles parade	Jack Russell
Take your own line	
Open sweepstake	
Go to bed jumping	
Working pony	

The show was the Blean Beagles' main financial support. Mrs Neasham ran a tombola stall. For the show's printed schedule, there was a firm in Folkestone which could do stencils with pictures, which made the whole programme much more descriptive.

Other events

Terrier Show, held in July. Foot Point-to-Point – run in early September. Sue Sorrell: *'We used to run around that little field adjoining Dargate. Chris Hill – from Seasalter – he did an enormous amount.'*

The Sponsored Ride was at the end of September. A 10 to 15 mile ride, the route devised by John Dawes, through the rides of woodland. It was affiliated to the beagles and different projects were supported. The year the venture started in 1977, all the proceeds went to the Hernhill Craft Centre. Usually, 20% of all profits made would go to the beagle funds.

The Sponsored Ride was held annually. A ride up through the fields and woods of the Blean. The trail was marked with white fertilizer bags tied on to trees. John Dawes was often found pruning the overgrown rides through the woods. I helped him many times (on visits to Kent). The best way to do this was with secateurs and pruning sheers – from horseback – to get the height right. Although beagling was usually done on foot, for those with horses this was a very agreeable day out.

Chapter Thirty-nine
Early eighties – after Jean died

There was a gaping vacuum in Betty's life after Jean died. It meant she had to get used to great changes in many areas of her life.

NORMA CURLING: *She didn't complain but she used to get lonely there, after Jean died... You see, until Jean died, she never ever slept in a house alone. During the War she slept up at Mount Ephraim. And when Jean was away, Betty went to Mount Ephraim. When Jean died, I think she went to Mount Ephraim for a couple of nights. Then Anne and Willie used to come and spend the night there* [at Waterham]. *And I remember they took it in turns and Betty saying,* **'Well, they never meet in bed these days, because of me.'** *And gradually they weaned off, gradually phased it out and got her on her own. She had the men in during the day.*

They wanted Betty to go over and live at Mount Ephraim, but she said no way was she **'going to be shut up in a sitting room, with a lot of elderly relatives, all twittering'**. She wanted to be independent. Betty had her own way of managing things Jean had always done for her. She was pragmatic.

WILLIE: *After Jean died, Mother had to become more domestic – did her own cooking and had a lady in two mornings a week, to help her tidy the place up.*

Tried to persuade her to move, but she was determined to stay there as long as she could. That's why she always saved her money up because, if she'd had to go into sheltered accommodation, she'd got her eye on that place in Lenham where your grandmother lived, next door there [English Courtyard]. *Mother thought that was brilliant, she was going up there. So she saved every bean she'd got,* **'Because I was going to go hunting two days a week by taxi, and it was going to be bloody expensive!'** *I persuaded her latterly to buy an annuity – after Jean died, which helped. It brought her about £10,000 a year, guaranteed, because sometimes the shares performed and sometimes they* *didn't. The majority of her income went on keeping the hounds going. So she ran the farm, officially as a hobby farm, so therefore didn't have to do any proper accounts. It was classified as a hobby farm.*

Jean Fraser had set up a trust which benefited Willie.

SHIELA JUDGE: *After Jean Fraser died Betty was very lonely, I think. I used to go over whenever I could. She used to say:* **'Come over. Come over.'** *I couldn't always get there. I was in and out of hospital. The car didn't perform. I used to phone and say, 'Look, I can't get there.' She'd be really upset but I'd go whenever I could.*

Geoffrey Neame, one of her young beaglers, used to go and see her every Thursday for years. He would drink her whisky. She would smoke his fags.

GEOFFREY: *After Jean Fraser died she was very much on her own. There were lots of visitors. For years I always used to go in the summer, once a week, once a fortnight. 7.00ish or sometimes later. Sometimes we would wander around the garden but mainly we'd just go indoors in the kitchen. She'd get out the whisky bottle and I'd get out the fags and we'd carry on till, um, I'd say, 'Master, I'm only staying half an hour, literally half an hour'. Normally I'd be there three or four, leave at about Eleven! She was managing OK at that stage.*

I once popped round in the morning and she hadn't got her false teeth in! A couple – two on a bridge. I was absolutely shocked to bits!

Betty was now in her 80s. Her eyesight was going as she had cataracts. Also after her shooting accident, a lot of debris and dust had gone in her eyes, and that had not helped.

Driving

One day Betty was on her way through Sittingbourne on the way to the Isle of Sheppey. She was driving her Land-Rover and trailer. She drove straight over a brand new roundabout – which hadn't been there the week before, and she was weaving about all over the place. A policeman flagged her down and wandered over. Everyone always knew who she was. *'Ah, 'morning Mrs McKeever,'* said Sgt Watchus.

'*Do you realize that you're weaving slightly?*' He didn't always have a full rapport with her.

'**Oh, don't be ridiculous!**' Speculating on her eyesight, he asked her to read the number on a car 50 yards ahead, on the other side of the road.

Betty could not even see the car! and answered, '**I've no idea. It doesn't really matter, does it?**' So she started trying to remember local numbers and make one up!

JOE: *Well, one weekend I think it was, she went up to Sittingbourne to the vets. Apparently she was going up a one way street and there happened to be a police car followin' her, I think they actually thought she'd had a bit too much to drink. She was wandering about the road and they stopped her. And they made her get out, like… The police found out she wasn't drunk or anything and asked her to read a numberplate. She couldn't. They said, 'You're going to leave the Land-Rover here.'*

I remember her telling me: '**I'm not leaving the bloody Land-Rover here!**' *she says. She made them drive it back to Waterham, and brought her back.*

I think she had to go to court to get the licence taken away from 'er. She knew the JP. '**Will I be all right to drive my pony in to get my money from the bank then? I will be allowed to park him in the warehouse?**' *And there was all roars* [of laughter] *about the Courthouse! I can imagine it, you know. Unfortunately, or fortunately, it was a good thing to have her stopped.*

Her plea was biblical, '**Paul was stricken blind on the road – and he saw again!**' The magistrate, Bill Foster, knew her. Betty was let off the charge – but her driving licence was taken away.

JOE: *She wouldn't admit to herself that she couldn't or wasn't supposed to be on the road. It was a godsend in some ways. Colin then – he was running her about more than I was, but of course you had to drive her everywhere… If she was out in a car on the road, she owned the road. I used to be with her at times when she used to drive, honestly [after her sight was bad] well that was a good thing.*

Of course, after that, she really hated the police. Terrible to have your licence taken away, but honestly, it was better for her own sake as well as for the car's.

Port Lympne

In August one year, when I was visiting Kent with my husband Colin and our three very young children; we all went on a jaunt, with my parents and Aunty Betty to Port Lympne Zoo, all piled into the Rancho.

It's not often on a family day out such as this, that it rains so hard that you get invited into the elephant house, right behind the elephants, just to shelter from the weather! The elephants were chained by one leg only and their size was very imposing. Betty was getting quite blind at this stage and so hadn't noticed whose house we were sharing, until she suddenly interrupted herself and said, **'I see elephants!'** She immediately got chatting with the keeper about how one feeds elephants. A memorable day.

Out shooting one day with Chip Stevens at Luddenham, Betty said she couldn't see. A flight of ducks came over and instinct came in, Betty shot the first six!

SIMON CURLING: *Betty set up a horse and trap to travel around in, down Waterham and Thanet Way. She didn't need a licence, test or health checks. Then she had an upset on the Thanet Way and that idea got quietly dropped.*

Slotty

Slotty had retired from the City in the 1960s and continued to keep himself active and sailed regularly from his beloved Whitstable. Ivy shattered her leg one day, falling off a horse. This took a long time to heal, so Slotty organized and built for her a stairlift, long before these items were generally used.

But in May '83, he suffered fourteen strokes. and was never the same again. So he had to be looked after by his batman, Brunton.

SHIELA JUDGE: *When her brother Slotty had a stroke and was dying, Betty was really worrying to see him laying there like that. I went over there one day when she'd come back from seeing him and it was the first time I'd ever seen her nearly in tears – heart-broken.* **'I couldn't let an animal lay like that,'** *she said.*

SIMON CURLING: *Betty told the 'Stag to France' story and got a hand squeeze from Slotty, because she got the year wrong. He was clearly registering things.*
'When I go, don't let it be like that.'

Slotty Dawes died, 8 December 1985, two and a half years after all those strokes. Following all those years of being such a close couple, Ivy followed him and died nine months later in 1986.

Slotty gave Whitstable Yacht Club its rescue boat, the *Slotty Dawes.*

HUGH CURLING: *Slotty spent a great deal of time trying to persuade Betty to go into Lloyds. She always refused. When Lloyds blew up, she was most annoyed that Slotty wasn't around to see it!*

Rudolf

Calling at Waterham one day, Norma found Betty sitting at the top of the stairs, putting on her stockings. **'I've had quite a week. My husband died'** – most matter of factly. Rudolf and Betty had not met since the 1930s. They had never divorced. In fact, she was rather annoyed with him, as she had wanted to leave him some pieces in her will. Rudolf had lived out his days in Dublin, biding-in with his partner Sydney Parr, who pre-deceased him. They were both buried in Mount Jerome.

WILLIE: *Father died in '87, I suppose – or '86. I've got it in a Bunyan's 'Pilgrim's Progress' which came through the McKeevers. My daughter Margaret came over with me for the funeral. Tom was at University and couldn't get away, but Margaret came. (My grandmother lived until she was 99, and died in mid to late '70s. '78 – somewhere about there.)*

Jean had always sorted out the presents before. All the complications of wrapping them at Christmas.

JAMES DAWES: *If Aunty Betty was giving you something, she'd ask you to get things out of the car, and she'd have a selection of old books or tools or something. Never wrapped anything up. Just sort of handed out and said 'Happy Christmas'. Things that were no longer any use to her, or books that she'd read. She wouldn't buy things for people, but they were nice things that she gave them.*

When we were children, she gave us a wonderful carpentry set in a box – I have it still.

Young children were often given quantities of stuffed animals. The one they invariably chose as their favourite, was the one Betty had given. Lucy Edgar 'Pussy'. Sophie Dawes 'Hunting Hare' – with green beagle coat. Kate Mineyko 'Brown Teddy'.

Betty understood how important one's feet were. **'Always make sure you have decent shoes to wear.'** She would say: **'My Father had these boots made round me when I was young, and they still work.'** She always had them handmade.

By this period she was able to get her shoes made by the National Health. Betty described walking in to be fitted by 'a Glorious Indian Gent', with his 'hareem' of three 'concubines' – or nurses! She had worn out her first fitted pair of National Health shoes, because she did everything in them. She walked miles in her shoes, beagling, shooting, farming, and for other outdoor activities; instead of just politely strolling round as an old lady should. Her Asian found the use Betty got out of her shoes bemusing and told her that Muslims would take off their shoes indoors.

Betty McKeever was getting to be quite a local celebrity in Kent now and she had been listed in the *Guinness Book of Records* for some years.

She was very knowledgeable on many different subjects, especially countryside ones. At various times she gave talks. She was interviewed a couple of times by local TV stations upon her life, her hunting, and her vigorous and robust views. She was on Radio Kent, interviewed by Peter Cook, in August 1983.

Another radio talk she gave was on the subject of English lavatories. Quite amusing, and well researched around and about.

Several times the W.I. asked her to speak. The lecture she gave on the old days in Hernhill is mentioned in chapter six. Another talk she gave the W.I. was on 'What they used to wear'. The petticoats, drawers, corsets, the combinations and the bodices. All very interesting and a different way of life for the women living in them.

The evening before travelling north for a holiday to Scotland one year, John and Jill Dawes found themselves marking out the trail for Betty's Sponsored Ride – to be held the following day; tying up the fertilizer bags to trees with orange string. They were in Betty's Land-

Rover. Jill was in front, with Betty in the middle and David Sorrell driving, John was behind. At twilight they got stuck in a bog and the Land-Rover tipped sideways. .

'**Oh good!**' said Betty. She could have been flustered by the situation and bothered by the great lurch, but being her, she just enjoyed it! She then sat patiently where she was – while the others had to deal.

Betty fishing in lochan at West Tempar

Chapter Forty
West Tempar

My sister Janet had developed a muscular disease in her early twenties called Myasthenia Gravis. This was very difficult for her but for some strange reason, she always felt a lot better being high and inland – especially in Scotland. Her aim was to live up in the Highlands and run a country house for guests, perhaps with a group of friends. Then she met Andrew Mineyko, a Scottish Pole, who taught Spanish in Manchester, and who was looking for any excuse to go back to Scotland.

Janet and Andrew got engaged in 1983. They looked for and found for sale, an old hunting lodge, West Tempar, in Rannoch. It was exactly the house they wanted, up in the Highlands, and would be perfect to run for guests. Janet had actually stayed in it previously – on a holiday let. It was ideal.

The Scottish system of buying a house means that each contender to buy, puts in an offer, then waits. The best offer will then be chosen by the vendor.

JANET MINEYKO: *When Andrew and I were engaged, we finally scraped all our pennies together and put in an offer for West Tempar House. Aunt Betty was interested, as the Mount family [her daughter-in-law Anne's step-mother Jane Mount] had once owned it. Andrew Mineyko came down to Kent for the weekend. The family endlessly talked wedding and West Tempar. The wedding was due to take place the next time that Andrew came to Kent.*

We were at rather a low ebb as we knew that someone else was after West Tempar, and would have offered more money.

On Saturday, Mother declared that neither subject (the wedding or the buying of the house) was to be mentioned. Andrew and I went beagling near Teynham, a few miles away – on Mount family land.

It was a cold and dark day. Hardly anybody was out beagling. Aunt Betty took one look at the despondent Andrew, shouted **'Hello, Solidarity!'** *and demanded to know the situation vis-à-vis*

West Tempar. Andrew explained that there was a rich Australian woman also after it.

'Oh!' exclaimed Muriel Shaw, from the other side of Aunt Betty, 'we're interested in West Tempar.' She turned out to be the only other serious contender for West Tempar! Obviously Andrew and I spoke to Muriel and to her friend Brian Peek. He was not too keen to go to the Highlands of Scotland, as his mother and interests were in Kent. Muriel's mother lived in Edinburgh and her purpose in wishing to own the house was – 'somewhere to read a book'. We explained our plans of having paying guests – our chance of a lifetime.

Afterwards, Aunt Betty button-holed Muriel Shaw and Brian Peek, and went on at them about how they **'must give a newly married couple a chance'.**

As a result, Muriel Shaw rang the estate agents' office and withdrew her offer, as long as we got the house. She was in a position to offer much more money than us. She has subsequently been to stay at Tempar and 'read a book'.

I always feel that we bought this house, due to Aunt Betty.

It seemed incredible for Janet and Andrew to meet, in deepest Kent, the only other person who was interested in a lonely house, deep in the Highlands of Scotland.

Betty liked having relations in Scotland – even if they were in the 'hills' – the mountains (unfamiliar to her), and in 1984 she was brought North by John and Jill Dawes for one of her visits to West Tempar.

JANET: *It was summer and Aunt Betty felt hot. She decided to join us swimming in Dunalastair water. She had not swum for 12 years, so did not have anything in which to swim. So she gingerly took to the water wearing a pink frilly bath-hat, an old-fashioned vest and a hugh, knee-length, pair of black bloomers* [she could no longer buy the beige ones]. *She began to try to swim, with which the vast amount of air, which was trapped in the bloomers, up-ended her 'duck-tails all'! The bloomers rose above her, and her head went under water.*

She surfaced coughing and spluttering. **'Oh! Oh! I must have forgotten how to swim! I didn't know you could.'**

The rest of us, suffering from suppressed giggles, were totally unable to explain what had really happened. John Dawes had a rubber ring with him, from the time he had badly broken his hip. This was thrown over, and she puttered about with it happily thereafter.

The visit lasted ten days. Aunty Betty fell asleep once for twenty minutes after lunch, but otherwise never drew breath!

Andrew took Betty to fish on the lochan. He said, 'Watch the end of your line, Aunt Betty'. Much to the surprise of others she was obedient and did so, and caught a fish.

In the summer of 1987, Betty went on her last visit to Scotland. She was 86 and nearly blind. Also her legs were unsteady. Willie took her around Glasgow Garden Festival in a Bath chair. They then went to stay at West Tempar with the Mineykos. There was a fellow guest staying at Andrew and Janet's hotel, a Mr Scrimgeour – who was looking into acquiring Rannoch Lodge.

Inevitably, Betty knew his grandfather, who was actually Selby-Lowndes, but known as Colonel Barker. This famous master had once damaged his hip and so ridden side-saddle. Betty had lent him her habit skirt, to keep his knees warm. He had been 'quite a one with the ladies'.

Betty knew more about his grandfather than Mr Scrimgeour did! Betty and Willie went on to take a last haunting look at Banff. They visited Whitehills, the Kirkyard and Colleonard, which was a wilderness and falling down.

On Sunday we went to Inverness and William inspected the Fraser grave where he had had Jean, her mother and Aunt's names added and all the lettering recut. We then had tea with Jean's cousin nearby.

They also went to Aultmore and Scattertie, to Bowie Bank and Duff House which was empty and being renovated. It had all changed so. Banff was full of supermarkets.

Betty found the changes dispiriting. She wrote to Janet about her daughters:

I hope that when the girls are older you will take them to Banff. I don't think I ever want to go there again. I will keep

my memories of so many wonderful times. Thank goodness these parts [Kent] remain much as I knew them. A few more electric lines and roads, but people much the same...

If you live as long as I have and I hope you will never be able to enjoy the north as I have done. [Betty was showing her age.]

In 1987, to complete the exodus North, John and Jill Dawes sold Sonstoll, and moved up to Rannoch, having bought the estate of West Tempar, and the old farmhouse.

During her 'swimming' visit north three years previously, Betty had stood on Tempar Rock, looking down on the property and farmhouse, and said to John and Jill, **'Your neighbours won't be here long. You should be able to swap Sonstoll for West Tempar.'** They loved Scotland and went there frequently, but had not had the idea of moving up there themselves. But to cut a long story short, they did just that. In 1987 they swapped the Sonstoll property for the West Tempar estate, within £1,000. Betty was sad when they moved north and she hotly denied giving them the idea!

Since Sonstoll had been built in 1962, Betty had always had Christmas lunch at her nephew's family. She had twenty-five Sonstoll Christmases. The people who bought Sonstoll from them in May 1987, had previously lived at the renovated Thread Cottage next door, and got to know Betty well.

Dan Heister – a lecturer in International Law at the University of Kent, and his wife Elizabeth, a partner in a firm of City solicitors – knew the Christmas ritual well.

Mary Dawes asked Betty to come to her for Christmas, as John and Jill were no longer there, but Betty replied, **'I'll be going to Sonstoll for Christmas Dinner as usual.'** The Heisters had obviously found that buying the house was not sufficient. Christmas must continue as before. On a beagling day, when they hunted around Sonstoll in September, Dan Heister had been chatting to her. *'Well, Betty, are you going to come to lunch at Sonstoll?'*

'Of course I am,' was the brief reply. Betty was absolutely delighted by their invitation. (This meant that Dan always took her home afterwards. As a result, he never kissed his daughters goodnight at Christmas. He sat in the kitchen at Waterham, listening to Betty's stories and no doubt, drinking a glass of whisky.)

Betty continued going to Christmas dinner annually at Sonstoll, as per usual, until she died.

Chapter Forty-one
Blean Beagles [5]

In 1987 out beagling, Betty was looking over at Throwley which had belonged to Lord Sondes in the old days. His property had been broken up some 20 years before. Betty told J N P Watson of *Country Life*:

> **Since the departure of the big landowners, every little wood in this part of the country seems to be let to some shooting syndicate or other, and in many places we're no longer welcome until the end of January. Then there's Kent's massive urbanisation and the hazards of the M2, the Canterbury bypass (A2) and the railways which were electrified in 1960.**

Joan Sayer retired from being the Hunt Secretary of the Blean in 1980 or 1983. Joan had been Hunt Secretary since 1934 and a whip since 1920. She was getting old too, but was still one of the most regular followers, as she had been since she was a girl. In her time she had won many foot races for the Blean. Norma Curling has been hunt secretary ever since.

Chris Hill and Guy Hindley were huntsmen in the '80s. They carried the horn or whipped-in, turn and turn about. Dr Laurie Kay also hunted the hounds on Thursdays. Kings' School Canterbury still used beagling as one of their activities.

Martin Browne and Dominic Reagon both whipped in and helped in the kennels. Paul Stern hunted some Saturdays also. Simon Hitches whipped-in.

All these people may have hunted the hounds, but Betty was still Master. She had a marvellous knack of communication with all animals. She brought the best out of her hounds by a few gentle sounds of encouragement, and without ever raising her voice. Betty's zest for life and interest in people continued to be remarkable.

STUART SILLERS: *When Mike Bax stopped hunting was really when things lost it. He was a very good huntsman.*

Some huntsmen were 'naturals'. Some of them could learn and some couldn't. Most of us had been brought up to it, or been at a college which had a pack. Simon [Curling] *was at school at Stowe which had a pack*

For Betty's 70th Year Celebrations, she had hired a chap called Nick Valentine. A professional kennel-huntsman for the season. Other years [the huntsmen] were amateur. The hounds were looked after by a chap on the farm – Colin. They were treated like pets and got all the attention. A couple of years after, Paul Stern, a farrier from Rolvendown (Kent/Sussex) hunted the beagles for the '80–81 season.

We used to put [Betty's] buggy in with the hounds in the horse trailer. The youngest whip would go in the trailer with the hounds and the buggy. Her eyesight wasn't all that brilliant, but she used to get about pretty well. She always seemed to know where the hare had gone. Sixth sense or something.

She'd certainly got strong views on how things should be done. It wasn't always easy to suggest other ways of doing things. But they were her hounds, so fair comment.

The hunting wasn't really anything terribly exciting. Since she died the Joint Masters have done a lot to open up new country.

In Geoffrey Neame's farm of Newlands, they had the Meet [more than once] before Christmas. So it was difficult to have good places to go. She had to arrange it all, but was not so much on the ball by then, and wasn't in a position to see different people.

One day we had an early morning Meet, right at the beginning of the season, at Dargate. Not a terribly exciting place but close to the kennels. We tried to hunt for a couple of hours, then went into the farmhouse to report to Betty how we had got on.

Although it was 9 o'clock in the morning, we were given beer or a glass of whisky. We had all had an early start and a drink and all fell asleep one by one! And she was carrying on a conversation quite happily with herself, while we were snoring our heads off! Of course by that stage, she couldn't really see what we were up to.

Speagles

Betty had a springer spaniel (brown and white) for shooting. Unfortunately it managed to get in with the hot bitches. So there was at least one litter of cross-bred spaniel/beagles. *They were extraordinary looking things, more like spaniel than beagle really, but they had got beagle characteristics. A spaniel with a long tail.* [This was] *when Chris Hill hunted them – late '70s early '80s – at least one litter, maybe two. They were the most awful looking things you've ever seen, ghastly! They'd got the worst characteristics of both beagle and spaniel. They were taken out hunting but were as mad as anything and absolutely useless! One or two of them lasted a couple of years. They disappeared after that. Only the Blean could have had a spaniel-cross hunting, known as 'the Speagles'!*

In the eighties, Betty still had her 'session' after beagling.

MARK JOHNSON: *I've been whipping-in since the early '80s. The Master used to invite us back to tea. She always had a long table in the kitchen with 60-packet of silk-cut cigarettes and also a bottle of whisky, so we'd all join in. She was very much a fun person to be around. A great character – super person. She had been there for decades and decades, and she'd seen a lot of history and everything. We held her in great respect, certainly.*

Whisky was poured – up to the thumbnail.

The Isle of Sheppey became more and more popular for beagle meets. There were fewer cars, railways, and other distractions. However, Betty always thought there were too many hares on the marshes of Sheppey.

MIKE BAX: *She always filled her buttonhole with the early flowers of Spring – late in the hunting season, and would get more and more as the day advanced.*

1983 – 50 days hunted

1985 – 50 days   ''

1986 – 48 days   ''

Colonel Richard Webb was Hunt Chairman until 1976. Arthur Finn took over and he became Chairman of the Blean Beagles. Arthur's father, Tom and his brother Bill Finn had each been Chairman of the Beagles in their day.

Mr Baldwin was Show Chairman. Mr Ken Barton took over in 1976 and was Chairman of the Blean Beagles until his death in 1982.

Betty was by this time, not only the longest-serving Master of all time, but she had a clear quarter-century lead over any other person alive. In 1984 she was described 'as a woman who holds an unchallenged position at the head of field sports in the country' by the *Faversham News*.

One of her main rivals in length of Mastership was the 10th Duke of Beaufort. He was Master of the Beaufort Foxhounds for a record 60 years, from 1924 until 1984 when he died, hunting for 3,895 days.

In the late '80s and following her hip replacement, Betty started finding it difficult walking the five miles or so for a day's beagling. In the end she did a couple of seasons in a golf buggy.

PETER GOODWIN: ... *later memories of Betty in the hunting field when she would be in her electric wheelchair cruising the lanes and tracks, knowing from many years' experience just where a hunted hare would be most likely to run.*

However, she could easily be persuaded to abandon her wheelchair in the nearest gateway or gap, where it would be collected later by possibly one of the whips, before transfer back to the beagle trailer. Betty would then join Kit in the car, who would have prepared for this with an ample supply of sandwiches, coffee, sherry and possibly cherry brandy.

I would now continue to drive, but under direction from Betty as to exactly which route I should take and where I should stop and scan the countryside. We could sometimes see more of the hare than hounds did, but very sadly, one just had to report on these movements as Betty's sight was by now so poor.

The Boxing Day Meet was held at the Fremlins Brewery in Faversham. It became more of an event latterly and was a special occasion. People would come over from far afield especially for it, and to honour Betty. '*Throughout her unprecedented term as Master, she missed only one Boxing Day Meet in Faversham due to a shooting accident.*' wrote the *Faversham Times*.

Until there is a law to stop me I shall carry on hunting. Hares are hunted by foxes every night, it is part of nature.

Betty continued following her beagle pack all her life and at the end she had 24 couple of beagles. By the time of her death in 1990, her EIGHTY-FIRST season as Master of the Blean Beagles had started. This is a record that will never be beaten.

Betty at Faversham Brewery Meet of the Blean Beagles

Chapter Forty-two
A legend in her own lifetime

50 years a Master! – Celebration Meet

30th December 1959

Presentation: A silver beagle. A picture of herself riding Lucky Day in the 1930s.

Letters from Betty to John Dawes (then living in New Zealand with his family):

Dec: 15th 1959...The Beagles are giving me a picture and silver hound for my 50 years on Dec: 30th. It is shrouded in mystery but I know that much & Jean is excited about it.

Feb: 24th 1960.
My dear John and Jill,
Thank you both so much for your very nice Christmas present of the butter, most welcome as we were a large party.
Also thank you so much for joining with all the others and giving me such lovely presents on my 50th season I do wish you could have been with us all that day. We were 185 people & had a good hunt to finish.
The picture is so good & also the silver hound. I have been trying to write all my thank yous, hence this delay.

One hundred and eighty-five people attended.

60 years a Master! – Celebration Meet

January and February 1969. This was hosted by John and Jill Dawes at Sonstoll.

Presentation: A new armchair was Betty's present – upholstered in beagle green. The family gave a footstool to match. There was also a silver hare on a plinth:

Presented to Mrs J B McKEEVER M.H.
after 60 years of Mastership
of the Blean Beagles
by supporters and friends
1909–1969

The speech: Joan Dawes, Betty's sister-in-law. 200 people
attended. **'Here you see me in my country seat.'**
Huntsman: Noel Watson

4 January – The Non Event!

MY DIARY [I as an 18-year-old kept a diary]: *January 4th,
Saturday. 8.45 Breakfast. Buttered bread all morning for sandwiches then Aunty Jean rang up to say that Aunty Betty had bron-
chitis and was not able to come to her presentation of being master
of the beagles for 60 years! Catastrophe! Red hot telephone for the
next hour. Roll and apple for lunch then handed out cherry brandy
to hundreds of people at meet. TV and press there. The armchair
and hare trophy displayed and Daddy made an announcement.
Went beagling. No kill. Round in circles. All to tea (130 people).
Sandwiches and smiled for ages. 1½ hours clearing up...*

We put much of the food – the cakes (baked earlier that week)
and the sandwiches into the deep freeze. It all came out again, four
weeks later.

5 February – The Event

MY DIARY: *February 1st Saturday. 9.00 Breakfast. Buttered
bread for sandwiches, arranged the frozen ones and put out all
the glasses. Read, gave quarter of a loaf of bread to the ponies.
Consommé soup for lunch. Joan Sayer came early. Brushed trousers
and changed. Had the Presentation Meet for Aunty Betty's 60th
year as Master of Blean Beagles (she turned up). Also about 200
people. Handed round cherry brandy and Granny Dawes* [Joan]
presented. Washed up. Beagled – (nothing killed). Took Ranger
[black Labrador] *on hunting crop most of time. Back, tea. Showed
Susan Sorrell around house. All little children crawling over me.
Washed up (hundreds). Drinks. Everyone left. Grand tidy...*

NOEL WATSON: *The lawn meet at Sonstoll to mark Betty's 60th consecutive season as Master of Hounds was truly a great affair with hundreds of spectators out to mark this very special occasion, including a camera TV team from Southern News. After imbibing a number of high octane stirrup cups, the TV crew set up their camera at the top end of a nearby orchard, commanding a good view of the proceedings. I drew the orchard first after moving off and almost immediately we found a hare which ran within ten yards of the camera, with the beagles in hot pursuit. The TV director rushed out waiving his arms and trying to stop the hunt. 'That was a perfect scene,' he said, 'But unfortunately we had just run out of film. Could you organise the hunt for a re-take when we've re-loaded!' I just gaped at him before leading the hounds back on line. As is their custom when first found, the hare ran a full circle before returning to the orchard and clapping down, relying on her camouflage. The beagles, however, stuck to her line and again put her up. Again the hare ran within ten yards of the now loaded and manned TV camera, with Blean Beagles screaming behind her. As I flogged passed the camera the director shouted, 'That's just great! It's in the can. Thank you very much.'*

John Dawes and Betty at 60 years presentation

70 years a Master! – Celebration Meet

27 October 1979 at 11.00. Hosted by Bill and Mary Dawes at Mount Ephraim.

Presentation: A large glass punchbowl engraved with a scene of Betty beagling as a girl on one side and on the other, the Master as an old lady. The bowl was engraved by Hilary Virgo. Betty was also given a much-needed new hound trailer and photograph albums of the years of beagling.

A perpetual cup was given in the name of the Blean Beagles to the Peterborough 'Harriers and Beagles'.

The speech was made by Captain Ronnie Wallace, MFH, former Master of the Heythrop. He was also Secretary of The British Field Sports Association (now The Countryside Alliance).

One well-wisher sent a dollar for every mile he had run.

About 500 people attended.

ARTHUR FINN [chairman]: *70 years celebrations I ran and there was a subscription, a book and a presentation.*

Beagling followed. A hare was found but thrown off before Crockham. The day ended with tea at John and Jill's house, Sonstoll.

Joan Sayer, Betty, Chris Hill & Martin Browne at the 70 years Celebration Meet

75 years a Master! – Celebration Meet

1 November 1984. Held at Sonstoll, hosted by John and Jill Dawes.

Presentation: Four albums of photographs of beagling over the years, and a large bottle of whisky. Joan Sayer was given a presentation too.

The speech: taken over by John Dawes as Arthur Finn, the Chairman was taken ill. Betty's nephew *'went rifling through her drawers'* and said that the Blean Beagles were different from most packs. Mrs McKeever *'has installed a certain amount of old world custom over the years'*.

Two hundred people attended.

The 'antis' who attended the event were offered a drink at the Meet by John Dawes, *'which was accepted by one member, to the total indignation of some of his colleagues'*.

JOHN: *When I was making my speech the 'antis' began spraying the hounds with 'antimate', so they were asked to leave, which they did.*

John Dawes and Arthur Finn prepared the photograph albums. Tea was at Mount Ephraim afterwards.

80 years a Master! – Celebration Meet

14 October 1989. Held at Mount Ephraim and hosted by Sandys and Lesley Dawes.

Arthur Finn as Chairman of the Blean Beagles ran the event. *'The 80 years celebrations I ran, but there was no organized subscription, but a book of those who attended at her request.'*

Huntsmen – Chris Hill and Guy Hindley. Whips: Robert Balicki, Martin Brown, Simon Curling, Mark Johnson, Simon Hitches, Geoffrey Neame, and Dominic Regan.

Presentation: Betty specified that she did not want a gift this time. There was a Presentation Book.

The speeches: Maurice Berry and Arthur Finn.

This Meet was smaller than some of the others – as it was by invitation only. Mignon Allen's son was told by Arthur: *'You are not invited, but I cannot prevent you coming.'*

STUART SILLERS' HUNTING DIARY: *14th October. 12 noon. Mount Ephraim, Hernhill, Faversham. A quiet meet at the Mount for Betty*

McKeever's 80th Mastership Anniversary. The proceedings were low-key, with Arthur Finn, Hunt Chairman and Maurice Berry, oldest farmer making speeches. The orchards round about were then drawn with the unfortunately easily predictable lack of success. It wasn't Chris Hill's fault, just an awful hunting area. After two hours of this, a large bunch of antis then appeared, mostly just very annoying, following hound closely, but not really nasty. And not a vast amount of noise. Only one had a horn. The police were called and were unusually good, escorting the antis from the orchard and keeping them on the road. Sandys Dawes had to be called upon, as the land-owner, to say who could be allowed to follow. The proceedings then drew to a close on New Zealand banks. We all repaired to the Mount for a delicious tea.

Two hundred and sixty-six names were in her presentation book, which was inscribed as follows:

On the 14th October 1989 at
The Opening Meet of the
Blean Beagles held at Mount
Ephraim, Hernhill, there was a presentation to mark
Mrs J B McKeever's
completion of her 80th Year as Master of the Hounds.

For a full list of all the names, see Appendix Two.

Chapter Forty-three
Late eighties

Both beagling and farming got a bit much for her towards the end of her life. Mary Dawes didn't know how she coped. Things ran down, especially after Jean Fraser died in 1982.

Chris Hill, the huntsman was nice to her, but the beagling was lacking the zest a younger Master would have had.

In the last three years or so, Betty took to her golf buggy to get around. Walking was difficult and she was practically blind but she was not deterred. *'Run over my feet with a motorised trolley!'* said John Hills.

Cooking

Breakfast was the big meal. Betty learned to make it herself. Porridge, followed by bacon and egg, then toast. This would do her all day.

Mrs Anne Hadlow did come and help. The Labour Exchange would send people round. Betty would take them on, then they would last – a few days, a few weeks.

Waterham – particularly the kitchen, was ingrained with grime. Although Betty had a daily, she was not used to running the house herself.

The kitchen was very old and indescribably dirty. There was a stone sink and a few cheap rickety old units. She had her precious Charles II chairs at the wooden kitchen table. It was quite something that Betty had learnt to cook at all. She would buy herself ham, bacon, and sausages.

JOE: *Some mornings you'd go back in there, when she was on her own, walk into that. Terrible it was. It was all – well, when you saw the cooking that went on in there, it was all black round the clock, you know.*

I know I was in there at times, when she had her gall bladder out. After that she had to put something on – sugary stuff – a box of this red stuff, two or three spoonfuls. She'd scatter it over the bowl [of porridge] *eat it away, no bother at all. And her burnt bacon and sausage and egg, whatever was going. You couldn't see across that room for smoke. No, she was no house person, nothing to do with cooking or housework.*

Betty had never learnt to throw anything away. As a result of this the office became entirely full of paper and she had to move into the dining-room. This was a pretty old room of a fair size. But by the end of her life, it was more than three-quarters full, and choked up with papers.

JOE: *She was having to move out of that 'cos she never threw a thing away. Oh, no, it was always there. Paper all over everywhere. I donno' how she knew what was what. I know we used to go in there sometimes because of these ponies.*

Towards the end, she couldn't [really] look after herself but there was no way she was going to go anywhere to be looked after. She had one or two people come there for an interview, be like Jean Fraser was, but I'm afraid none of them – come up to expectations!

Betty would have been fairly unliveable with at that stage. Sue Sorrell had been a close friend over many years who did some secretarial work – and other things too.

SUE: *I did get into her system where I actually managed to do the VAT, and we managed to do it successfully, and there were no come-backs. Because of all the various sales of straw and horses.*

Doing the VAT for her, which you can imagine. There is the dining-room table, with all the papers, and Betty's system very much in her head. Battling through VAT and then after a certain amount of time.

All right Sue. Right we've done enough of that. We've done enough of that. Let's go down into Whitstable and have some oysters.

So we used to trot off and have half a dozen oysters.

I didn't do a lot of 'looking after her'. I was the chauffeur. Shopping was always interesting in Whitstable. We used to go into the delicatessen, and Budgens. But mainly Whitstable; into the delicatessen to get her pin-oatmeal. She used to like going and getting a fillet steak. Miss Fits (Delia) Wheelers to get oysters and seafood. She liked the idea of the Miss Fits.

Had very well-cooked bacon for breakfast. If she was feeling flush, we'd go into the delicatessen and have proper bacon. But if she was feeling she ought to be good, we'd go in to Rooks. Then we'd have a few weeks of Rooks and she'd realize she didn't really like their bacon after all, so she'd be back to the Deli.

Mushrooms, she used to like mushrooms. Bacon and mushrooms and sausages. And always soup. We always bought tinned soup. When Jean was active in the kitchen, it was always home-made soup.

For a dinner, the whole of the VAT used to be cleared off the dining-room table. And increasingly, as she got older, the more papers, the more difficult it became to entertain and have dinner parties. The dining-room table was completely full, it was quite difficult.

X-ray

MIKE BAX: *Some years after her shooting accident, Betty had to go in and have an X-ray. (This may have been for cataracts.) Anyway, on the X-ray of her skull were large numbers of black spots, which the hospital couldn't understand. They came out and said, 'Mrs McKeever, can you explain to us, why you've got the most extraordinary bone formation on your head, and it's covered in black spots?*

'Oh Lord! Those aren't black spots, those are lead shot.'

And sure enough a whole lot of lead shot was still lodged there, in her skull.

Sarah Bax, Mike's daughter has strong memories of Betty from when she was a young girl.

SARAH: *We went to a pub where there were beermats all over the walls and Jean Hilton did a beagling tea.*

She told my friend Cassia and I this incredible story. We were so bored at tea, with all the grown-ups. She told an incredible story about someone who was drinking. A great big man who loved his drink and was always fairly red-faced, with bulging eyes and was overly merry and boisterous. He drank so much one day that he just blew up, like a balloon and started floating to the ceiling, burping. And suddenly – exploded!

Cassy and I were amazed. We had been watching 'James and the Giant Peach', and reading the book, and so completely believed an 'exploding man' story.

She was almost mystical. She did have very illuminating eyes. You could really see that she had experienced life to the full, got the best from life. But she seemed to be very down to earth and in touch with the world.

Betty although extremely old, still had her interest in the cultural things in life.

SHIELA JUDGE: *One day I went round there and there she was.* **'Oh, I repainted the sittingroom.'** *She had too – done it beautifully.*

Rather do carpentry to anything else. Mind you – I saw some pictures she'd painted when she was young. She did the most beautiful paintings of wild birds and things, and flowers. I mean, everybody used to think she was just whisky and beagles. The music she collected. She had a big collection of classical music on cassette. Her books were very good. She used to lend me books and I had some of mine over there. Books we used to pass between us. She wasn't just beer and skittles. She wasn't just hunting – one of these hunting women.

Madly keen on her garden. When her eyesight went at the finish, it drove her mad 'cos she said, **'I can't see whether I'm pulling out weeds or flowers.'**

[In November 1985]
I managed to go out with the Blean Beagles on Saturday. I had been laid up for over three weeks. I got flu and had a patch on my lung, which was ill to clear up, and Ned McMelan kept me in the house for ages.

Royal Progression

Norma Curling, who started beagling 34 years ago, had joined the secretarying of the Blean Beagles in 1970 with Joan Sayer and Jean Fraser.

NORMA: *Gardening – Betty was a very keen gardener. You could never get away without going around the garden. She used to go out there, fiddling with the garden and she was pretty blind. How she managed I don't know.*

You'd think she was just one of those Huntin' shootin' fishin' types, which of course she was, but it wasn't just that.

She was always fantastically interested in people. In the last few years when Betty could no longer drive, I would take her to the Kent County Show. She was going round on a golf buggy by then. It used to be taken down in the horsebox the day before, and parked behind the cattle sheds.

We would go down, pick up the golf buggy and progress around the showground. And people would appear. A bit like a Royal Progression. I have been to a Garden Party to see what happens. People would approach her from the side and say, 'Mrs McKeever, how lovely to see you,' or 'Mrs McKeever, how are you?' I'd very often know who they were. I'd have to introduce them, so I'd say, 'Betty, It's so and so'. Sometimes I didn't know who they were. Anyway there was no problem 'cos she'd say: **'You'll have to tell me who you are, my sight isn't very good these days.'** *And the minute they told her – it could be village people or work people – she just knew them. Betty knew their parents and all about them. She had this phenomenal memory for remembering people – and incidents. I can't do that sort of thing. She never stopped talking.*

Getting away

Towards knocking-off time, both Joe and Colin used to steer clear of their employer because otherwise they would be there for an hour. She was lonely.

JOE: *It was* **'Shall we have a drink Joe? Go and get the whisky bottle. Pour mine out. Have one yourself.'** *And this would go on and on, and sometimes you'd leave there late – good job I'd only got this to walk home round here!* **'Have another one, Joe.'** *And she'd go on about these old tales.* **'You remember, Joe, you remember so and so.'**

And honestly I didn't, you know. And she'd go way on and you'd keep edging towards the door. Colin would be the same. He says, 'You try to get out the door, but no'. She must have been lonely. Well, its sad and all that. I know, it wasn't very nice, the sort of way that you was trying to get away.

Colin West would take her into Whitstable regularly on a Friday. They would get back, unload, then have a few whiskies.

Gale – 1987

In 1987 there was a great gale which hit Kent badly. Colin West, in his half of the pair of cottages, was in bed when his gable-head blew in and the bricks fell down on to the bed alongside him! It wasn't quite so bad on Joe's side.

Colin came round to Joe's: *'He was yellin' and hollarin' "Hey, you want to come out? Bloody house is comin' down!" So I said, "No".'*

When Colin had explained that his end had come in, Joe went out to look, then walked across the road to Waterham. He could hardly keep upright, the wind was so strong. Joe was worried about the big old chestnut tree alongside the house, which was swaying away. He had a latch-key, so unlocked the door and called up.

Betty didn't know what the matter was, as she was half asleep and hadn't heard the gale. Joe wanted to know if she was all right.

JOE: *She said* **'Yes of course I'm all right. Why wouldn't I be?'** *'That bloody tree?'*

'Well,' *she said.* **'It's O.K.'** *So I left her and walked home. She seemed so unconcerned. She never got up or anything, stayed in bed and that was it!*

Admittedly, it was blowing the tree away from the house, so if it had gone, it would've gone away from the house. Poor old Colin, all the slates off his side of the house. We were lucky, we lost a few odd slates. Very selective, like. Up at New Zealand, a lot of trees went – and up through the wood.

The big barn also fell down in one of the two big gales.

Clive Donnery, who worked for P & O for thirty-five years asked me if Betty had ever travelled to India? I explained to him that she hadn't, but her father and grandfather had.

CLIVE: *Well, perhaps that was it. I felt the way she could quote P & O ships names was better than I could do. I didn't know her well. But she talked at length about P & O. She always seemed well informed about it.*

'Holding a glass of whisky in one hand and a cigarette in the other, she booms out her stories in her deep throaty voice,' wrote Mike Field of *Horse and Hound*.

Muriel Wilson became friendly with Betty in her latter days.

MURIEL: *We listened to hours and hours of stories. She wouldn't let us go home, my husband and myself when we went to visit. She always invited us to another dram.*

We were going to go on the coach to the Derby. It was around the 3rd May, 1989 (the Derby was the 6th June). She had invited my husband and me to go as guests. My husband died. So she came to the funeral and we all had lunch in my son's house and she was sitting there, and she said. **'Now Muriel, now that you've planted Wally, what do you plan to do next?'**

So I said I hadn't thought about it. Betty said **'Well you're still coming to the Derby.'**

'I don't think so.'

'Yes' *she said,* **'Your son Douglas can bring you and we'll all go together. I've got a chair for you.'**

I said 'What for?'

'Well, I'm going to be in a Bath chair. I'm bringing one along for you, too.'

So when we got to the Derby, she hauls out this Edwardian Bath chair with this long thing. It's not an ordinary wheelchair like we've got now. She had someone to push her, and she got Douglas to push me. He didn't want to, he felt embarrassed.

Anyway, we drove along from the place where the charabanc was parked, round to the paddock. Betty was in a Bath chair and I was in a wheelchair, and as we came along, everyone made way for us. So we got a marvellous place at the rim – to look at the horses.

'And now we'd better go and have a leak.'

I said, 'What! You can't get up and walk. All these people are saying 'Sorry', they're so sad for us.'

'Oh no, there's no problem at all. Get up and take a stick.'

'We walked along to the do da further back and our places were still kept for us. Then she decided she wanted to go in the stand (before they had the new one). And she walked up the great flight of steps to the top. She walked up the whole blinking lot!

She had a great time going to the Derby – on Smith buses, 1989, the year before she died.

[One time out and about] ... *she opened the door of her motorcar.* **'I'll squat down here.'** *We were parked right on the edge of the major road. She couldn't squat because it was a bit*

difficult to get up and down, so she hauls up her skirts and pulls down these pink seeleneese bloomers to her knees – shocking pink! I said, 'I don't know you. I'm not with you! I'm going to stand by the road to see if anyone's coming.'
'It's nothing they haven't seen before. Don't worry.'

With the antis – she said **'Well I've disposed of them.'** *Two of them that came down – she practically converted them later on.*

She didn't want to be buried. She wanted to take her last journey in the hounds. She wanted to be chopped up and given to the hounds to eat. I was shocked to the core! She said the Government in all its wisdom won't allow that. She said the most outrageous things.

She had a story about the Queen Mother. How she met her and talked to her and how she met her years later. The Queen Mother knew exactly who Betty was and what she had said – years and years before.

Bernard Lever told of his wife Annie's exhibition of her paintings in Sussex.

BERNARD: *Betty insisted upon coming and brought a small pack of red nosed male beaglers with her for the run.*

She arrived in the most marvellous coarse tweed suit with matching tweed hat and sensible shoes.

Being short sighted, she planted herself in the middle of the gallery on a shooting stick and proceeded to inspect all the pictures on the walls – through field glasses!

NORMA: *Her eyesight was so bad. She went to Miss Starbutt the eye doctor, who told her, 'With your cataracts, I can't really do anything. If I could do anything, I would.'*

Yet she had this funny sight out of the sides – at the edges – would see something at an acute angle quite clearly.

Betty gashed her leg one time and it was festering. She used a broom as a crutch – under her armpit.

Hip

NORMA: *She was allergic to penicillin. In the Autumn of 1986, she had a replacement hip. It cost £500. Betty had the operation at St Saviors, Hythe. She got a bladder infection as they were clumsy with catheter.*

She had no antibiotics. At the (Cottage) hospital at Whitstable, she was looked after for a fortnight.

Simon Curling and Geoffrey Neame visited Betty in hospital. They brought a bottle of whisky and the ward was youthful and noisy.

NORMA: *After she'd had the hip operation Betty had a Red Cross or hospital bed, and she moved downstairs at Waterham and slept in the drawing-room. She found it very convenient so just staying down there* [with just bare boards, otherwise she might trip. She dealt with her infirmities rather well].

She could get upstairs and went upstairs to bath and did that regularly. Like a large bedroom downstairs, but rather cut the drawing-room up for sitting in, and for us doing anything in.

So we'd end up sitting in the dining-room – if there were other people there. All those lovely chairs – their backs were broken and everything. The paperwork had started taking over. The dining-room table had disappeared years ago.

Every so often you could go down there – because she used to have a Christmas dinner (after Christmas) *for Willie and family. You'd go down there and find the dining-room table suddenly cleared in time for Betty's dinner party.*

JOE: *Well, she had a replacement hip, didn't she. She used to be a bit sore with it, but not much. She used to get around remarkably well with it. I've had mine done and it's marvellous. I think she didn't have much bother with hers.*

Vicky Constance did some sewing for Betty after she had lost weight almost overnight in old age. Vicky re-lined and altered her suits. Then she had them cleaned. The difference was absolutely remarkable, as tweed rejuvenates and the original colours come to light.

Vicky also reknitted the feet of Betty's stockings – the parts which wear out first. Knitting was no longer viable for Betty after she lost most of her sight, as she couldn't see if she'd dropped a stitch.

One day Betty went down to have lunch with her niece, Jean Rowntree in West Sussex, with Willie and Anne driving her. Somewhat inevitably they arrived a day early!

Jean said, *'It doesn't matter. Lovely to have you. Come on in. Now the problem is there's no lunch organized for you. Now what have we got? I've got a nice piece of roast beef – if you don't mind chatting for 45 minutes.'*

'Oh no,' says Aunty Betty, **'I do like my bit of roast beef.'** The mistake had been hers.

SHIELA JUDGE: *The vet was always out there. He told me he went in one morning. She was washing in the kitchen. Waved a towel at him.* **'Come in you silly old man.'** *I mean – we all knew Jimmy well. He was a Calvinistic Scot, also.*

'OK, OK, I'll wait outside.'

Then they went over to the marshes and looked at a colt or a pony, and coming back, there were lots of mushrooms and she said to him, 'I must have some of these. I can't waste them all.' So she ups with her skirt and kilted the mushrooms, and Jimmy's eyes were getting redder and redder. Betty with her ruddy great drawers – she didn't care! She stomped along with [skirts held up] *and wasn't worried at all.*

WILLIE: *She had trouble with waterworks. Had an infection – about 18 months before she died.*

SHIELA JUDGE: *She was put on water tablets.* **'Expect me to take three a day. I'm not messing about with that. I take 'em all first thing in the morning, get it over with.'**

So if you went out with her early, she kept disappearing into the hedge!

We bought some lovely ponies off her. We knew the vet. He was our vet – the one we went mushrooming with. He's dead too now.

Betty gave a lot of information to Sheila Judge for her book on the history of Faversham. This she would like to dedicate to Betty. One chapter in there is on sport and hunting in Faversham. *'She more or less dictated it. That does come from her.'*

COLIN WEST: *I used to look after the old girl – latterly. I'd go round – looked after her, mopped after her. I literally looked after her. Because she was in her eighties. Pick up the you know – whatever. Good old girl. She was a hard old bastard. A real character.*

Betty never shut the door when she went to the loo – off the kitchen. And Colin would go in to help put her knickers on and pull her woollies up.

'It was a good life. A bloody good life. I'm fifty-five.' Colin would nanny her, do the books and drive her around.

Lilian McKeever had been abroad and came back just in time to see her grandmother again. Betty showed Lilian around the garden and talked about her roses – her wonderful scented roses.

She was always a natural hunter. On a beagling day, when Betty was old and blind and in her last year, Dan Heister remembers meeting her in her golf buggy, motoring up and down Thread Lane, Hernhill – hunting hunt saboteurs!

Betty beagling in her golf buggy with John Dawes

Chapter Forty-four
And at the end

A month before Betty died, Norma Curling came to visit her and say that she was going on holiday for three weeks.

Betty, who knew she didn't have much longer, and who would always look at a fact full in the face told her, **'I've had a wonderful life. if I had the choice, I wouldn't change a bit of it.'** They did not meet again.

Waterham was burgled. Betty was present but could not get up the stairs. There were two or three people. They stole £30,000 or £40,000 worth of goods. She was most upset at having the book, Crammond's *Banff* stolen. It was part of her ancestry and irreplaceable for her. This awful incident, six weeks before her death, not surprisingly took some of the heart out of her. After that, Betty slept with her shotgun under her bed and the family were worried that she would actually shoot a burglar.

A couple of weeks before Betty died, she took Arthur and Anne Finn, Willie and Anne, and Mary Dawes out to dinner at the Marine at Tankerton.

It was an epic evening.

MARY DAWES: *The Stories. Well, she knew she was being preposterous. They got more and more outrageous. There was a whole new set of stories that no-one had heard before.*

There was a chap who had a mausoleum built for himself. He was put into it after his death, and he had had so much to drink that his body exploded and burst in the mausoleum. [In fact, this was Mad Jack Fuller, who had drunk quantities of port and been buried sitting upright.]

An Irish aristocrat, a countess in Ireland, who insisted on being buried with all her rings on. Thieves got into the grave somehow. Couldn't get the rings off so they cut off her fingers.

One of the party suggested at about 10.30, 'Shall we go?' but they didn't. All the hotel staff were hovering, hanging on her words. They all knew her of course. These were Betty's final stories as far as Mary was concerned. Each more preposterous than the last – and she knew it.

Once a week or once a fortnight, Willie collected his mother, and took her home to have a family supper at Renville. They did the same as usual that week. Willie returned her back home. Betty sorted sheep on the Monday.

On the Tuesday, she had been out talking to her neighbour Queenie Butcher from her buggy.

Sheila Judge: *'What she actually did, was walked out then sat down, over and out. That's what she'd want.'* It was a heart attack.

Joe found her when she died.

JOE: *Yes, Yeah. I remember seeing her that evening, I was doing some sheep out the back of the farm there.*

But that evening, I suppose it was about half-past five or six o'clock, I saw her like, and I spoke to her and she looked her normal self to be quite honest. And then to go round there in the morning and find her laying there like that. I wouldn't imagine that she'd been indoors long, like, before it happened, because she – her little old hat that she normally wore, was laying on the ground over there, and, if I remember rightly, she still got her shoes on. Yeah, because I thought there was something wrong directly when I went round there, because normally we'd have...

In the kitchen, I mean to say, me and Colin had a key to get into the house. I went to unlock the door, and found it unlocked. So she hadn't locked it up, like, so it had been open all night. Yes, when I touched her, you know, she was stiff, like sort of thing, obviously she'd been there a long time.

Betty died in the fullness of her years on Tuesday, 18 September 1990. She was 89 years old.

Chapter Forty-five
And afterwards

There was an autopsy or post-mortem held after – as Betty had died alone.

Boulty was rung up and told that Betty had just died. He was then informed of the funeral details. *'You'll be there? It's just family and old friends. I suppose really we can call you an old friend?'*

'I think so,' he answered quietly.

Her Cremation Service was held on Friday, 28 September, at 2.30. This was held at the big Crematorium at Charing and was attended by some family members and very close friends, but the main 'do' was her Memorial Meet.

Memorial Meet

This was held on Wednesday, 31 October 1990 at 12.30, high up on Betty's favourite pastures of New Zealand. It was a golden Autumn day.

> WILLIE: *At her funeral do on New Zealand – 300 to 500 people. We had a whip round for 'Shaftsbury Homes and Arethusa' and collected £600 to £800 at that do. Collected just by people putting money in fertilizer sacks.* [John reckoned it was close to £1,000.]

> SARAH BAX: *I remember going to the sprinkling of her ashes when I was 10. I didn't know what to expect. Dad said something, so I said, you know – 'You were wonderful. We'll never forget you.' She was always very comforting to be around, with mesmerizing blue eyes. She had this amazing serenity. I think because she was so in touch with nature and the beagling. Animals – that side of life.*

Betty's oft-expressed desire to have 'just one more day's hunting' by being cut up and fed to her beagles, was modified to a more permissible method. This was done by pouring her ashes into a cross-shape on the hill, and then the beagles 'drew' over them.

Willie gave a talk about his mother.

'A manly and unaccustomed tear' was shed by Noel Watson as he remembered that Betty had offered one of her kidneys to him when he was ill.

NOEL WATSON: ... *along with the tears of seemingly all rural Kent, when Betty McKeever's ashes were laid in Cruciform on the side of New Zealand Hill overlooking the Thames Estuary, to the ringing accompaniment of Mike Bax (my successor) blowing the 'Gone Away', loud and clear on that bleak winter's afternoon a few years ago. We then all went beagling and enjoyed a splendid tea at Mount Ephraim. Betty's funeral service, like her, was unforgettable.*

Blowing the 'Gone Away' was something Mike found was one of the hardest things he had ever done. He blew on the presentation silver hunting horn.

The occasion was replete with pagan symbolism. It was a commemoration – a fine outdoor memorial to sporting life. An occasion which gave identity to the North Kent rural commununity.

We all ended up with a day's beagling – and Betty was very much with us.

Obituaries were written on Betty in 1990 from:

Horse and Hound, 27 September and 4 October
Daily Telegraph, 22 September
Faversham Times, 26 September
Faversham News, 28 September

Betty remained in the *Guinness Book of Records* until 1997.

There is now a memorial tablet set up to her on New Zealand, flanked by trees.

The beagles have had another lease of life since having been taken on by six joint-masters full of youthful enthusiasm.

Joint-Masters appointed in 1991:

Anne McKeever
Michael Bax
Simon Curling
Guy Hindley
Geoffrey Neame.

Rene Simon joined them in 1994.

ARTHUR: *'The Blean Beagles are thriving – but having problems kennelling.'*

After Betty's death, everyone moved up a generation and a farm. Willie and Anne now live at Waterham and their son Tom is farming Bifrons, Patrixbourne.

Willie has cleared up the Waterham yard and buildings substantially. He has put up some new sheds and rears Christmas geese. He has special chickens and Anne runs all the sheep on the farm.

By Betty's death her land, both owned and rented, was in a bad state. Willie has fettled up the land successfully, going in for a considerable amount of scrub clearance and fencing.

MARY DAWES: *Willie is a good tenant and increasing his acreage.*

JOE: *But when we finish' with them ponies, we had to sell them at the end after she died. Willie didn't want 'em. I mean to say, there was ninety of them odd, that we had to get rid of . 'Cos Willie didn't want any more to do with them.*

There were 86 ponies left when Betty died. Willie kept half a dozen back before Christmas, half a dozen back for eighteen months/two years then he cleared them all up.

Furniture

When Berkeley was sold up after her mother's death there was a share out. Betty brought back furniture and bits and pieces to the farm and put them all up in the Oast.

The furniture was kept in the dust and damp. Betty's great-niece Wonky once asked if she might have a chest-of-drawers. The answer had been an unequivocal **'No!'**

JOE: *Some of the things got used but it was a bloody shame really. There was some good stuff there, and it was all left up there. Honestly, all the rats were running through it! A lot was books and things like that. It all got ruined. It wasn't until Willie came here and said, 'Do you know what, I've had someone out.' (I don't know where they came from, Folkestone or somewhere – to do with this antique business.) Honestly, they were taking away some of them chairs, that only had three legs on them. All the upholstery and that had gone, but, 'Oooh,' he said. 'They was going mad over them as genuine antiques!'*

WILLIE [in 1997]: *Colin [West] was left the house for his lifetime, without any rent – I think it's a shilling a year.*

Joe [Butler] was left his house in perpetuity for his lifetime, without any rent. The last of the family living there. Hardy, very hardy. He comes and helps me at busy times. He helps Anne in the garden occasionally. He retired when he was 65. He's 68 now, he never worked anywhere else. In fact we were very proud. Before he retired, I put him in for the '50 Years', the Kent County Agricultural Society Medal. You put them in for it after they've done 25 years. Nobody had put Joe in, and I'm a member of the Society. So before he retired, he'd done 50 odd years. Mother had just died. 'Cos he started on the farm Easter '42 – after he'd finished school.

JOE: *How it' s worked out, in retrospect is marvellous! She left me this house. Well, it's not mine, just to live in, like. So, it's worked out marvellous, really.*

COLIN WEST: *What you're losing now is humanity. All you're doing is work, work, work, now – then a paypacket. A real joker. Missed her more than I did my mother. Wasn't that bad?*

In Willie's cupboard until a couple of years ago when he found it, was an envelope labelled **'Please open and action, in case I snuff it'**!

Betty had written this before she had her hip done in St Savior's, Hythe. Inside were two bequests:

One was a barber's gold pen-knife – to go to her godson.

The other was to go to her great-niece Diana, who now lives in New Zealand. This is a sharkstooth and pearl necklace which was given to Mopsie in 1908 when she went to New Zealand – a Maori necklace. Betty thought it ought to go back to New Zealand.

Her generation had practically all gone, but Joan Sayer still hung on and then she also died, in 1993.

So what can we make of the life of one sturdy Kent lady, who made for herself her own corner in history? Perhaps this:

In 1998 my sister-in-law, Annie Dawes attended the Eridge Pony Club's One Day Event, accompanying her daughter, Sophie with her pony. Annie stood next to another mother doing the same thing, who told her, *'My daughter is riding Blean Monarch, a super Welsh pony. It was bred by the late great Mrs Betty McKeever.'*

Memorial Meet on New Zealand with marshes and Sheppey in the background

Appendix One
A history of the Blean Beagles*

The Blean Beagles are well known in North-East Kent. They have been an established pack for many years, with a reputation for showing good sport.

The pack is also renowned for having been under the same Master since 1909, a record which takes some beating.

Hounds are kennelled at Waterham Farm, Hernhill, which is the home of the Master, Mrs Betty McKeever.

There are twenty-six couples, marked 'B.B.' They are mostly pied hounds, with some lemon and white, and one or two blue-grey saddle hounds, a type that crops up unexpectedly, after missing one or two generations.

They hunt the country from Dover along the A2 – then Chilham, Challock by Pilgrims' Way to the Maidstone/Sittingbourne Road and the Isle of Sheppey. All this country is bounded by the sea on the North.

Like other Kent packs, their country has been reduced by new coast roads, motorways, and the electrification of the railways, but luckily, much of their hunting is over marshland, which remains undeveloped – and a lot of arable.

Hares are plentiful, and every season there are some great Hunts, often ending on the beaches and mudflats.

The Blean have a lively history. There has been a pack here for well over one hundred years, and many amusing stories are still told about earlier days.

In 1853 it was a Farmer's pack, nominally Harriers, of hounds of all makes and shapes. The Kennels were then at Church Farm, Hernhill, the home of the farmer Mr Merton Mercer. The hounds were trencher fed, and on hunting mornings Mr Mercer would ride

* Mrs Sheila Judge typed this out, which was then corrected in Betty's handwriting. Mrs Judge deserves much credit for actually writing it in Betty's lifetime – and keeping it. This tract was written in the late 1970s.

all round the village, blowing his horn lustily until the hounds and huntsmen assembled. Merton Mercer was renowned for his rather wicked sense of humour, and there are still tales told of his more bizarre jests.

The pack continued in this manner until 1883, when for some reason it was dispersed. Lord Sondes then formed a new pack of Beagles and Harriers, which flourished under his patronage until 1894.

At that time the country extended beyond and round Canterbury to Nackington, Throwley and Challock, and was open and unspoiled.

In 1894 Mr Dawes, of Mount Ephraim, took over as Master. The pack were 'riding Harriers', and became known as the Blean from this date.

The pack continued happily, showing good sport, until 1907, when Mr Dawes went to New Zealand and hounds were given to Mr John Buckland, as noone could be found to hunt the pack.

On his return from New Zealand in 1908 Mr Dawes once again started a pack, this time of Beagles. This was known as the Blean Beagles, and the name has remained unchanged since then. Mr Dawes was at this time also Master of the Tickham Hunt, and he registered the Blean in his daughter Betty's name from the beginning.

At this time George Alcock was huntsman to the Tickham, and between 1910 and 1914 he collected Beagles from everywhere. Hounds were given by Miss Guest from the Inward Beagles, one of these was noted because it was whiskered. The well-remembered Welcome was a blue and white hound, while those obtained from the Stoke Place pack were pied.

This assortment Mr Dawes welded into a pack which he hunted himself, assisted by his daughter. On highdays, holidays and birthdays she was allowed to hunt them herself, the best foundation for future sport. At that time some of the Field were riding to hounds, and continued to do so for years, almost up to the second world war.

During the 1914/18 War hunting was curtailed, but the pack was maintained.

After the war, Betty Dawes was Master in practise, as well as in name. In 1921 her brother, then Captain Sandys Dawes, was Master of the Tickham, and brother and sister hunted the two packs almost next door to each other. Sandys Dawes was Master of the Mid-Kent Staghounds for 22 seasons [from 1927], and was well known as a

Master of Hounds throughout the county, having been associated with the Ashford Valley and Romney Marsh.

By this time, at the Blean, a selective breeding programme was in progress, and the pack improved accordingly. The success of this was proved in Peterborough in 1928, when Ballyboy won the unentered Dog Hounds. Other winners were the stallion hound Rollicker, and Conqueror; and Ballyboy was Champion in 1928.

In 1920 a committee was formed, and the Blean became a subscription pack, and continued to thrive and show good sport until the second war, when the hounds were perforce reduced in number, and only a nucleus kept.

During this time, hunting was stopped, but when the war finished, breeding recommenced and the pack was soon hunting as well as ever.

It is thought that the persistent recurrence of the odd blue and white hound, after a miss of one or two generations, is due to the inbreeding that was inevitable in the war years.

With a pack in the same family for such an uninterrupted length of time, it is not surprising that many local stories have grown around the Kennels.

Romulus, the grandsire of Champion Ballyboy, was, for some reason, reared by one of the stable cats. When he was an adult, it was noticed that he had a curious whorl of hair on each flank. This was attributed to the way in which the cat washed and cleaned him as a pup.

There are many more stories of this kind, fascinating to listen to, and giving the pack a character entirely of its own.

It is not possible to think of the Blean without thinking of their Master. The Blean Beagles and Mrs Betty McKeever are synonymous to most people. Pack and Master have literally grown up together, for Mrs McKeever has been Master since the age of nine, when the pack was started.

Coming from a family well known in Kent as first rate sportsmen and horsemen, Mrs McKeever has ridden and hunted all her life.

She can relate how she was blooded, at four years old, when hunting with the Tickham. She was riding side-saddle on a small pony, hounds killed in Lees Court Park, and she was blooded by George Evans, an amateur huntsman who was hunting hounds for Mr Rigden, the Master at that time.

In her earlier days as Master of the Blean she rode to hounds. On her fiftieth anniversary as Master, the hunt members presented her with a portrait of herself [in the 1930s, riding Lucky Day] as a girl [young woman], dressed in the Hunt uniform of green, with white collar and black cap. She is painted riding side-saddle, following the pack. It is a very distinctive painting, and much treasured.

Mrs McKeever is now in her seventies, and makes no secret about it. Age does not appear to hinder her at all. She is more active than many youngsters, foot following her beagles and walking miles across wet, muddy marshes in all weathers.

She is an outspoken, direct person, standing no nonsense, and with a great reputation for fairness in all things.

The Blean Beagles Horse Show, which she organises yearly, started from a very small beginning, and has now become one of the most popular Shows in this part of Kent.

As well as the Beagles, Mrs McKeever runs a small mixed farm, in which she has a great interest, knowing all her stock, their breeding and value. She is even better known for her Blean Hills Stud, a stud of remarkably good Welsh ponies, carrying some top class blood lines.

These make ideal ponies for young children, and also good show ponies.

The Blean Hills prefix is frequently seen in the first three of the lead rein and 12.2hh classes.

There are also some useful T.B. stock bred on the farm, from a strain that has belonged to the family for years.

When asked about the future of the Blean, Mrs McKeever is optimistic. The hunt is in a healthy financial state, and there is no reason why they should not continue to hunt, and provide sport. Despite new roads and motorways, the marshes are still there for hunting, and she is a welcome guest with hounds in many places.

The Blean also have a strong supporters Club, which arranges social occasions and other fund-raising events.

Many people working on the Waterham Farm, and in the Kennels, have been associated with the family for several generations, and that is a good sign of well being on any estate.

The Blean is unique in that it has such a long association with one family. In this corner of Kent, both the Hunt and the family are regarded with justifiable pride and affection.

It is a Kentish pack that has been maintained in the best of Hunting traditions, by a Master who comes from one of the good old Hunting families.

The story of the Blean Beagles is surely worth recording, for such stories are becoming increasingly rare.

Appendix Two
Attendance at the 80 year Celebration Meet

The following friends were present:

Miss Barbara Amos
Miss Mignon Whitacre-Allen
Leslie Atkinson (Huntsman of West Street Hunt)
Mrs Leslie Atkinson
Mr and Mrs Nigel Berry, Simon, Thomas and Nicholas
Mrs Clare Bryant
Mr and Mrs Henry Bryant
Miss Nora Bearsby
Stuart Boult, Natalie and Adam
Guy Beck
Mrs Veronica Bramhall
David Beeny
Mrs Brunger
Robert Balicki
Mrs Flora Bensted
Mr and Mrs Pat Browne
Miss Queenie Butcher
Mr and Mrs Maurice Berry
Mrs Sheila Burley
Mr and Mrs W M Brockman
Mrs Marjorie Bryant
Mr and Mrs Julian Berry & Emily
Martin Browne (Whip)
Mr and Mrs Alec Bray
Mr and Mrs Simon Barnes
Mr and Mrs Tom Borman
Mr and Mrs Birchenough

Mr and Mrs Reg Butler

Joe Butler

Mrs Margot Buchanan

Mrs Hugh Curling (Secretary to the Hunt)

Hugh Curling

Simon Curling

Mrs Sally Clifford-Cox

Dr Betty Curling

David Chantler & Andree

Mrs Tods Chantler

Mr and Mrs Ray Cutchee

Mr and Mrs John Clarke

Mrs Jack Cantor

Mr and Mrs Paul Crook

Mrs Rosemary Cleverdon MFH

Bob Connelly (*Faversham Times*)

Mrs Lizzie Cook

Mrs B Churchill

Mr and Mrs Sandys Dawes, Jenny, Julia and Alice

Mrs Mary Dawes

Mrs Gwen Day

Mrs Jean Douglas

Mr and Mrs James Dawes & Sophie

Mr and Mrs George Dawes

Georgie Dawes

Christopher Dawes

Michael Dixey

Mrs J M Elworthy

Geoffrey Elworthy

Mr and Mrs Colin Edgar, Rupert, Lucy and Philip

Mr and Mrs Simon Elworthy

Arthur Finn (Chairman of the Hunt)

Mrs Pam French

Mrs Olive French

Miss Felicity Fawcett

Mr and Mrs Windham Fletcher

John Funnel, MIH

Mike Freed

Mr and Mrs Richard Fuller

Mr and Mrs Mike Field (*Horse & Hound*)

Mrs Marjorie Funnel

Frank Goodhew

Mrs Betty Gaskain

Mr and Mrs John Goulden

Brigadier and Mrs David Groves

Peter Goodwin

Mr and Mrs Paul Grugeon

Miss Katie Garfit

Miss Susan Glew

Kit Houghton (*The Field*)

Mrs A D M Hilton

Chris Hill (Huntsman)

Mr and Mrs Bill Henderson

Alan Hayes

Guy Hindley (Huntsman)

W Hughes d'Aerth

Mr and Mrs Brian Hindley

John Hills Senior

John Hills Junior

Miss Marjorie Hills

Paul Hayler

Mr and Mrs Derek Howard

Geoff Ingleton

Mr and Mrs George Janes, Susannah and Thomas

Mark Johnson

Mrs Pam Jaquet

Mr and Mrs John Johnson, Georgina and Thomas

Mrs Elizabeth Kama

Mr and Mrs Jasper Knight

Mr and Mrs Hugh Kelsey

Mrs James Linington

Mr and Mrs Bruce Lushington

Andrew Lea

David Manners (*Faversham News* and the *Kentish Gazette*)

Mr and Mrs John Mills

Major P B P Mitchell

Mr and Mrs Guy Minter

Mrs Susan Milner and Alexandra

Frank Middleton (Chairman Wye College)

Mrs Freda Morrison

Willie and Anne McKeever

Mr and Mrs Andrew Nicol and Lucy

Mr and Mrs David Neame, Jessica and William

Mrs John Nesham

Mr and Mrs Basil Neame

Geoffrey Neame

Rebecca Neame

Mr and Mrs Christopher Neame

Mrs Margaret Ockenden

Mr and Mrs Reg Older

Mrs Pip Prideaux-Selby

Mr and Mrs Gavin Prideaux-Selby

Mr and Mrs Nigel Prideaux-Selby and Tom

Mrs Diana Potter

Mr and Mrs Andrew Parry and Arthur and Edward

Oliver Prichard

Mr and Mrs M Richmond

Dominic Regan

Miss Liz Riley

Sandy Rogers

Mr and Mrs John Regan

John Fairfax-Ross

Mrs Jean Rowntree

Mr and Mrs Ralph Stevens

Gerald Smith

Victoria Softly

Mrs Peggy Stevens.

Miss Joan Sayer

Millie Stankawitch

Mr and Mrs David Sorrell

Mr and Mrs Mike Taylor & Rowena

Mr and Mrs Max Tultberg

Alf Taylor

S P B H Ward

Mrs Doris White

Granville Wheler

Mr and Mrs Charles West

David Willis

Colin West

Stewart Wood MFH

Mrs Stewart Wood MFH

J B McKeever 1909–1989

Appendix Three
Contributors

BARBARA AMOS
Cousin to Hugh Curling and Mary Dawes. A rider. Born 1908, a decade younger than Betty, and still alive.

MICHAEL BAX
Beagled from school at Kings' Canterbury in the 1960s. Carried the horn until 1980. Chartered surveyor from East Kent family. Now a Joint-Master of the Blean Beagles.

STUART BOULT
'Boulty' – Born 1912. Was haulage contractor in Ramsgate (beagled from there) then made bullion bags. Married Sue late in life and has young family. Blean Beagles whipper-in for five years in the 1930s. Retired to Sutton Valance. He died 11 November 1999.

JOE BUTLER
Born in the early 20s. Farm worker at Waterham all his life. Saw Betty out.

ANNE CLINCH
Worked as groom for Betty from 1961 until 1963 when she married from Waterham.

HUGH CURLING
Beagled since the early 1920s. Farmer and chartered accountant. Ex-Mayor of Faversham. Long term supporter of beagles. Cousin to Mary Dawes.

NORMA CURLING
Wife of Hugh. Friend of Betty's. Blean Beagles secretary. Hosted many Meets at Perry Court.

SIMON CURLING
Son to Hugh and Norma. Beagled as a boy and young man. Moved away, later returning to Kent and becoming Joint-Master of the Blean Beagles after Betty's death.

JAMES & ANNIE DAWES
Author's brother (in marine paint – city gent) and sister-in-law (PG's racehorses).

JILL DAWES
Married to John Dawes, author's mother. Daughter of Gordon Mitchell, Master of Mid-Kent Staghounds. Gave many meets at Sonstoll, in Betty's home parish.

JOHN DAWES
Betty's nephew, author's father. Son of Betty's brother Sandys. Worked for Betty 1941–42 on farm. Served, Officer, Royal Scots Greys – decorated. Returned to Kent in 1961. Farmer and Lloyds insurance broker in London. Retired to West Tempar, Scotland.

MARY DAWES née FINN
Married Betty's nephew Bill Dawes. Hostess – gave Lawn Meets at Mount Ephraim. Brewing and farming family. Her Mother was Joint-Master of the Tickham with Sandys.

ARTHUR FINN
Local farmer. Cousin to Mary Dawes. Huntsman and Chairman of the Blean Beagles.

PETER GOODWIN
Whipped in for Blean Beagles, before and after World War II. From Canterbury where he worked in a garage. Moved to Heathfield, Sussex and ran a garage.

MIKE HICKS
Beagled with Betty in the 1950s. A journalist and writer, he wrote several articles on Betty (one in French!) and on hunting. He now lives in Ireland.

SHEILA JUDGE
Local historian at Minster, Sheppey. A generation younger than Betty. Had Welsh ponies from her. Friend of Betty's in old age. She wrote a book on Faversham including a chapter on hunting dictated by Betty.

WILLIE MCKEEVER
Betty's son from marriage with Rudolf McKeever. Born Waterham 1931. World War II boyhood in Banff. Always a farmer except for three years in Army at Transport. Branch Chairman of NFU.

JANET MINEYKO née DAWES
Betty's niece, author's sister. Cordon-bleu cook. Witness. Lived in
Kent 1961–83. Hotelled in Scotland. Ran guest house in Rannoch.
Married a Scotto-Pole, Andrew Mineyko. Produced at least half
the contents of this book.

GEOFFREY NEAME
Was a Kings' schoolboy (1970s) and huntsman. In marquee business.
Joint-Master of Blean Beagles after Betty's death.

ANDREW & RANDALL NICOL
Brothers. Nephew's of Mary Dawes on the Finn side. Scotsmen.

SANDY ROGERS
Keen beagler. Friend of Betty's. TA officer – HAC. Faversham resident.

JEAN ROWNTREE née DAWES
Betty's neice and Slotty's daughter. First married army officer.
Eventer and horse trainer,

STUART SILLERS
Beagler in the 1980s

DAVID & SUE SORRELL
Divorced couple who separately looked after Betty in old age.
Beaglers. Friends of Betty's from around the 1960s. Sue did Betty's
paperwork.

NOEL WATSON
Huntsman for the Blean Beagles in the 1960s

MURIEL WILSON
South African beagler. Friend of Betty's in old age. Widow of Wally.

Many thanks to my main conributors and also to these others:

France Bale	Cyril Cox	Dan Heister
Jane Bax	Elizabeth Curling	Mark Johnson
Sarah Bax	Jill Dawes II	Barnard Lever
Nora Bearsby	Lesley Dawes	Pauline Lewington
John Beach	Sandys Dawes	Anne McKeever
Wonky Beeny	Clive Donnery	Tom McKeever
Sue Boult	Colin Edgar	Lilian Spencer
Tony Broughton	Lucy Edgar	Alan Warner
Vicky Constance	Rupert Edgar	Colin West

Appendix Four
Sources

Bailey's Hunting Directory 1937–38; Country Life – J N P Watson;
Farmers Weekly – Peter Cook; *Faversham News; Faversham Times;*
William Fawcett, *Blean Beagles & Tickham Foxhounds; Fine Homes
& Exclusive Property,* December 1984, Allison Walnman 'Mount
Ephraim'; *Guiness Book of Records;* Hernhill Women's Institute *Betty
McKeever speaks to Hernhill* (tape); *Horse and Hound,* 22 June 1979,
Stuart Newsham, 12 October 1989, Mike Field, October & November
1990, obituaries; ITV local news; *Kentish Gazette;* 7 February 1969,
Gregory Blaxland; Radio Kent; *The Daily Telegraph,* 22 September
1990, obituary; Westrays.

Mrs Good, racing in a Blean Beagles Point-to-Point in 1922